SOCIAL JUSTICE EDUCATION

SOCIAL JUSTICE
EDUCATION

Inviting Faculty to Transform Their Institutions

Edited by

Kathleen Skubikowski, Catharine Wright,
and Roman Graf

Foreword by Julia Alvarez

STERLING, VIRGINIA

COPYRIGHT © 2009 BY STYLUS PUBLISHING, LLC.

Published by Stylus Publishing, LLC
22883 Quicksilver Drive
Sterling, Virginia 20166–2102

Library of Congress Cataloging-in-Publication-Data
Social justice education : inviting faculty to change
institutions / edited by Kathleen Skubikowski, Catharine
Wright, and Roman Graf ; introduction by Julia
Alvarez.—1st ed.
    p.   cm.
    Includes index.
    ISBN 978-1-57922-360-1 (cloth : alk. paper)
    ISBN 978-1-57922-361-8 (pbk. : alk. paper)
    1. Social justice—Study and teaching—United
States.   2. Educational sociology—United States.
3. Critical pedagogy—United States.   4. Education,
Higher—United States.   I. Skubikowski, Kathleen M.
II. Wright, Catharine, 1961–   III. Graf, Roman, 1960–
    LC192.2.S63   2009
    370.11'5—dc22   2009026011

13-digit ISBN: 978–1-57922–360–1 (cloth)
13-digit ISBN: 978–1-57922–361–8(paper)

Printed in the United States of America

All first editions printed on acid free paper
that meets the American National Standards Institute
Z39–48 Standard.

Bulk Purchases

Quantity discounts are available for use in workshops
and for staff development.
Call 1-800-232–0223

First Edition, 2009
10   9   8   7   6   5   4   3   2   1

We would like to thank our family, friends, colleagues, and students past and present for their inspiration.

Special thanks to Maurianne Adams, Barbara Love, Francie Kendall, and Carol Rifelj for their support at the very beginning of this project and Lisa Shepard for her assistance at the end.

Thanks as well for the support of the Mellon Foundation and Middlebury College.

CONTENTS

PREFACE   *ix*

FOREWORD: RAPUNZEL'S LADDER   *xiii*
Julia Alvarez

PART ONE: THEORETICAL PERSPECTIVES ON SOCIAL
JUSTICE EDUCATION

I   A SOCIAL JUSTICE EDUCATION FACULTY
     DEVELOPMENT FRAMEWORK FOR A POST-
     GRUTTER ERA   *3*
     Maurianne Adams and Barbara J. Love

2   LEARNING THROUGH STORY TYPES ABOUT RACE
     AND RACISM   *26*
     Preparing Teachers for Social Justice
     Lee Anne Bell

3   ACADEMIC ACTIVISM AND THE SOCIALLY JUST
     ACADEMY   *42*
     Glen David Kuecker

4   FROM SCIENTIFIC IMAGINATION TO ETHICAL
     INSIGHT   *56*
     The Necessity of Personal Experience in Moral Agency
     Arthur Zajonc

5   CHANGE TO SOCIAL JUSTICE EDUCATION   *70*
     Higher Education Strategy
     Karen L. St. Clair and James E. Groccia

PART TWO: COLLABORATIONS

6   BEYOND DIVERSITY   *87*
     Social Justice Education Across the Curriculum
     Kathleen Skubikowski

7   CIVICS WITHOUT CYNICS   *100*
     A Campuswide, Ethics-Based Approach to Social Justice
     Pedagogy
     Meryl Altman, Neal Abraham, Terri Bonebright, and
     Jeannette Johnson-Licon

8   ON COMMITMENT   *117*
     Considerations on Political Activism on a Shocked Planet
     Vijay Prashad

PART THREE: SOCIAL JUSTICE PEDAGOGY ACROSS
THE CURRICULUM

9   MATHEMATICS OF, FOR, AND AS SOCIAL JUSTICE   *131*
     Priscilla Bremser, Chawne Kimber, Rob Root, and Sheila Weaver

10   VALUED CONTINGENCIES   *148*
     Social Justice in Foreign Language Education
     Roman Graf

11   SHAKESPEARE MEETS SOCIAL JUSTICE   *163*
     Incorporating Literature in the Social Sciences
     Carolyn F. Palmer

12   WRITING FOR SOCIAL CHANGE   *177*
     Building a Citizen–Scholar Discourse That Combines Narrative,
     Theory, and Research
     Catharine Wright

13   DELIBERATIVE DIALOGUE AS A PEDAGOGICAL TOOL
     FOR SOCIAL JUSTICE   *194*
     Kamakshi P. Murti

     AFTERWORD: OBLIQUE I AM   *215*
     Zaheena Rasheed

     CONTRIBUTORS   *221*

     INDEX   *231*

I n 2004 the three of us came together to propose to the Mellon Foundation a project focusing on faculty development in social justice education. The project would be inter-institutional, involving six liberal arts
colleges. Its goal would be to bring into conversation colleagues taking individual steps—in their classrooms, departments, and administrative
offices—to make the academy more socially just. We ourselves experience
higher education in a range of different ways: as teachers and administrators,
as tenured and adjunct faculty, in the humanities, languages, and the arts.
One of us has 20 years' experience incorporating social justice praxis in her
teaching and faculty development work; another is the founding Director of
Middlebury's Center for Teaching, Learning, and Research; and the third is
Middlebury's first Dean for Institutional Diversity. In fact, it is the collaboration of these offices of diversity and teaching and learning that lies at the
heart of both our grant work and this book.

Under a year-long grant, at Middlebury College in September of 2005,
we hosted an Institute on Social Justice Education for the deans and directors of teaching centers and diversity offices at six participating schools:
Scripps, Vassar, Denison, Middlebury, Furman, and DePauw. Institute
workshops were led by Maurianne Adams and Barbara Love, with whose
work we were familiar from attending the National Conference on Race &
Ethnicity in American Higher Education (NCORE). At the Middlebury
Institute, participants investigated the following principles as guidelines for
administrators and faculty doing social justice work at liberal arts colleges:

- Like diversity, social justice is a process and an idea that needs to be
  fostered continuously. It addresses issues of equity in our society and
  attempts to negotiate them among diverse interest groups.
- If the academy wants to become more socially just, it needs to be
  informed by a social justice pedagogy.
- A social justice pedagogy is a pedagogy aware of its positionality
  within the power structures of academic institutions and makes this
  positionality transparent and thus open to inquiry and change.

- At its best, social justice pedagogy highlights collaboration within and outside the classroom, transforming the traditional "omniscient" professor/teacher into an informed collaborator in the common pursuit of knowledge.
- This transformation requires that social justice pedagogues realize their own privileged position of power within the system and continuously negotiate it.

As these principles suggest, pedagogical change, curricular change, and institutional change go necessarily hand in hand: The socially just classroom needs a socially just academy in order to flourish.

In her introductory essay to this volume, "Rapunzel's Ladder," Julia Alvarez asks, "What would it look like, an academy that has social justice at its center?" We offer this volume as a response to Julia's question, challenging ourselves and our readers to reconstruct our classrooms, our administrative functions, and our self-awareness—our very relationship to education and its role in the 21st century.

We begin, in the first of three parts, with **Theoretical Perspectives on Social Justice Education**, and move in part two to exemplary cases of inter- and intra-institutional **Collaborations**, both horizontal—among colleagues—and vertical—among students, faculty, and staff. In part three, **Social Justice Pedagogy Across the Curriculum**, we arrive at the heart of our institutions: the classroom. Contributors in this section present transforming praxes in disciplines ranging from writing to mathematics, from the languages to the social sciences. And finally, Alvarez's wish for a socially just academy in a more socially just world finds itself echoed in the narrative of Middlebury College first-year student Zaheena Rasheed, whose essay "Oblique I Am" closes this volume. Zaheena's essay reminds us that, in Alvarez's words, "the new arrivals in the field of time meet head on . . . the challenges they will be facing as the next generation at the helm of our human family" (xiv).

In the first section, **Theoretical Perspectives on Social Justice Education**, we have put in dialogue voices from social justice education, political activism, contemplative traditions, and systems analysis. In the section's opening, foundational chapter, Maurianne Adams, Professor of Education and chair of the Social Justice Education Graduate Program at the University of Massachusetts Amherst, and Barbara Love, Associate Professor of Education in the same program, expand on the guiding principles listed here, providing a context for the theories and practices that follow. Then Lee Anne Bell, the Barbara Silver Horowitz Director of Education at Barnard College, focuses on a "framework for teaching about racism through the arts using the metaphor of story and story types." This project challenges new teachers as they realize their own positionality and become agents of educational change. In the third chapter, Glen David Kuecker, Professor of History at DePauw University, explores the tension, "if not contradiction," between the critical pedagogy necessary to a socially just academy and the "realities of education in a capitalist society." Arthur Zajonc, Professor of Physics at Amherst College and Academic Program Director of the Center for Contemplative Mind in Society, then highlights the role of imagination in scientific progress and the importance of direct insight, as fostered by contemplative inquiry, in our moral development. In part one's final chapter, Karen St. Clair, Director of Emerson College's Center for Innovation in Teaching and Learning, and James Groccia, Director of the Biggio Center for the Enhancement of Teaching and Learning at Auburn University and former President of the POD Network, theorize about systemic change in institutions of higher education, focusing on models of change in liberal arts colleges.

In part two, **Collaborations**, our authors demonstrate how, theoretically, institutionally, disciplinarily, and in individual classroom praxis, intra- and inter-institutional collaborations can challenge and change liberal arts colleges whose mission statements increasingly call for a response to diversity. In the first chapter, Kathleen Skubikowski, Associate Professor of English and Director of the Center for Teaching, Learning, and Research at Middlebury College, asserts that, in order for diversity to transform the institution, social justice pedagogy must inform teaching and learning across the curriculum. Then, in a collaborative chapter, DePauw University faculty and professional staff—Professor of English and Women's Studies and Faculty Development Coordinator Meryl Altman, Professor of Physics and Astronomy and Executive Vice President Neal Abraham, Professor of Psychology Terri Bonebright, and Director of Multicultural Affairs, Jeannette Johnson-Licon—describe how an already-existing, visible, and well-funded ethics initiative functions as a vehicle for developing faculty across the curriculum. Vijay Prashad, George and Martha Kellner Chair in South Asian History and Professor of International Studies at Trinity College, concludes this section by problematizing multiculturalism and envisioning the next steps toward social justice in liberal arts colleges. He, too, offers theoretical and practical suggestions for collaborating vertically throughout the institution.

The contributors to part three, **Social Justice Pedagogy Across the Curriculum**, offer us learning environments that are active and engaged, open to controversy and safe for disagreement, and that balance emotional and cognitive components of learning. Professors of Mathematics Priscilla Bremser of Middlebury College, Chawne Kimber and Rob Root of Lafayette College, and Sheila Weaver of the University of Vermont demonstrate that addressing social justice questions both serves mathematical learning and supports instructors integrating service-learning or community-based learning and social justice issues in mathematics courses. Roman Graf, Professor of German at Middlebury College, concurs that a social justice approach to foreign language learning and instruction, with its pedagogical transparency, activates and improves student learning. He argues that, by making cultural contingencies transparent, students learn to avoid stereotypical engagements with the "other." In the next chapter, Carolyn Palmer, Associate Professor of Psychology at Vassar College, describes how incorporating the arts into the social sciences can create a "safe space" for both faculty and students to explore new perspectives on social justice issues. Middlebury College Lecturer in Writing Catharine Wright explores how inviting a hybrid discourse in formal and informal writing assignments encourages students to connect the personal and theoretical as they study complex social issues. Finally, Kamakshi Murti, Professor of German at Middlebury College, finds that "Deliberative Dialogue" provides a space for multiple perspectives, where students in the classrooms of any discipline can come to "voice" and hear each other.

This book is a step in an ongoing process that opens the doors of academia to all students in the 21st century. It intends to lay the groundwork for future collaborative work among colleges and universities, administrators and faculty, students and teachers, and ultimately between the academy and society at large. As Julia Alvarez points out in her introduction, "Rapunzel's Ladder," "the ultimate . . . wish of social justice education is a world that is also socially just."

Kathleen Skubikowski, Catharine Wright, and Roman Graf

FOREWORD: RAPUNZEL'S LADDER

Social Justice Education:
A Way Down From the Ivory Tower

Rapunzel, here is a ladder for you to climb down from the ivory tower. It is a phrase woven out of three words, strong enough to hold anyone who feels stuck in an old paradigm: *Social justice education.*

When I first heard the term, I felt one of those "ah-ha!" moments. So there was a name for the unease I had long experienced in the classroom as a student and later as a teacher. A name for why I often felt like an outsider in the academy.

Now I understand why. Though the academy welcomed me, the content of the education that I got as a student and which, later, I was asked to pass down to my own students often did not include people like me. Or it labeled us in ways that marginalized us. Or it disappeared us altogether under the righteous blanket of "universality." As a female, as a Latina/Hispanic, as a scholarship student, and later as a non-Ph.D. faculty member with a mere Masters in Creative Writing, I felt institutionally marginal.

What's more, most of what I was learning in those pre-multicultural days, including how I was being asked to learn it, did not include my own style and story, my ways of perceiving and moving in the world. I learned to live a double life in those ivory towers, to impersonate the exemplary minority who was lucky to have been chosen, who could be cited as a credit to the institution, not to mention a check mark in that critical box of diversity that schools were scrambling to fill at the time. But all the while, I was plotting my escape.

It was not until the day I gave up tenure to become a full-time writer who now teaches on the side that I felt a baffling sense of both terror (I was leaving behind the structure that had been the only home I knew in this country) and relief (I was released from a home that had never felt like home). Perhaps the best way to describe my unease is to compare my academy self to Goldilocks in the house of the three bears. The dimensions of every piece of furniture did not acknowledge or accommodate my proportions. The windows were far too high for me to see out of or to open. I gasped for air in that stuffy space, wondering why no one else was complaining. What's more, I lived in fear of being found out and—the scholarship student's nightmare and later the untenured's terror—of being thrown out.

Having made my confession, I worry about overstating my case. I was, after all, nourished in academia. Even when the institutional structures and canons lagged far behind, there were always individual teachers and texts and classmates and courses and colleagues who taught me a way around things or made exceptions. But the fact that an alternate way was considered an exception branded this bending of the status quo as "problematic."

What's amazing to me is how many of us felt the same way. Not just women, not just Latinas, not just minorities, not just scholarship students. Institutions, bless them, often start out as responsive living structures. But the problem is that they become codified, claustrophobic, limiting, and we have to keep reinventing them. And they resist reinvention. In fact "they" dig their heels in and fight back.

And yet, a learning institution has, as its raison d'être the mandate to be a place of constant, vibrant revision; a place where knowledge and tradition can be held up to the scrutiny of time to ensure that they are still useful to the needs of the world, can still nurture our spirits, can still respond to who we are now and who we must become in order to survive. Here, too, the new arrivals in the field of time meet head on with the challenges they will soon be facing as the next generation at the helm of our human family.

In evaluating my own education, I want to walk softly and throw away the big sticks. Why? Because it matters too much that this be a space for all of us. There is no future in blame, which just ends up being more of that old bifurcated thinking, a reactive *us*-ing and *them*-ing that makes a battleground of learning, a space where someone will be left out.

And my life in academia was never a matter of cruel imposition, colonizing of my mind; it was more of an absence. Small omissions, fine points, miniscule matters of tone or perspective, which might seem like splitting hairs to bring up now.

But the devil (I was taught) is in the details. Indeed, it is in those fine points that we can make a difference. Strand by strand, we can plait a ladder down from our ivory towers, and ask ourselves what would an education look like that holds itself accountable to the very values it seeks to promote? An education that is not just about proficiency in content. An education whereby we create community and conscience. An education that can do what Keats claimed only for poetry: embody negative capability, that ability to entertain dualities and "to be in uncertainties, Mysteries, doubts without any irritable reaching after fact & reason . . ." Education as "a vale of soulmaking."

The essays in this volume challenge us with those questions, theoretically, institutionally, and personally. They all start from the premise that an education that puts Rapunzel in a tower, removes her from her roots, her family, her community, and her own self does not do justice to what education is all about. In fact, such an "education" does violence, however unwittingly, to that effort to comprehend, connect, question, and make whole which is the very life of a learning institution. How create an academy that takes on its acknowledged role of helping form an integrated self, body, mind—in a word: a soul? After all, we call schools *alma maters*, mothers of our souls.

Before I leave you to these thinkers and educators who have lived with these questions in a conscious, committed way far longer than I have, I want to go back to a defining Rapunzel experience in my own education. All through my American schooling, I had a serious academic problem: I couldn't take exams. I'd show up, all right, over-prepared, and determined that this time it would be different. But as I began to read the questions, a terror would seize me that I couldn't seem to control.

Back then (early 1960s), we didn't have a term for what was going on. Now, no doubt, I would be diagnosed as suffering "panic attacks." When I finally finished my formal education, I packed away my exam phobia in that Pandora's Box of memory where we happily leave behind our past damaged selves, hoping they'll crumble away into dust and disappear.

But recently I was forced to revisit that time in my life. I was working on a nonfiction book on Latina adolescence, *Once Upon A Quinceañera: Coming of Age in the USA*, and my editor suggested that I include some of my own experiences as a teenager coming of age in my new country. I tried writing about that time without bringing *it* up, but somehow I could not avoid dealing with a problem that had marked my whole adolescent life.

Learning about social justice education has helped me see this problem in a new light. Granted that my extreme response had a lot to do with my own temperament, with the fact that when the problem began, we were recent political refugees from a grim dictatorship and had barely escaped with our lives. But could my academic breakdown also have been a way my psyche was registering its bafflement at finding itself, like the canary in the mineshaft, in a noxious environment? Could it be that my spirit was responding to an education that was asking me to leave out too much of who I was? That my young Rapunzel self, who had not yet heard of social justice education, was scrambling down from that ivory tower before the witch's scissors descended and cut off all my hair?

When my family arrived in this country in 1960, fleeing the dictatorship of Trujillo in the Dominican Republic, education became a matter of survival. School was the place to learn the skills that would allow us entry into an alien culture. Those were the early days of the Civil Rights Movement, pre-bilingual education, pre-everything but the old assimilationist model of immigration. From the start, my American education was not about adding to and, therefore, expanding my heritage or preserving my native language, but replacing it with something *better*. In fact, the harassment in the playground confirmed that fact. My sisters and I were pelted with pebbles, taunted as "spics," told to go back to where we came from.

Our rescue came in the form of boarding school. My older sister and I won scholarships at Abbot Academy, an elite prep school north of Boston. Abbot Academy was just beginning to concern itself with bringing diversity to its all-white, Anglo-Saxon, Protestant student body. But diversity was that early, well-meaning but ultimately condescending variety of "diversity," a kind of missionary pedagogy in which a few girls from different backgrounds (Jewish, African American, "foreign") were given the privilege of being converted into Abbot girls. All the while, our difference was held up as proof of the liberal-mindedness of the institution.

At Abbot, education became not just classroom learning but a total immersion. I was soaking it in: how an elite fleet of girls dressed, talked, worked, played, lived, learned. Since Abbot was a prep school, the main mission of our education was to prepare us for college. This goal was always before us as the reason we were learning. Sure, the inscription on the front gates read, *Enter Into Understanding That Ye May Go Forth Into Nobler Living*, and this might be what we ultimately hoped for, but who could see that far summit for all the ivory towers looming before us? One of them would end up being the college Abbot helped us get into.

What now seems odd is that the skills we were being taught in the classroom—to be smart, ambitious, competitive—went against the feminine virtues and social graces promoted by the school and outlined in our Abbot "Blue Book." We were to behave in a manner befitting young ladies—with all the mind-numbing implications of that phrase in that pre-women's-movement time. But what seems even odder was that no one remarked this gulf. No one seemed to acknowledge that each of us was being asked to be a divided self.

If this was so for our Anglo classmates, it was even more so for my sister and me. An even larger gulf was growing between what we were absorbing at Abbot and our Dominican Catholic culture and *familia*. In fact, almost everything I was learning was bringing down a whole belief system and way of life.

Take the content of just two courses. In European History, we were learning about the corrupt practices of the medieval Catholic church: the Inquisition, rival popes, the selling of indulgences. I was shocked and shaken. I didn't know *how* to take in these new facts and integrate them with what was still the guiding faith of my fathers and mothers and my own life. How to throw out the baby of unexamined dogma but not the bath water of a spiritual life?

In American History our teacher lectured on the Monroe Doctrine, presenting the eight-year (1916–1924) Marine occupation of my country as an effort to rescue an unruly people from debt and bloodshed. I wasn't totally sure what *unruly* meant, but it didn't sound good. Had my father been lying when he talked about those same Marines as invaders who had put in place the 31-year dictator who had forced my family to flee the country?

And it wasn't just the content of my courses that distressed me. It was the whole competitive style of learning that set us against each other to see who would come out on top. I had grown up in a familial culture, where I didn't operate as a sole agent, but was always a part of a "we," a community effort. Even after we came to this country and were living as a nuclear family in Queens, my sisters and I were a unit, constantly talking in our shared bedrooms, trying to make sense of what was happening to us in this country.

I wish I could report that I was a young Joan of Arc at Abbot, holding firm to my faith and pride in my culture and language. But no, I began to feel that as the gatekeepers of the dominant culture, my teachers were right, and I was wrong. Since this was boarding school, there was no matrix of home and culture and community that I could return to daily to affirm and feed that other self. Moreover, I was terrified I'd lose my scholarship, be sent home in shame to my parents, end up in a worse place—that other rougher, public-school playground where the kids threw stones and didn't allow me entry into even rhetorical understanding, but hollered that my spic sisters and I should go back to where we came from.

And so, by sheer effort, I disciplined myself to become a good student. I was going to make my parents proud. I would vindicate us by showing the Americans that we were not just an unruly lot. Thinking back, I feel a pang for that young Rapunzel—how much was riding on her education! Where was the freedom of spirit or fun of learning? Not to mention the outright contradiction of vindicating "us" by becoming "them"! This past summer at our fortieth-year reunion, my Abbot roommate recalled how every day I'd draw up a detailed schedule which I would follow religiously: 6–6:15 A.M.: wake up, get dressed, brush teeth; 6:15–6:30 A.M.: study vocabulary list, reread English assignment, review Latin translation, and so on.

But although I could follow a rigorous schedule and be transformed in the crucible of the classroom, back in my dorm room at night, it was a different story. I had trouble sleeping, worrying about all I had to learn or what I had already learned that was a mortal sin to have learned. I was terrified that the devil would come after me. In fact, all through high school, I slept with a crucifix under my pillow, a crucifix I was careful to keep hidden from my roommate, who already teased me enough about being a nut and a grind. I had come from a country and culture steeped in Catholicism and *santería*, demons and spells, beliefs and practices now termed "primitive superstitions." I could not so easily cut myself from these deep roots, which indeed had their negative aspects, but were also the only way I knew to feed my soul and nurture my spirit.

Soon, these demons—whom I renamed "the furies" in order, I think, to contain them, to make them literary—began to stray from the private space of my bedroom at night. They'd show up at the most inopportune time: the moment of reckoning when I had to be at my most competitive: exam time. I'd sit down to a test, and a sense of dread would descend on me. A distracting voice would start up in my head, *You're going to mess up!* I would try to ignore the voice, to force myself to concentrate, but panic would seize me, my breath would come short, my head would begin to spin. The discomfort was so great that finally I would bolt out of the room, leaving behind my dumbfounded teachers and disgusted classmates.

I felt ashamed. I couldn't explain what was going on. Why was I self-destructing in this way? "You don't have any reason to worry," my teachers kept reassuring me. I had high grades going into finals. Finally, the administration found a way to calm the furies. All through my time at Abbot, I took my final exams in the infirmary, and until we got the problem under control, my mother drove up to school and sat on the other side of the door waiting to take me home when I was done.

Now I see how unprepared I was to receive an education that did not take into account all it was destroying inside me. Something in me was refusing to make that leap to the other side of that widening gulf my education was creating between an old life and a new self. Why my mother had to be there, to reassure me that I could still have "us" even if I succeeded as a "me." My spirit was up in arms.

In his insightful and controversial memoir, *Hunger of Memory* (Bantam Books, 1983), Richard Rodriguez writes of a similar painful gulf in his education. As the young Richard becomes increasingly successful in school, he learns to keep his home life and culture "repressed, hidden beneath layers of embarrassment." It's only now as a grown man writing his memoir that he acknowledges "what it has taken me more than twenty years to admit: *A primary reason for my success in the classroom was that I couldn't forget that schooling was changing me and separating me from the life I enjoyed before becoming a student*" (p. 45).

As his memoir attests, Rodriguez is haunted by his education. Researching the literature on pedagogy, Rodriguez finds a description in Richard Hoggart's *The Uses of Literacy* of the type of student he became: "the scholarship boy." (This term enlightens Rodriquez, much as the phrase, "social justice education," did me.)

The scholarship boy is a student who has come "up" from the lower ranks. (Hoggart, a Brit, was writing in the 1950s.) He moves between antithetical environments, his home and the classroom. With his family, the boy has "the intense pleasure of intimacy, the family's consolation in feeling public alienation. Lavish emotions texture home life. Then, at school, the instruction bids him to trust lonely reason primarily" (p. 46). Unlike his upper-class or middle-class classmates, the scholarship boy goes home and "sees in his parents a way of life not only different but starkly opposed to that of the classroom . . ." (p. 47). Hoggart describes the increasing toll his education exacts on the scholarship boy:

> He has to be more and more alone, if he is going to 'get on.' . . . He will have, probably unconsciously, to oppose the ethos of the hearth, the intense gregariousness of the working-class family group. (p. 47)

Add to the scholarship boy's social and economic class difference, an ethnic, racial, cultural, and language difference and you've got . . . an anxious student; an over-achieving boy; a girl running out of exams. This does not sound like the education of a student but like the breaking of his spirit:

> Here is a child who cannot forget that his academic success distances him from a life he loved, even from his own memory of himself. . . . To evade nostalgia for the life he lost, he concentrates on the benefits education will bestow upon him . . . Without the support of old certainties and consolations, almost mechanically, he assumes the procedures and doctrines of the classroom. . . . Success comes with special anxiety. (p. 49)

Where my own experience differs from that of Richard Rodriguez, and what has made him a controversial figure with many Latinos and educators, is his belief that this is an inevitable process. But to think so is to have totally absorbed that other, dominant point of view. Granted, as Rodriguez himself acknowledges, education always contains loss. It is painful to leave behind our gated gardens, our little security-blanket ways of thinking, our historical and cultural and familial biases. It hurts to expand the self, to forge a soul. But education need not be a violence against the self, a core Rapunzel self held hostage forever.

And this is precisely the challenge to social justice educators who write in these pages and labor in the classroom to create more inclusive models: how to grow the spirit with the mind, how to help our students not just with content but with the process of integrating that content into an *alma* whose *mater*, after all, the academy says we are.

As for my own story, this problem not only marked the course of my American education, it determined the course of my life. What I mean is that without this problem, I probably would not have sought out those courses (creative writing: all the "exams" were take home!) and teachers (writers, many of whom were disaffected with the academy, exceptions themselves) who would allow me to express what I had learned in a way more simpatico with my temperament and background. I probably would not have embraced a major (English) in what was, after all, a second language if I had not found in that major a "minor" (creative writing) where poetic license was the rule.

And so, my breakdown in the educational process proved to have a happy ending. To the academy's credit, I was allowed to stay on the strength of recommendations from my teachers who found enough merit in my writing and hard work to overlook my inability to perform under pressure. As my education "progressed" in college and later in graduate school, I regressed less and less. Happily, this was not just a matter of my own maturity, but the academy itself was changing, loosening up, challenged by the student activism of the 1960s, the Civil Rights Movement, the women's movement, affirmative action, the culture "wars" in departmental curriculum and faculty. In the student-centered, open-classroom movement of the late sixties and early seventies, professors began encouraging creativity among students, even in traditionally conservative disciplines, like the sciences. (I recall writing a series of poems on the Vermont landscape for my geology class.)

Years later, these examination fears showed up again when I came up for tenure. Again I was being tested, forced to perform and prove myself for visiting evaluators. (What is the place of tenure, a ranking system that encourages hierarchy and preservation of the status quo, in an academy committed to social justice education?) Granted that these evaluators were colleagues, whom I knew would be fair, that my department was "behind me," that I had great student evaluations and a first novel coming out with a good publisher. But since when had hard work and a well-laid groundwork stopped my furies?

What saved my soul that semester and garnered me tenure, I still believe, was that I had recently married. Rooted at last in my own home and life, I could withstand the pressures of performance. Many times during that "tenure semester," I'd ask my husband, "What if I don't get tenure?"

"Don't worry, we'll figure something out. No matter what, we'll have each other." This was another version of my mother posted outside the performance door! I came through—not exactly with flying colors—but this time intact, body and soul.

And yet, like Richard Rodriguez, I've remained haunted by my education. Curiously, I not only stayed in the academy by becoming a teacher, I also returned to teach at the two schools that were the most significant in my own education: Abbot Academy (now absorbed into Phillips Andover Academy) and Middlebury College. It's almost as if I needed to go back, in part to understand what had happened to me there, but also out of a sense of responsibility to those coming after me. If nothing else, I could contribute what had been missing for me—the presence of others like me. As Sandra Cisneros writes at the end of *The House on Mango Street*, "I have gone away to come back. For the ones I left behind. For the ones who cannot get out."

Indeed, as Richard Rodriguez acknowledges, "if because of my schooling, I had grown culturally separated from my parents, my education finally had given ways of speaking and caring about that fact" (p. 72). I came "home" to the academy because that was the only home I knew in my new country, where I became an American self. Abbot Academy and Middlebury College were my alma maters, mothers of my soul, however problematic that mother-daughter relationship was. The academy was also where I found my calling, where I learned to navigate this craft of writing through the Scylla and Charybdis of *either-ors*, and integrate all those disparate selves, if only on paper, with the promise of more.

In fact, even after I gave up tenure, I found a way to come back. The academy, which had always seemed so gated and exclusive, fashioned a place for me as a writer in residence. It turns out there is no witch in Rapunzel's tower, or if there once was a witch, she doesn't live there anymore. More and more, administrators, faculty, and especially students, who are increasingly diverse themselves, are demanding an education that reflects and does justice to the multiplicity and richness of the world we all live in. With the rapid advances in technology, that world is now literally in their dorm rooms, before them on a screen, at their fingertips. With this incredible broadening of possibility comes an even greater challenge for educators: how to help our individual students so that they do not lose their way, swept up in this deluge of information. How to help them integrate all they are learning into a meaningful whole, a whole they will keep making and remaking for the rest of their lives. For there should never be an end to education, a segregation of learning into a determined set of years in our lives. As I like to tell my workshop students, one of the best reasons to be a writer is that you are always having to learn new things.

There are those who worry that bringing such issues as social justice to the academy threatens to politicize neutral ground. That the value of academic discourse is in its impartiality. (Another righteous term like "universality" that stifles all further discussion.) In fact, the academy already has deep-seated and often unconscious biases that should be examined, discussed, held up to the light. As Chaucer's Wife of Bath reminds us, "Who peynte the leon, tel me who?" In other words, if the picture of the hunter slaying a lion had been painted by the lion, what would the scene look like?

What would an education look like that includes both the lion's and the hunter's points of view? In a pluralist society, indeed a pluralist world, how can education not do justice to this multiplicity if we are indeed preparing our students for their lives in this complex world?

At the close of each meeting of the board of Shelburne Farms, a local non-profit sustainability farm and learning center, we always have an agenda item called, "blue sky." This is a time when we cast aside bureaucratic concerns about funding, adherence to precedents, and instead, "dwell in possibility," as Emily Dickinson once wrote, allow the institution—through our dreaming—to re-imagine itself.

One of my wishes for this collection is that it serve as this kind of blue-sky inspiration for educators, administrators, students, the community at large. What would it look like, an academy that has social justice at its center?

It would be inclusive, providing a welcome home for traditionally excluded others so that the concept of "others" becomes moot, and the focus is community, participation, comprehension.

It would put a student's whole well-being at the center of the process, remembering that in addition to passing on information, the academy is also helping to form and inform a whole person, a humane being who is always learning, always enlarging his or her understanding of the world.

It would allow for play because learning is fun, and labor done with passion can be exhilarating, liberating.

It would commit itself to change by looking at the ways it might consciously (or unconsciously) be promoting and prolonging stereotypes or biases which ill serve its mission to educate each and every one of its members.

It would reconsider the ways in which it promotes hierarchy and resistance to change in order to preserve a status quo through its process of tenuring.

It would embody the principles it professes to value. For instance, putting in place environmental practices that it teaches in its classrooms must be observed if we are to survive as a planet.

It would find ways to connect the classroom with the local and global community so that students do not experience learning in a gated community disconnected from the world.

It would never forget the others, the vast majority of the world's population who don't yet have the opportunity and the luxury of an education. It must hold itself accountable to them, remembering that the ultimate blue-sky wish of social justice education is a world that is also socially just.

Rung by rung: this is how we begin climbing down from Rapunzel's tower.

Julia Alvarez
Middlebury College
Middlebury, Vermont
August 31–September 1, 2009

PART ONE

THEORETICAL PERSPECTIVES ON SOCIAL JUSTICE EDUCATION

A SOCIAL JUSTICE EDUCATION FACULTY DEVELOPMENT FRAMEWORK FOR A POST-*GRUTTER* ERA

Maurianne Adams and Barbara J. Love

T he June 2003 Supreme Court finding for *Grutter v. Bollinger et al.* permitted postsecondary admissions policies to include race and ethnicity as narrowly tailored "plus" factors in efforts to increase campus social and cultural diversity. However, in affirming the educational benefits of diversity, the role of this Court's majority decision goes beyond permitting admissions policies to be tailored toward campus diversity. The Court reiterated its view, established in *Brown v. Board of Education* (1954), that "education . . . is the very foundation of good citizenship" and that "effective participation by members of all racial and ethnic groups in the civic life of our Nation is essential if the dream of one Nation, indivisible, is to be realized" (*Grutter v. Bollinger et al.*, 2003, pp. 331–332). It also affirmed expert testimony concerning the educational benefits of diversity: namely, promoting cross-racial understanding, breaking down racial stereotypes, enabling students to better understand cross-racial differences, and providing classrooms that are "livelier, more spirited, and simply more enlightening and interesting" based on "the greatest possible variety of [student] backgrounds" (p. 330, referring to Bowen & Bok, 1998; Orfield & Kurlaender, 2001). The Court affirmed the "overriding importance" of diversity in higher education in "preparing students for work and citizenship" and in "sustaining our political and cultural heritage" (*Grutter v. Bollinger et al.*, 2003, p. 331).

This decision is heartening for faculty and administrators who have long sought to enhance both the presence and role of underrepresented racial and ethnic groups on predominantly White college campuses and to facilitate their interaction with traditionally privileged social groups. It affirms a line of reasoning and evidence that all students benefit from thoughtfully designed, socially diverse instructional settings. The research cited by the *Grutter* (2003) Court goes beyond the merely physical desegregation affirmed by the *Brown* (1954) Court and links the benefits of diversity to programs of study that facilitate productive and long-term relationships across social and cultural differences (Chang, 2005; Gurin, Dey, Hurtado, & Gurin, 2002; Nagda, Gurin, & Lopez, 2003; see also Milem, 2003, and Zúñiga, Nagda, Chesler, & Cytron-Walker, 2007).

The substantial research cited in support of the *Grutter* ruling is part of a larger tradition of research on the benefits to all students of social and cultural diversity in higher education reaching back to the 1950s and school desegregation in the wake of *Brown v. Board of Education*. This research tradition disconfirms the naïve belief that merely admitting students from previously underrepresented racial and ethnic groups will in itself be educationally and socially salutary. Instead, it documents specific conditions that must be met if intergroup contact is to become educationally beneficial. Known collectively as the "contact hypothesis," these conditions include equal group status within educational settings, shared educational goals, intergroup cooperation, opportunities for sustained rather than incidental or random intergroup interactions, and the support of institutional authorities for the educational benefits of social diversity (Allport, 1954; Brewer & Brown, 1998; Brown, 1995; Pettigrew, 1998).

Following desegregation in the late 1950s and the social movements of the 1960s and 1970s, colleges and universities have developed core requirements that not only address issues of diversity but foster interaction among multiple perspectives (Humphreys, 2000). Faculty have designed undergraduate courses and curricula on diversity and social justice in which the curricular content, the course pedagogy, and the students who enroll make possible the civic and educational benefits of diversity described here. Faculty and campus administrators have understood that beyond the moral, demographic, and political rationales for increasing access to higher education for students from underrepresented social groups, there are compelling educational reasons to rethink the curriculum and pedagogy to assure reciprocal benefits for all participants within these demographic changes (Adams, 1992; Chang, 2000/2001; Clayton-Petersen, Parker, Smith, Moreno, & Teraguchi, 2007; Milem, 2003). The body of empirical research and curricular writing that builds on the benefits of diversity, multiculturalism, and social justice in higher education is large and growing, providing valuable resources for faculty and administrators who are working toward social and cultural equity and inclusivity at the level of interactions, whether between individual students or within classrooms, disciplinary curricula, and entire postsecondary institutions (most recently, see Adams, Bell, & Griffin, 2007; Bauman, Bustillos, Bensimon, Brown, & Bartee, 2005; Milem, Chang, & Antonio, 2005; Ouellett, 2005; Williams, Berger, & McClendon, 2005).

The implications of this literature are challenging for faculty, most of whom have been trained in lecture-mainly classes or discussion sections within relatively homogeneous classrooms. For many, the knowledge and skills necessary for effective undergraduate teaching were not core components of their doctoral preparation and professional apprenticeship. Instead, many faculty, at four-year institutions as well as community colleges, teach in ways that reproduce their own successful academic experiences as products of demographically homogeneous campuses. It is not surprising that such faculty may be ill prepared to teach in classrooms populated by students whose backgrounds, culture, educational socialization, and birth-languages may differ from theirs.

The National Center for Education Statistics documents the widening demographic gap between the increasing racial and ethnic diversity of students in higher education (from 15% in 1976 to 30% in 2004) and the relative homogeneity of the faculty (e.g., faculty from underrepresented groups at 15% in 2003) (NCES, 2006). To better prepare traditionally trained faculty for demographic and cultural changes in their classrooms, many campuses have created centers for teaching, offices for diversity, and graduate programs that offer inclusive teaching opportunities in diverse classrooms. This is the larger national context for the social justice education approach presented in this chapter.

A Social Justice Education Framework

Our social justice education perspective is based on an analysis of the processes of schooling that reproduce overarching societal structures of domination and subordination. By this we mean that schooling often reproduces patterns of social and economic inequality that have historical roots and that characterize contemporary society. These patterns of inequality are based on social and cultural differences, used as explanations and justifications for the domination of some social groups and the subordination of others. In our view, social and cultural differences often are used to rationalize and justify inequality that, in our view, results not from these differences but from the domination and subordination that are based on and shape those differences. The social justice framework includes an analysis of domination and subordination at different societal, institutional, and interpersonal levels. It includes an analysis of the ways in which structures of domination and subordination are reproduced in the classroom, following patterns of social and cultural difference in the larger society.

A social justice education framework recognizes that the patterns of domination and subordination are manifest throughout and across social institutions. Among these institutions, education plays the dual role of reflecting these stratified relationships as well as reproducing them through access to curriculum as well as course content and pedagogy. But education also offers a unique opportunity for interrupting these unequal relationships, both by helping people understand social inequality and by modeling equitable relationships in the classroom (for further discussion, see Adams, Bell, & Griffin, 2007).

As social justice educators, we start from the understanding that schooling presents educators with choices, either to ignore and reproduce unequal social relationships or to recognize, interrupt, and transform those relationships. These choices are reflected not only in access to schools and curricula but also in course content and pedagogy. As students in different disciplines learn new course content, they also learn to prize certain knowledge and devalue other knowledge or ignore it entirely. Thus, a social justice perspective on course content enables us to scrutinize a curriculum in order to see the implicit judgments about social relationships embodied by what is included in or excluded from the curriculum.

Similarly, a social justice perspective enables us to recognize the patterns of domination and subordination that characterize the larger society and thus are reproduced in teacher-student or student-student relationships, as well as opportunities to develop reciprocal and equitable relationships. This perspective explores the reproductions of race, gender, class, and other identity-based power inequities and analyzes these in the context of other power relations in the classroom. Such an analysis enables us instructors to clarify the specific kinds of relationships we choose to model and endorse in the classroom.

We share this social justice education framework with our faculty colleagues not because we expect them to include it explicitly in their curriculum, but because we want to convey our view that potentially every component of teaching and learning can be informed by this social justice perspective. We are not asking our colleagues to teach social justice content. Rather, we are asking that our colleagues develop a social justice analysis of their own teaching practice.

A Four-Quadrant Analysis of Teaching and Learning

Teaching and learning are fluid, interactive processes that can be characterized in many different ways. To compress our social justice framework into a single heuristic, we conceptualize teaching and learning processes as falling into four interactive quadrants, each one of which can be analyzed from a social justice perspective. These four quadrants are based on (1) what our students, as active participants, bring to the classroom, (2) what we as instructors bring to the classroom, (3) the curriculum, materials, and resources we convey to students as essential course content, and (4) the pedagogical processes we design and facilitate and through which the course content is delivered (Adams & Love, 2005; Marchesani & Adams, 1992). Appendix 1.A provides a worksheet that accompanies the model (Figure 1.1).

As an overall organizer, this model enables us to take snapshots (i.e., our students, ourselves, our subject matter, our pedagogical process) of an extraordinarily complex moving picture which, in real life in the classroom, is a dynamic process by which each quadrant interacts simultaneously with the others. Focusing on each quadrant individually cannot itself reveal the complex interplay among and within these dimensions as they occur in real-time classroom interaction, but it does enable us to consider the characteristics of each quadrant before setting them back into dynamic interaction. The use of this teaching and learning model reflects both our need for order and

FIGURE 1.1
Dynamics of Multicultural Teaching and Learning

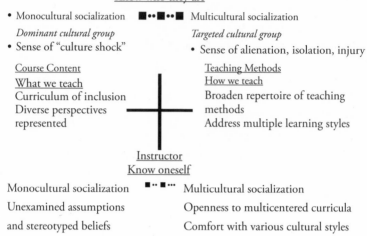

our recognition of the complexity of the multiple and layered dynamics of teaching and learning.

Quadrant 1: What Our Students as Active Participants Bring to the Classroom

In our experience with faculty colleagues, we find they prefer to begin the conversation with stories about their students rather than about themselves. Focusing on our students is often the way we talk with each other about the challenges and opportunities in our teaching, and starting at this point helps us examine our assumptions and, perhaps, misconceptions about our students, especially when their visible social identities differ from the visible social identities of the faculty. We encourage faculty to focus on dynamic interactions with all students, to notice whether those interactions differ with students who hold different social identities.

Faculty may describe classroom situations in which students interact or fail to interact with each other on the basis of their social identities and the stereotyped expectations that attach to those social identities. The scenarios described by one faculty member may be familiar to others. For example, students assembled in small groups for projects may reproduce the patterns of residential separation along racial or class lines that occur in their home-towns and neighborhoods. In small groups, women may take notes while men speak and take up greater physical and psychological space. Women may appear less comfortable challenging the authority of the teacher; the same may appear with students of color or international students. Male faculty may describe feeling more comfortable with challenges from White male students than from Black men or from women. These situations often refer forward to Quadrant 2, in which we ask faculty to explore their own social-ization and their unexamined assumptions about the "other," who, in this case, might well be their students.

Before doing so, however—especially if we are working in seminars with faculty who appear uncertain how to interpret and deal with classroom sce-narios such as these, and who may belong to social groups that have tradi-tionally had the dominant role in higher education—we might use one or more of the following questions to probe faculty analysis of who their stu-dents are and what their students bring to the classroom:

- Can you give examples of possible student-to-student interactions (or avoidance) based on their social identities?
- What have you noticed about and how have you accounted for differ-ences in ways that students of different or the same social identities may understand their own and each other's ways of communicating?
- What differences have you as faculty noticed in students' differing cultural and individual learning styles and communication and inter-action styles?
- What happens when you ask students to reflect on their differing per-spectives or their interactions on "hot button" social issues?
- What strategies do you utilize to plan for different levels of skill in, readiness for, and comfort with the subject matter in your classes?

In faculty seminars in which "knowing one's students" remains the pri-mary or exclusive focus for discussion and analysis, we introduce various organizers to engage faculty with considerations such as learning style and/or cognitive and social identity development (Adams, Bell, & Griffin, 2007, chapter 17; Anderson & Adams, 1992). *Learning style models* help faculty to design a range of learning environments that match some preferred cultural or individual student learning styles while at the same time stretching others.

Cognitive development models help faculty to understand the different levels of complexity with which students take in and process knowledge and to anticipate the tendency of some students to dichotomize complex questions, reducing multiple perspectives to simple either/or, right/wrong choices, although other students (often in the same classroom) work with the inherent messiness of real-world social issues and appreciate the multiple, differing perspectives held by their peers (Adams, Bell, & Griffin, 2007, chapter 17; King & Shuford, 1996; for application, see Adams & Marchesani, 1997). *Social identity models* enable faculty to understand and account for the possibility that students connected by seemingly same social identities may express very different responses (e.g., denial, anger, pain) to social issues in the classroom (Adams & Marchesani, 1997; Hardiman & Jackson, 1992; Wijeyesinghe & Jackson, 2001). Information about social identities is not important only to the instructor. It is also important for students to know about each other's social identities, as well as about their own, as a context for understanding their different perspectives on social justice issues.

Quadrant 2: *What We as Instructors Bring to the Classroom*

We believe that the teacher (i.e., professor, instructor, facilitator, mentor, and/or coach) is an integral contributor to classroom dynamics and not, as in more traditional accounts of teaching and learning, separate from considerations of subject matter and pedagogy, or from teacher-student interactions. Faculty enter the profession with knowledge and skills developed in a range of academic disciplines. This academic-discipline-based knowledge and skill, although obviously necessary for successful classroom teaching, is not sufficient for what we refer to as a social justice education perspective. Faculty begin to gain perspective on their social position in their classrooms (as distinct from, but interacting with their institutional authority) in many different ways. Faculty may reflect on their social interactions with people who are different from them. They may have noticed domination and subordination within the larger society and within the academy, or their own stereotypes about others and the roots of those stereotypes in their earlier experiences within their extended families, neighborhoods, schools, religious education, and workplaces.

Some faculty appreciate the opportunity to reflect more systematically on this prior socialization in a structured setting with colleagues; others find it troubling or are dismissive of the idea that they are perceived by their students in contexts of social group membership as well as in their institutional roles. Sometimes we find that faculty appreciate seeing self-knowledge exploration as an ongoing process modeled by the two of us as co-facilitators, so that they, too, can think about how to model self-awareness for their students. For example, we may choose to suggest how our approaches have been shaped over the years by our academic backgrounds—one of us in curriculum studies, the other in English literature—or that one of us was born in Philadelphia and the other in Dumas, Arkansas, or that between us we have taught a total of 80 years in public schools and universities and small private colleges. We may give examples of experiences that shape our choices as classroom facilitators, such as having been born and raised in the rural working class and urban professional middle class, being a European American and an African American, being Baptist and Jewish, and with English as our sole language, with local dialects and accents that signal racial, class, and geographical differences. These and other of our social identities and experiences have positioned us in relation to our students, to our colleagues at our home institutions, and to the faculty whom we join in seminars that explore a social justice perspective on our teaching practice. Various organizers, such as models of social identity awareness, models of socialization processes, self-awareness, and knowledge of social justice (content) issues are all components of this second quadrant on participant self-awareness (see chapter 16 in Adams, Bell, & Griffin, 2007; and Weinstein & Obear, 1992, for further discussion).

Social identity awareness includes analysis of one's multiple and interacting social identities (such as race and ethnicity or gender and sexuality) as well as one's identity statuses (i.e., dominant or subordinate) and the impact of those identities and identity statuses on various dimensions of one's classroom practice (e.g., subject matter, pedagogical process, interactions with students). Socialization awareness includes analysis of how we come to know ourselves as persons holding the particular identities we wear and the socialization impact on us of institutional and cultural systems, structures, and practices (see Harro, 2000a, 2000b; and Love, 2000, for texts that help generate discussion). Social justice issue awareness includes analysis of the consequences of societal structures of domination and subordination on the life chances and opportunities of people from different identity groups based on race, gender, class, sexuality, (dis)ability, religion, and primary language.

This includes an examination of the ways that power and privilege are connected to those identities and how power and privilege are reflected in the classroom and in the academy (see Goodman, 2001; Pharr, 1988; Wildman, 1996; Young, 1990, for useful texts to prompt discussion). Social justice facilitation issues include assessing readiness (in terms of support, passion, awareness, knowledge, skills), establishing effective learning environments, choosing appropriate leadership roles, and attending to a variety of leadership tasks (Adams, Bell, & Griffin, 2007, chapter 5).

Here are some areas in which we encourage faculty to engage in deeper analysis, using questions they have raised or classroom scenarios they have described or the data generated from one of the self-assessment instruments:

- Awareness of the ways in which power and privilege based on social group memberships affect student learning and teacher–student interactions
- Awareness of the ways in which power and privilege based on social group memberships are compounded by the power and privilege connected to faculty's educational status and institutional role
- Knowledge of the many different consequences for students and for faculty of their different histories of social domination and subordination, such as (limited) access to schooling, residential segregation, and (reduced) access to employment, health care, and legal protection
- Knowledge and skills to create intervention and action strategies for students, peers, and self, such as interrupting racist jokes, heterosexist innuendoes, and collegial evaluations of each other based on stereotyped assumptions (Delgado Bernal & Villalpando, 2002)

Faculty participants may understandably express frustration and anxiety when faced with the daunting task of developing their own self-awareness, correcting misinformation and misguided stereotypes, and developing new cross- or intergroup communication skills to better "read" the social dynamics of diversity and social justice within their own classrooms. As facilitators, we agree that this is indeed a formidable task. It is also a lifelong task, whereby our goal is not to be "experts" but seen by ourselves and our students as "works in progress." To strengthen the participant group's sense of shared challenge and common cause, we utilize a checklist and self-assessment we have devised based on a compilation of bias issues that in the past faculty members have reported to be most fearsome or formidable (Bell, Love, Washington, & Weinstein, 2007; Weinstein & Obear, 1992; see Appendix 1.B). Participants are often reassured by knowing that others before them faced the same fears and anxieties, and they are inspired to share stories that document their own experience or that illustrate their own fears. We treat this checklist as "fears," whether or not the items represent experiences that have actually happened.

Quadrant 3: The Curriculum, Materials, and Resources That Convey Course Content to Students

We encourage faculty to work in cross-departmental, cross-disciplinary, and cross-institutional settings that encourage cross-fertilization and multiple perspectives among participants. Faculty appreciate the opportunity to talk without fear of repercussion at their home institutions over the challenges they face in developing inclusive curricula or in identifying sources of institutional support. We asked questions designed to prompt insight and information, such as:

- What specific course content, exploratory issues, examples, and perspectives can be brought into your formal curriculum to enable students to see their social group perspectives and experiences as valued and represented?
- What are the ways that the curriculum can decenter the dominant worldview and incorporate multiple perspectives that reflect underrepresented peoples' viewpoints?
- Might these multiple perspectives be conveyed through her-/histories of the field, contributors to the field, the application of theories to under- or misdocumented populations, and the identification of new information sources for the field?
- What strategies or models do you as instructor use to examine your curriculum for inclusivity (e.g., the readings, films, videos; written, oral, visual assignments and outside projects; modes of assessment and examinations for final grades; collaborative and group communication skills; perspectives, information, and examples presented in lectures)?

We acknowledge that the task of reconceptualizing academic fields in order to make the teaching more inclusive is a daunting one, and one that may alienate more traditional colleagues. At the same time, we provide examples of how dramatically fields such as history, literature, and sociology have changed in recent decades and encourage faculty to look at the many journals within academic disciplines that focus on social justice, diversity, and teaching. Although it has generally been easier for faculty in the social sciences and humanities than for faculty in mathematics and the natural sciences to find curricular and pedagogical resources on inclusivity, diversity, and social justice, this situation is rapidly changing, with new resources that support the efforts of faculty in science and math to create more inclusive curricula, such as in ethnomathematics and new mathematics epistemology (Powell & Frankenstein, 1997; Steinbring, 2005), multicultural mathematics education (Hines, 2003; Leonard, 2008; Nasir & Cobb, 2007), and inspiring math literacy in the context of civil rights (Moses & Cobb, 2001).

We have found that faculty participants provide valuable, creative, often ingenious, curricular resources for each other as they talk about the challenges and opportunities for more inclusive curricula across their various disciplines. As part of our agreement prior to participation, we encourage faculty participants to commit themselves to carry out one specific curricular "change" project in the following year, and this prior commitment proves a powerful incentive for change. We suggest guidelines to help faculty identify specific elements in their curricular change project, one step at a time, and urge that participants see their curriculum change projects as works in progress (see Appendix 1.C).

Quadrant 4: The Pedagogical Processes Through Which the Course Content Is Delivered

An overarching principle of social justice education practice—that how we teach conveys powerful messages about what we teach—may sound counterintuitive, given the content-focus of most academic disciplinary and professional training. This focus on pedagogical process often poses a challenge for faculty trained in traditional lecture-and-listen, question-and-answer modalities within established academic disciplines. We try to provide rubrics and examples to develop interactive pedagogical strategies by which all students participate in their own learning and the learning of their peers. This is central to our core principle of active learning. We offer concrete examples of ways in which students can be helped to acknowledge and engage with contradictions to their current ways of knowing, and to develop more complex, informed perspectives on their own beliefs and the beliefs of others. Active learning occurs through interactive classroom dynamics that offer opportunities for students to question their previously held beliefs about themselves and about socially different "others" in light of new perspectives and information.

Faculty who are open to social justice education frameworks usually are aware that their teaching about social justice issues is not neutral. The challenges raised by inclusive curricula are emotionally loaded for students as well as for faculty and are linked to strongly held—and sometimes vehemently differing—beliefs, values, and feelings. It is often difficult for faculty, rigorously socialized in a tradition of objective, factual discourse, to acknowledge that strong feelings attach to different beliefs about and perspectives on "the facts."

Our social justice education framework includes attention to both the micro levels, of classroom and interpersonal interactions, and the macro levels, of institutional and systemic change. One level requires the knowledge and skills useful to faculty interested in teaching more inclusively. The other requires recognition of the complex nature of institutional structures, and the knowledge and skills as well as the support and alliances necessary to enact effective, sustainable institutional change. We encourage faculty to identify obstacles and opportunities within their campus and to identify and build support for this process as an ongoing endeavor. Most faculty are able to identify potential allies, both on the faculty and elsewhere on their campuses.

We further encourage faculty to link their individual goals with the articulated goals of their departments or campus in order to garner more sustained institutional support for their change efforts. For example, campus resources such as community service-learning programs, residential life programs, or campus outreach programs can be possible sources of networking and support, as can centers for teaching improvement and offices for diversity or multicultural affairs. Where colleges and universities exist in geographical proximity to other institutions, these networks can be developed across different campus networks.

Finally, we encourage faculty to use web-based communication, including bulletin boards, listservs, and e-mails as powerful tools for the exchange of ideas and resources that can make a difference and provide ongoing support for their change efforts.

We believe that working directly with faculty, both on the microdynamics of diversity in their classrooms and on the macrodynamics of change toward social justice in their institutions, is a challenging but also a rewarding endeavor. Although some faculty may express the view that creating more-inclusive classrooms and institutions is overly daunting, we have found that many faculty—whether beginning faculty or faculty well established in their careers—find the effort both professionally and personally rewarding. It is professionally rewarding when faculty find that many of their disciplinary peers are similarly rethinking their classrooms, their academic disciplines, and their institutional contexts. It is personally rewarding when faculty find that their teaching becomes more effective for all students and allows them to engage a wider range of students in learning.

References

Adams, M. (1992). Editor's notes. In M. Adams (Ed.), *Promoting diversity in college classrooms: Innovative responses for the curriculum, faculty, and institutions. New directions for teaching and learning, No. 52* (pp. 1–5). San Francisco: Jossey-Bass.

Adams, M., Bell, L. A., & Griffin, P. (2007). *Teaching for diversity and social justice* (2nd ed.). New York: Routledge.

Adams, M., & Love, B. J. (2005). Teaching with a social justice perspective: A model for faculty seminars across academic disciplines. In M. L. Ouellett (Ed.), *Teaching inclusively: Resources for course, department, and institutional change in higher education* (pp. 586–619). Stillwater, OK: New Forums Press.

Adams, M., & Marchesani, L. (1997). Multiple issues course overview. In M. Adams, L. A. Bell, & P. Griffin (Eds.), *Teaching for diversity and social justice: A sourcebook* (pp. 261–275). New York: Routledge.

Allport, G. W. (1954). *The nature of prejudice*. Reading, PA: Addison-Wesley.

Anderson, J. A., & Adams, M. (1992). Acknowledging the learning styles of diverse student populations: Implications for instructional design. In L. L. B. Border & N. V. T. Chism (Eds.), *Teaching for diversity. New directions for teaching and learning, No. 49* (pp. 19–33). San Francisco: Jossey-Bass.

Bauman, G. L., Bustillos, L. T., Bensimon, E. M., Brown, M. C., & Bartee, R. D. (2005). *Achieving equitable educational outcomes with all students: The institution's roles and responsibilities*. Washington, DC: Association of American Colleges and Universities.

Bell, L. A., Love, B. J., Washington, S., & Weinstein, J. (2007). Knowing ourselves as social justice educators. In M. Adams, L. A. Bell, & P. Griffin (Eds.), *Teaching for diversity and social justice* (2nd ed., pp. 381–394). New York: Routledge.

Bowen, W. G., & Bok, D. (1998). *The shape of the river: Long-term consequences of considering race in college and university admissions.* Princeton, NJ: Princeton University Press.

Brewer, M. B., & Brown, R. J. (1998). Intergroup relations. In D. T. Gilbert, S. T. Fiske, & G. Lindzey (Eds.), *Handbook of social psychology* (4th ed., pp. 554–595). Boston: McGraw Hill.

Brown, R. (1995). Reducing prejudice. In R. Brown (Ed.), *Prejudice: Its social psychology* (pp. 236–270). Oxford, UK: Blackwell.

Brown et al. v. Board of Education of Topeka, Shawnee County, Kansas, et al. (1954). 347 U.S. 483, 98 L.Ed. 873, 74 S.Ct. 686.

Chang, M. J. (2000/2001). The educational implications of affirmative action and crossing the color line. *Amerasian Journal, 26,* 67–84.

Chang, M. J. (2005). Reconsidering the diversity rationale. *Liberal Education, 91*(1), 6–13.

Clayton-Pedersen, A. R., Parker, S., Smith, D. G., Moreno, J. F., & Teraguchi, D. H. (2007). *Making a real difference with diversity: A guide in institutional change.* Washington, DC: Association of American Colleges and Universities.

Delgado Bernal, D., & Villalpando, O. (2002). An apartheid of knowledge in academia: The struggle over the "legitimate" knowledge of faculty of color. *Equity & Excellence in Education, 35*(2), 169–181.

Goodman, D. J. (2001). *Promoting diversity and social justice: Educating people from privileged groups.* Thousand Oaks, CA: Sage.

Grutter v. Bollinger et al. (2003). 539 U.S. 306.

Gurin, P., Dey, E., Hurtado, S., & Gurin, G. (2002). Diversity and higher education: Theory and impact on educational outcomes. *Harvard Educational Review, 72*(3), 330–366.

Hardiman, R., & Jackson, B. W. (1992). Racial identity development: Understanding racial dynamics in college classrooms and on campus. In M. Adams (Ed.), *Promoting diversity in college classrooms: Innovative responses for the curriculum, faculty, and institutions. New Directions for Teaching and Learning, No. 52* (pp. 21–37). San Francisco: Jossey-Bass.

Harro, B. (2000a). The cycle of liberation. In M. Adams, W. J. Blumenfeld, C. Castañeda, H. Hackman, M. Peters, & X. Zúñiga (Eds.), *Readings for diversity and social justice* (pp. 457–463). New York: Routledge.

Harro, B. (2000b). The cycle of socialization. In M. Adams, W. J. Blumenfeld, C. Castañeda, H. Hackman, M. Peters, & X. Zúñiga (Eds.), *Readings for diversity and social justice* (pp. 15–21). New York: Routledge.

Hines, S. M. (Ed.). (2003). *Multicultural science education: Theory, practice, and promise.* New York: Peter Lang.

Humphreys, D. (2000, Fall). National survey finds diversity requirements common around the country. *Diversity Digest.* Retrieved July 27, 2009, from http://www .diversityweb.org/digest/Foo/survey.html

King, P. M., & Shuford, B. C. (1996). A multicultural view is a more cognitively complex view: Cognitive development and multicultural education. *American Behavioral Scientist, 40*(2), 153–164.

Leonard, J. (2008). *Culturally specific pedagogy in the mathematics classroom: Strategies for teachers and students.* New York: Routledge.

Love, B. (2000). Developing a liberatory consciousness. In M. Adams, W. J. Blumenfeld, C. Castañeda, H. Hackman, M. Peters, & X. Zúñiga (Eds.), *Readings for diversity and social justice* (pp. 463–470). New York: Routledge.

Marchesani, L., & Adams, M. (1992). Dynamics of diversity in the teaching-learning process: A model for analysis. In M. Adams (Ed.), *Promoting diversity in the college classroom. New directions for teaching and learning, No. 52* (pp. 9–21). San Francisco: Jossey-Bass.

Milem, J. F. (2003). The educational benefits of diversity: Evidence from multiple sectors. In M. J. Chang, D. Witt, J. Jones, & K. Hakuta (Eds.), *Compelling interest: Examining the evidence on racial dynamics in colleges and universities* (pp. 126–169). Stanford, CA: Stanford University Press.

Milem, J. F., Chang., M. J., & Antonio, A. L. (2005). *Making diversity work on campus: A research-based perspective.* Washington, DC: Association of American Colleges and Universities.

Moses, R. P., & Cobb, C. E. (2001). *Radical equations: Math literacy and civil rights.* Boston: Beacon.

Nagda, B. A., Gurin, P., & Lopez, G. (2003). Transformative pedagogy for democracy and social justice. *Race, Ethnicity, and Education, 6*(2), 165–191.

Nasir, N. S., & Cobb, P. (2007). *Improving access to mathematics: Diversity and equity in the classroom.* New York: Teachers College Press.

National Center for Education Statistics (NCES), U.S. Department of Education. (2006). Digest of Education Statistics, 2005 (NCES 2006–005). Retrieved July 27, 2009, from http://nces.ed.gov/fastfacts/display.asp?id = 61 and http//nces.ed .gov/fastfacts/display.asp?id = 98

Orfield, G., & Kurlaender, M. (2001). *Diversity challenged: Evidence on the impact of affirmative action.* Cambridge, MA: Harvard Education Press.

Ouellett, M. L. (Ed.). (2005). *Teaching inclusively: Resources for course, department, and institutional change in higher education.* Stillwater, OK: New Forums Press.

Pettigrew, T. F. (1998). Intergroup contact theory. *Annual Review of Psychology, 49*, 65–85.

Pharr, S. (1988). *Homophobia: A weapon of sexism.* Inverness, CA: Chardon Press.

Powell, A. B., & Frankenstein, M. (Eds.). (1997). *Ethnomathematics: Challenging Eurocentrism in mathematics education.* Albany: State University of New York Press.

Steinbring, H. (2005). *The construction of new mathematical knowledge in classroom interaction: An epistemological perspective.* New York: Springer.

Weinstein, J., & Obear, K. (1992). Bias issues in the classroom: Encounters with the teaching self. In M. Adams (Ed.), *Promoting diversity in the college classroom. New directions for teaching and learning, No. 52* (pp. 39–50). San Francisco: Jossey-Bass.

Wijeyesinghe, C. L., & Jackson, B. W. (2001). *New perspectives on racial identity development: A theoretical and practical anthology.* New York: New York University Press.

Wildman, S. M. (1996). *Privilege revealed: How invisible preference undermines America.* New York: New York University Press.

Williams, D. A., Berger, J. B., & McClendon, S. A. (2005). *Toward a model of inclusive excellence and change in postsecondary institutions.* Washington, DC: Association of American Colleges and Universities.

Young, I. M. (1990). *Justice and the politics of difference.* Princeton, NJ: Princeton University Press.

Zúñiga, X., Nagda, B. A., Chesler, M., & Cytron-Walker, A. (2007). *Intergroup dialogues in higher education: Meaningful learning about social justice. ASHE-ERIC report series, Vol. 32.* San Francisco: Jossey-Bass.

APPENDIX 1.A

Four-Quadrant Model of the Dynamics of Diversity: Self-Assessment

(1) While listening to the presentation about the four quadrants of teaching and learning, reflect on what are for you the (felt) level of difficulty involved in imagining change in your own classroom on each of these four dimensions.

Use the scale for assessment:

1 = Low Level of Difficulty, 5 = High Level of Difficulty.
(low)   1   2   3   4   5   (high)

Knowing your students
(their social identities)

Knowing yourself
(your socialization)

More inclusive curriculum
(building in multiple perspectives)

Flexible teaching repertoire

(2) Note which quadrant poses the least difficulty for you, and which poses the greatest difficulty. Jot down what you believe are some reasons for these levels of difficulty, challenge, or sense of risk.

(3) Use the comparative levels of difficulty—and your sense of the reasons for them—to consider some of the specific challenges or obstacles (internal or external) that you may experience in attempting changes in any one of these four quadrants.

(4) Turn to the person next to you and talk about whatever insights you wish to share out of steps #2 or #3 in this activity.

(5) Brief open discussion about some of the challenges noted in your paired-sharing.

NOTE: As you think about your own "change plan" for later on, consider which quadrant you wish to focus on.

Adapted from L. Marchesani & M. Adams. (1992), "Dynamics of diversity in the teaching-learning process: A model for analysis," and M. Adams & B. J. Love (2005), "Teaching with a social justice perspective: A model for faculty seminars across academic disciplines."

APPENDIX 1.B

Self-Assessment of Vulnerabilities in Teaching

1. Write "yes" (I have felt this) or "no" (I have never felt this) next to each bullet.

- Confronting my own social and cultural identity conflicts
- Unexpectedly confronted stereotyped attitudes toward my social identity
- Felt guilty, ashamed, or embarrassed for behaviors or attitudes of others in my social identity group

2. Confronted my own biases [Respond "yes" or "no" regarding whether you feared these things would happen, whether or not they actually did]

- Being labeled racist, sexist, etc. by others
- Finding prejudice within myself while conducting a class
- Having to question my own assumptions in the midst of teaching
- Being corrected by members of targeted group
- Having to face my fears of targeted group while teaching or preparing to teach

3. Responding to biased comments [Respond "yes" or "no" regarding whether you feared these things would happen, whether or not they actually did]

- Having to respond to biased comments from targeted group
- Hearing biased comments from dominant group members in presence of target group members
- Having to respond to bias from members of my own social group

4. Doubts about my own competency [Respond based on fear]

- Having to expose my struggles with these issues
- Not knowing the appropriate terms or language
- Feeling uncertain about what I am saying

- Feeling like I can't unravel the complexities of the issue
- Being told that I don't know what I'm talking about
- Making a mistake

5. Need for learner approval

- Fear making students feel frustrated, frightened, or angry
- Leaving students feeling shaken, confused, and unable to fix things

6. Handling intense emotions in classroom, fear of losing control

- Not knowing how to respond to angry comments
- Having a discussion blow up
- Having anger directed at me
- Being overwhelmed by strong emotions
- Losing control of the classroom

Adapted from J. Weinstein & K. Obear (1992), "Bias issues in the classroom: Encounters with the teaching self," and M. Adams & B. J. Love (2005), "Teaching with a social justice perspective: A model for faculty seminars across academic disciplines."

APPENDIX 1.C

Dynamics of Diversity Change Plan

Refer back to your risk assessment in Appendix 1.A to focus on the quadrant that poses the greatest challenge and difficulty for you. Use that as a barometer to indicate where change would need to be most intentional.

Knowing your students (their social identities):

> What strategies or activities can I use to learn about my students' social identities?
>
> How can I help my students develop their own self-awareness of social identities?
>
> How can I enable my students to interact more effectively & consciously across their social identities?
>
> How can my students' social identities become a positive and intentional part of my classroom dynamics?

Knowing yourself (your socialization):

> How can I develop greater comfort in exploring my own social identities?
>
> How can I learn more about how my social identities affect my classroom comfort levels and presentation?
>
> What are the obstacles that prevent my developing a more flexible, interactive classroom pedagogy?
>
> What skills do I feel I should develop more fully to be a more effective classroom instructor & facilitator?

Inclusive curriculum (Building in multiple perspectives):

> What specific aspects of my course curriculum can I make more inclusive?
>
> How can I make my readings & resource materials more inclusive?
>
> How can I make my instructional examples more inclusive?

How can I draw upon the diversity in my classrooms to bring multiple perspectives into my course content?

Flexible teaching repertoire:

How can I begin to practice new, different instructional strategies?
How can I begin to develop new facilitative skills?
How can I remind myself to use a range of activities that may match or stretch different learning styles, as well as my own?
How can I encourage myself to try strategies that do not meet my own comfort zones?

Support and encouragement for change:

How can I establish the support I need from professional friends and colleagues?
How can I build the support I will need from my department and home institution?

Adapted from L. Marchesani & M. Adams (1992), "Dynamics of diversity in the teaching-learning process: A model for analysis," and M. Adams & B. J. Love (2005), "Teaching with a social justice perspective: A model for faculty seminars across academic disciplines."

2

LEARNING THROUGH STORY TYPES ABOUT RACE AND RACISM

Preparing Teachers for Social Justice

Lee Anne Bell

This chapter presents a theoretical and conceptual framework for teaching about racism through the arts using the metaphor of story and story types. Developed by the Storytelling Project at Barnard College in 2005–2007 (Bell, 2009; Bell & Roberts, forthcoming) and supported by funding from the Third Millennium Foundation, a creative team of artists, academics, public school teachers, and undergraduate students crafted the model we call the Storytelling Project model. In the second year of the project we field-tested the model in two high school classrooms and in teacher professional development in New York City. Since then, we have refined and presented the model at national conferences in higher education, where we have found that it can be flexibly adapted for use by college faculty in various disciplines and by staff in student affairs, community and adult education, and upper elementary/secondary classrooms.

Here I demonstrate the Storytelling Project Model, showing how it organized a seminar for students preparing for teacher certification while completing their liberal arts majors. First, I briefly talk about the context for using the model in teacher education. Then I present the model and the four story types: stock stories, concealed stories, resistance stories, and emerging/ transforming stories (see Figure 2.1.). Each story type is defined and discussed,

FIGURE 2.1
Storytelling Project Model

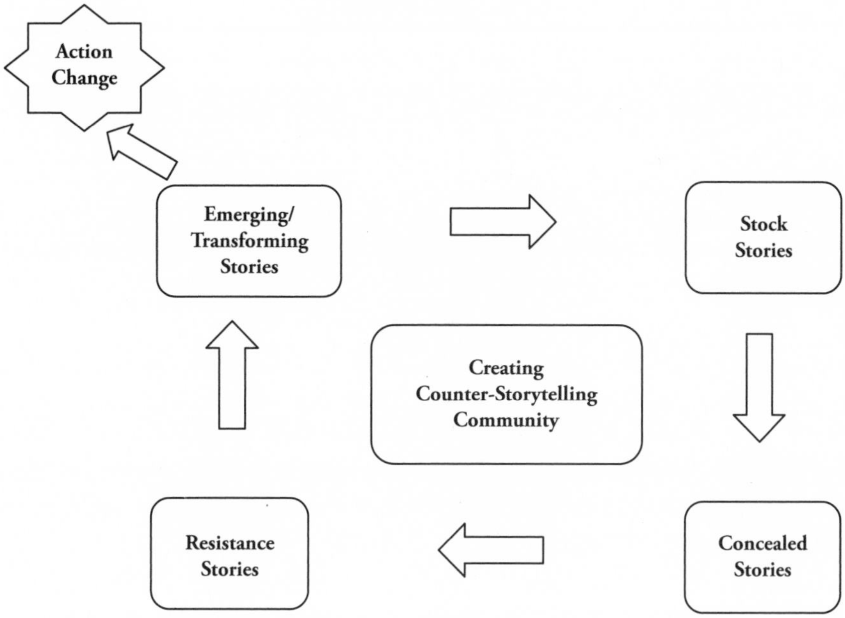

```
  ┌──────────┐
  │  Action  │
  │  Change  │
  └──────────┘
       ↖
  ┌────────────┐          ⇨          ┌──────────┐
  │ Emerging/  │                     │  Stock   │
  │Transforming│                     │ Stories  │
  │  Stories   │                     └──────────┘
  └────────────┘
       ⇧          ┌──────────────┐        ⇩
                  │   Creating   │
                  │Counter-Storytelling│
                  │  Community   │
                  └──────────────┘
  ┌────────────┐          ⇦          ┌──────────┐
  │ Resistance │                     │Concealed │
  │  Stories   │                     │ Stories  │
  └────────────┘                     └──────────┘
```

and illustrative excerpts from student papers are included. I conclude with a discussion of the strengths and weaknesses of the model for preparing undergraduates to promote equity and justice in the urban classrooms where they plan to teach.

The Context: Why Focus on Preparation for Anti-racist Teaching?

The United States is more racially, ethnically, and linguistically diverse than ever, and children of color, already a numerical majority in major U.S. cities, will soon be a majority of public school students overall (Villega & Lucas, 2002). In a sharp contrast to student diversity, close to 90% of teachers are White, middle-class, female, and English monolingual (NCES, 2007). Further, the already low numbers of people of color in teaching could drop by more than half unless active measures are taken to reverse this pattern (Dilworth, 2004).

The almost apartheid-like status (Kailin, 1999) of an overwhelmingly White teaching profession constitutes a serious crisis for education in our increasingly diverse nation. Although increasing the numbers of teachers of color is critical, preparing the White/Anglo majority of prospective teachers to become culturally responsive and knowledgeable about educational inequality is equally pressing. Strategies are needed to prepare all teachers to understand, analyze, and challenge racism and ethnocentrism in the larger society, because these affect school practices and procedures that differentially impact poor children, children of color, and children from diverse linguistic and cultural communities.

Although teachers from all racial and ethnic groups need education about racism and strategies to address it in their schools and classrooms, they often bring differing awareness and needs to this process. Even though teachers of color are less likely than White peers to deny the existence of racism or cling to naïve color blindness, they too can benefit from an opportunity to discuss and analyze their own experiences with racism in the broader society (Bell, 2003). White teachers, on the other hand, need to identify and examine their own socialization, the unearned advantages of White racial dominance, and conscious and tacit assumptions about race/racism. Teachers from all groups need skills for detecting bias in the classroom and curriculum, analyzing and confronting racism in school practices and helping students become future citizens prepared for fairness and justice in a multiracial democracy (Gordon, Della Piana, & Keleher, 1998).

The Storytelling Project focuses on race to explore both the overt and implicit knowledge that prospective teachers hold about race and racism, and to provide engaging strategies to teach knowledgeably, conscientiously, and ethically in communities they are likely to enter as privileged outsiders. Using the Storytelling Project Model in their seminar asks aspiring teachers to question the overt belief that they occupy racially neutral social positions and to expose how racism operates in this society and in the schools they will enter as teachers. It also asks them to think about the kind of society they wish for the future and to consider how they might teach toward this vision.

The Storytelling Project Model

Working within a social justice education paradigm that looks at diversity through the structural dynamics of power and privilege, the Storytelling

Project and the seminar discussed in this essay explore the potential of using story types and the arts as methods to enable teachers who are often positioned differently racially (and socioeconomically) than their students to constructively contend with racism in curriculum and school interactions. Through the model we at the Storytelling Project examine the role that storytelling plays in either reproducing or challenging the racial status quo through exploring both the power *in* stories and the power dynamics *around* stories as these shape learning and practice about race and racism. The model highlights how social location (i.e., positionality) affects the stories we construct and considers how in analyzing racial issues we might generate new ways to understand stories about race that account for power, privilege, and position. In particular, we explore the power of storytelling to expose and confront color-blind racism and to offer alternative tools to tackle racial issues consciously and proactively.

We focus on both diversity—how race is constructed as a form of difference—and social justice—the unequal ways in which social hierarchies sort difference to the benefit of some groups over others (Adams, Bell, & Griffin, 2007; Bell, 2007). Further, we offer creative strategies to teach about race and racism in ways that connect individual and psychological (i.e., micro-sociological) features with systemic/social features of racism (see, for example, Bell, Love, & Roberts, 2007).

We were drawn to story in developing the model because stories operate on both individual and collective levels and can thus build a bridge between the sociological/abstract and the psychological/personal contours of daily experience. As hooks notes, stories "can provide meaningful examples and ways to identify and connect" (hooks, 1989, p. 15). Thus, we see that story can be a potent vehicle for connecting individual experiences with systemic analysis, allowing us to unpack, in ways that are perhaps more accessible than abstract analysis alone, racism's hold on us even as we move through the institutions and cultural practices that sustain it.

Four key interacting concepts underpin our understanding of race and racism: race as a social construction; racism as an institutionalized system of hierarchy that operates on multiple levels; White supremacy/White privilege as key, though often neglected, aspects of systemic racism; and color blindness as a problematic notion that serves as both an ideal and barrier to racial progress. We also draw on scholarship in critical race theory (CRT). Like CRT scholars we see race and racism as central to our analysis of inequality.

Like them, we use the idea of counter-storytelling to denote stories that counteract or challenge the dominant story. However, we differentiate such stories into three types: concealed stories, resistance stories, and emerging/transforming stories. *Concealed stories* include narratives from minoritized groups that counteract the grand narratives (or stock stories) of the dominant group to reveal the strengths and capacities in marginalized communities that are so often ignored or devalued by mainstream society. *Concealed* and *resistance stories* expose and challenge normative White privilege and are usually related by members of marginalized groups, who usually see more clearly what those in the center take for granted, but can also be told by members of the dominant White group, who are in a position to expose the workings of privilege as insiders committed to working against racism. Emerging/transforming stories are new counter-stories people create, drawing from concealed and resistance stories, to challenge stock stories in the present.

At the center of the model is the creation of a counter-storytelling community, one in which we can build multiple connections among members to enable honest conversation about race and racism. We acknowledge the difficulty in telling stories that challenge dominance, especially in racially mixed groups, and want to be conscious about distributing risk fairly so as to constructively explore frequently painful questions about racism and how we are implicated in the systems that sustain it. We also want to foster hope and belief in our capacity to imagine and act to realize more just alternatives.

In order for storytelling in diverse groups to be meaningful and honest, we need to articulate the "terms of engagement" (hooks, 1989). In the Story-telling Project (STP) model, we ask the group to generate intentional guidelines that can support the counter-storytelling community and enable constructive dialogue about race and racism, emphasizing the need to acknowledge inequality embedded in the different social positions occupied by members of the group. How can we enable race and racism to be openly discussed, ensure that each person's voice and story will be respectfully heard, hold up and scrutinize all stories in terms of their relationship to systems of power and privilege, and interrupt practices of power that differentially privilege or mute particular stories (thus reproducing the system we hope to dismantle)? We set forth these intentions with the group and engage them in naming and practicing guidelines that support these intentions so that when conflicts or disagreements arise they can be used to facilitate thoughtful face-to-face exploration and resolution. We know that specific guidelines will likely differ from group to group. What matters is that guidelines be embraced by the group and conscientiously used to facilitate dialogue. Establishing such a community is an essential first step and foundation for effectively exploring the story types.

Illustrating the Story Types in a Seminar for Student Teachers

For the past three semesters I have used the STP curriculum and story types to frame a seminar for undergraduate student teachers. I structure the syllabus, readings and course sessions using the four story types, beginning with an exploration of what it means to build a counter-storytelling community where race and racism can be productively explored by people who are positioned differently by race. Seminar students use the story types in two ways: (1) as a set of lenses to examine and problematize their own socialization and assumptions about student and community assets in urban communities of color, the sources of problems facing urban schooling, the teacher's role, and the effects of racism on the institution of school, and (2) to think about and plan social-justice-oriented curriculum appropriate to their grade level/ subject, either implicitly, by using the story types to organize and plan curriculum, or explicitly, by teaching the story types directly to their students.

We begin by reading authors who problematize storytelling for both listener and teller. For example, we read an article that contrasts storytelling in three different groups (Sarris, 1990). In the first example, the author relates a Pomona Indian tale to a classroom of predominantly White, non-Indian students and notices how, semester after semester, what they remember and leave out of the story is shaped by the cultural lenses and experiences they bring to the telling. For the group in the second scenario, a classroom of Native students from the same community, the issue is not about understanding the stories they all know and share but about believing their stories matter in an often alien and alienating school context and coming to believe that they can speak back to the dominant story told by the mainstream curriculum. In a third class of minoritized students from different racialized groups, there is no shared cultural story; however, through juxtaposing stories they see the potential to develop a shared understanding of and shape a collective response to a system that denigrates them all. Similarly, a close reading of Toni Morrison's Nobel Prize acceptance speech (Morrison, 1993), which tells and retells a story from multiple perspectives, opens up our classroom to awareness of our positionality and power in stories we tell and destabilizes notions of a single "true" or "correct" story.

In our seminar we also look critically at empathy and question the capacity of those who are outside of an experience, particularly within hierarchical relations, to step into the shoes of the "other." We read excerpts from *Feeling Power* (Boler, 1999) in which the author defines the problem of passive empathy, challenging standard notions about this term. "These 'others' whose lives we imagine don't want empathy, they want justice. . . . What is at stake is not only the ability to empathize with the very distant other, but to recognize oneself as implicated in the social forces that create the climate of obstacles that other must confront" (p. 166).

These readings provide a frame for thinking about racial positionality and our responsibility (i.e., response-ability) to systems of oppression and lead to an examination of color blindness. We read an essay from *Seeing a Color-Blind Future* (Williams, 1998) in which the author explores the notion of color blindness through a story about her Black child's experience with his "color-blind" White teachers. This is invariably revealing for students because it so clearly illustrates the problems with color blindness. One White student teacher responds:

> I realized I had fallen into the stock story that I was not racist, that this was not my problem. I saw racism as something that I could help other people solve so they would not be discriminated against. I also hadn't understood until then how race (specifically) and privilege (generally) affected my relationships with people on individual levels, and the kind of difficult community building that is needed to lay these issues out on the table instead of only pretending they operated on some macro level, floating above our daily interactions.

Collectively, these readings open up the possibility for talking about race and racism with the recognition that White people are also racially positioned and inescapably implicated in the systems they wish to interrogate. The authors lay the groundwork for discussing ways to create community among a diverse group of people in which we are attentive to racial and other positionalities and strive to stay conscious of the hegemonic assumptions that often shape discourse. We develop guidelines both to construct our own learning community and to help students think about creating in their own classrooms the type of community where stretching beyond one's "comfort zone" (Griffin, 2007) is possible.

> My learning edge is pushing myself to be comfortable with all these discussions that make me uncomfortable, so that I can continually reevaluate my own racialized position with respect to that of my students . . . if I'm comfortable, change can't happen.

This discussion takes place just as student teachers are themselves entering a new elementary or high school placement, so creating a community and a classroom learning environment are very present in their minds. They become sensitized to noticing and looking at their own racial location, socialization, and experiences in relation to that of their students and begin to note ways that normative classroom discourse privileges and supports some students but silences or overlooks others. This connection is made by a Korean American student teacher who unearths and then compares her own early schooling experiences with that of a young student in her classroom as a way to try to understand and connect with her:

> I . . . remember that as a child I would yearn to see an Asian in my texts . . . a feeling of a longing to belong. In the classroom where I am student teaching, the majority of the texts have protagonists who are white. . . . On one of my first days [student teaching in 2nd grade], several girls asked if I was a sister to one of the Asian students in the class because, they said, "Your eyes look the same." The girl herself then proceeded to ask me if I was the same ethnicity as she and when I told her no [she was Chinese and I am Korean], she seemed disheartened. I felt as if she was looking to find something in me that is missing in the school. . . . This made me think about how important it is even for younger students to be validated in the curriculum.

Stock Stories

Having established norms in the seminar for recognizing racial positionality and talking openly about race, we move to a discussion of *stock* and *concealed stories* about race and racism, teaching and learning in urban schools. Stock stories are those told by the dominant group to rationalize the status quo by which they benefit. Such stories are passed on through historical and literary documents and celebrated through public rituals, law, the arts, education, and media representations. Because stock stories tell a great deal about what a society considers important and meaningful, they provide a useful starting point for analyzing how racism operates.

Throughout the seminar, student teachers use the story types to examine their own racialized narratives and locations, and to listen and learn from the stories of their students, families, and communities in order to critique stock stories about color-blind meritocracy. Through reading, observations in schools, analysis of popular culture, and autobiographical reflection, we look at stock stories about urban schools and communities and about youth of color—mainstream assumptions about what they need and deserve as evidenced in the material and human resources dedicated to their education. One student teacher, for example, reflects on the power dynamics obscured by stock stories about immigrant youth.

> Students who enter school speaking primarily Spanish, enter because succeeding in the United States demands some sort of working knowledge of English (and often fluency). Attendance is all but obligatory. The students who enter the school speaking English as their first language do so because they have made a decision to learn a second language. They have a choice. From the get go, the students speaking Spanish have no control over where they go, whereas the English-dominant students have agency and power in their world. . . . Working in a dual-language classroom in a country in which English is strongly reinforced as the "official" language, this message will always exist externally. All the more reason for what goes on in the classroom to be actively anti-racist, anti-oppression, and pro-social justice.

Concealed Stories

Concealed stories are the hidden (from the mainstream) stories told from the perspective of racially dominated groups, stories that can be uncovered by a critical analysis of statistics and social science data about the differing ways race shapes experience in our society. Concealed stories coexist alongside stock stories but most often remain in the shadows, hidden from mainstream view, and they provide a perspective that is often very different from that of the mainstream. Through concealed stories people who are marginalized, and often stigmatized, by the dominant society recount their experiences and critique or "talk back" to the mainstream narratives, portraying the strengths and capacities of their marginalized community, what Yosso calls "community cultural wealth" (Yosso, 2006) that are so often ignored or devalued by mainstream society. Levins Morales (1998) insists, "We must struggle to re-create the shattered knowledge of our humanity. It is in retelling of stories of victimization, recasting our roles from subhuman scapegoats to beings full of dignity and courage, that this becomes possible" (p. 13).

As students read articles and books that portray the history and struggles of communities of color to achieve a decent education for their children (e.g., Michie, 1999; Perry, Steele, & Hilliard, 2003; Valenzuela, 1999), they write about their own experiences of schooling and examine these alongside what they are reading and what they observe in their student teaching placements. This positioning of stories alongside other stories that challenge and talk back to them means that the "normative" story is up for question and analysis. White and middle-class students begin to see their own story not as right or normal but as one among many.

> The truth is that there is no such thing as an un-racialized situation. . . . The concealed story is that the colorblind mentality is detrimental to the goal of tolerance and equity. . . . to teach a child through your actions and words that their race doesn't matter is to belittle that child's very being, and the identity they have created for themselves up to this point. In addition, ignoring any influence of race prevents you as a teacher from identifying and challenging institutionalized racism.

The juxtaposition of stock and concealed stories also creates a more welcoming space for students of color in the seminar to explore their own racialized experiences and those of the students in their classrooms, relieving them of the pressure to engage in normative color-blind discourse.

> I have experienced being educated in a wealthy school and being educated in a not so wealthy school. For a few years I was in a predominantly white elementary school and I remember being in a classroom with about 20 other students. All the teachers were white and the school had state of the art facilities but what I remember most was how I was isolated (along with the rest of the minorities).
>
> I remember knowing that I wasn't like the rest of the kids. During recess, most of the minorities would play together. Although I was getting a great education, I was not socially accepted.

Together, students look at how stories about urban schooling are constructed to benefit some groups and disadvantage others and examine how such stories shape school policies, curriculum choices, grouping practices, relations with parents, and other issues. They analyze normative practices through questions such as, *In whose interest does this particular story operate? What concealed stories challenge or talk back to it?*

> Once I had begun to think about how power and privilege operate on personal, individual levels and as part of larger systemic machinations, it became a constant lens for me to use in analyzing my classroom and myself. I worried about the ways that I might be setting expectations at different levels, how my teaching might be missing or connecting with certain students, what it meant for me to be a white teacher in a classroom of students of color teaching and learning about racism, how the curriculum was or was not built off of their experiences, cultures, and interests, and a host of other concerns. These thoughts and conversations helped me to develop an entire way of thinking and looking at the world beyond the classroom and pushed my commitment to social justice in all areas of my life.

Resistance Stories

Resistance stories are the third story type of story in this model. These are stories, both historical and contemporary, that relate how people resist racism, challenge the stock stories that support it, and fight for more equal and inclusive social arrangements. Resistance stories include the reserve of stories built up through the ages about people and groups who have challenged an unjust racial status quo. They comprise stories of "sheroes" and "heroes" who have been excluded from history books (though sometimes included but vilified) but who have nevertheless struggled against racism. Too often, iconic stories of heroic individuals simplify resistance, sanitizing the collective struggles that drive social change, and thus fail to pass on necessary lessons about how social change actually comes about. Resistance stories teach about anti-racist perspectives and practices that have existed throughout history and thus expand our vision of what is possible in our own antiracism work today. *What stories (historical or contemporary) exist that serve as examples of resistance? What role does resistance play in challenging the stock stories about racism? What can we learn about anti-racist action from these stories?*

> As an educator, it is important to show students this system so that they are aware of what they're up against but also so that they know they are

not inherently at fault and can resist. Often what is left out is just as important as what is said. For example . . . much of what is left out from the Rosa Parks account speaks to the many levels in which [African American] culture is denigrated and history sugarcoated. The account leaves out details that could better encourage resistance to racism and also help to develop an empowering image of African Americans as resistors and activists within their community.[1]

As their critique develops, students begin looking for alternative stories and examples to inspire and guide them in their struggle to teach in a way that works for the interests of their students and against an unjust status quo. They use the story types to design lessons and discuss the importance of teaching resistance stories to youth to help them become critical thinkers who can analyze, and act as agents within, their own situations.

Emerging/Transforming Stories

Emerging/transforming stories are new stories deliberately constructed to challenge the *stock stories*, build on and amplify *concealed* and *resistance stories*, and offer ways to interrupt the status quo to work for change. Such stories enact continuing critique and resistance to the stock stories, subvert taken-for-granted racial patterns, and enable the imagination of new possibilities for an inclusive human community. Building on resistance stories, students begin to generate new stories in which they imagine alternative scenarios of racial equality and develop strategies to work toward the changes they envision. Guiding questions include, *What would it look like if we transformed the stock stories? What can we draw from resistance stories to create new stories about what ought to be? What kinds of communities based on justice can we imagine and then work to enact? What kinds of stories can support our ability to speak out and act where instances of racism occur?*

I believe that "truth" stories [those that counter stock stories], whether they hear/see one from someone such as a teacher or peer or whether they experience them for themselves, give students a chance to see and share the change and justice we want for the world, as well as to practice being agents themselves. "Acting in solidarity with others is a learned habit," and being able to participate in monologues or role-playing gives students their own voices and empowers them to see and share alternatives to the oppression they and others experience.

These four story types are intricately connected. Stock stories and concealed stories are in effect two sides of the same coin, reflecting on the same "realities" of social life, but from different perspectives. Resistance stories and emerging/transforming stories are also linked through their capacity to imagine and enact challenges to the stock stories. Resistance stories become the base on which emerging/transforming stories can be imagined and serve to energize their creation. Emerging/transforming stories then build anew as each generation engages with the struggles before them and learns from and builds on the resistance stories that preceded them. Story is the connective tissue of the model, and various art-based storytelling activities ground curriculum lesson plans.

Students write a concluding story paper in which they review the four story types to discuss what they have learned during the semester and what remains to be explored as they continue their growth as anti-racist educators. Using the story types as a framework and/or as content, they also design curriculum units in their respective subjects that support critical education. For example, some student teachers designed history units in which they introduce story types as analytic frames to examine classroom texts: They have their own students identify stock and concealed stories in history and search for historical examples of resistance to racism, then use this information as a basis for considering conditions today and their own responsibilities and opportunities for action. A student preparing to teach high school sciences designed a chemistry unit that looked at DNA to debunk the notion of racial categories and to help her students understand the social construction of race. Another student designed a middle school literature unit around concealed and resistance stories about racism in novels and poetry, drawing on contemporary youth hip-hop and spoken word.

Conclusions

Through the Storytelling Model we place diverse stories side by side as worthy of critical inspection and see that the mainstream story is not normative but one among many, and thus contestable. We learn to attend to stories from the margins as sources of crucial information our society needs if we are to realize our democratic ideals. The model offers a critical lens that can be applied to many areas of analysis and thus engages students in critical learning for social justice.

Although the Storytelling Project Model is effective at moving students to consider the problems of color blindness in teaching and to see the importance of understanding culture, institutional racism, and critical pedagogy to inform the creation of truly just classrooms, problems and contradictions remain. How far students get in the development of their analysis is very much shaped by where they begin. Many students simply do not yet have enough knowledge or models to apply a consistent critique. Without further support and learning, expanding their knowledge and awareness of racism and its historical and contemporary operations, it is not clear whether they will continue to develop a critical stance.

> I don't think that this will just happen one day, but rather will be a life-long process as a teacher. To be honest, it is very overwhelming to think of how much I don't know and how much I have to learn. However, reading about teachers such as Ms. Logan (Orenstein, 1994) and Mr. Michie (Michie, 1999) who were able to effect change in their classrooms, I am inspired and motivated to do the same because I see that it is possible.

Although students are inspired in the context of our course, how is it possible in one semester to build the awareness and knowledge to resist the constant recruitment back into the status quo that they will encounter in their lives and schools after graduation? Furthermore, even students who are the most knowledgeable, activist, and committed and who have sustaining systems of support often encounter a school culture that makes it exceedingly difficult to enact anti-racist curriculum and teaching practices.

Yet, without teachers who have a vision of what socially just teaching can be, there is little hope that we can create the kinds of classrooms and schools where all children see themselves as central to the curriculum and agents of their own lives. The Storytelling Project Model offers a framework that new teachers and others who work against racism in universities and communities can use to actively critique the *stock stories* about urban youth and schooling, to seek out *concealed* and *resistance stories* about their communities' history, struggles, strengths, and aspirations, and to develop *emerging/ transforming stories* to enact and sustain more inclusive and just educational practices.

Note

1. Refers to an essay by Herb Kohl (2004) in which the author challenges the typical representation of Rosa Parks' action, that she refused to vacate a White seat

on the bus because she was tired that day, by contextualizing her activism within a community of planning and support that was collective.

References

Adams, M., Bell, L. A., & Griffin, P. (2007). *Teaching for diversity and social justice* (2nd ed.). New York: Routledge.

Bell, L. A. (2003). Sincere fictions: The challenges of preparing white teachers for diverse classrooms. *Equity and Excellence in Education, 35*(3), 236–245.

Bell, L. A. (2007). Theoretical foundations for social justice education. In M. Adams, L. A. Bell, & P. Griffin (Eds.), *Teaching for diversity and social justice* (pp. 3–15). New York: Routledge.

Bell, L. A. (2009). The story of the storytelling project: An arts-based race and social justice curriculum. *Storytelling, Self and Society, 5*, 107–118.

Bell, L. A., Love, B. J., & Roberts, R. A. (2007). Racism and white privilege curriculum design. In M. Adams, L. A. Bell, & P. Griffin (Eds.), *Teaching for diversity and social justice* (pp. 123–144). New York: Routledge.

Bell, L. A., & Roberts, R. A. (forthcoming). The Storytelling Project Model: A theoretical framework for critical examination of racism through the arts. *Teachers College Record, 112*(9).

Boler, M. (1999). *Feeling power: Emotions and education.* New York: Routledge.

Dilworth, M. (2004, October). *Assessment of diversity in America's teaching force: A call to action.* Washington DC: National Collaborative on Diversity in the Teaching Force.

Gordon, R., Della Piana, L., & Keleher, T. (1998). *Facing the consequences: An examination of racial discrimination in public schools.* Oakland, CA: Applied Research Center.

Griffin, P. (2007). Conceptual foundations for social justice education: Introductory Modules. In M. Adams, L. A. Bell, & P. Griffin (Eds.), *Teaching for diversity and social justice* (pp. 48–66). New York: Routledge.

hooks, b. (1989). *Talking back: Thinking feminist, thinking Black.* Boston: South End Press.

Kailin, J. (1999). Preparing urban teachers for schools and communities: An antiracist perspective. *The High School Journal, 82*(2), 80–88.

Kohl, H. (2004). The politics of children's literature: What's wrong with the Rosa Parks story. In D. Menkart, D. Murray, & J. L. Roem, *Putting the movement back into civil rights teaching.* Washington DC: Teaching for Change.

Levins Morales, A. (1998). *Medicine stories: History, culture and the politics of integrity* (1st edition). Cambridge, MA: South End Press.

Michie, G. (1999). *Holler if you hear me: The education of a teacher and his students.* New York: Teachers College Press.

Morrison, T. (1993). Nobel Lecture: December 7, 1993. Nobel Foundation. http://nobelprize.org/nobel_prizes/literature/laureates/1993/morrison-lecture.html

National Center for Education Statistics (NCES), U.S. Department of Education. (2007). *Schools and staffing in the U.S.* Washington, DC: Author.

Orenstein, P. (1994). *Schoolgirls: Young women, self-esteem and the confidence gap.* New York: Doubleday.

Perry, T., Steele, C., & Hilliard, A. (2003). *Young, gifted and Black: Promoting high achievement among African American students.* Boston: Beacon Press.

Sarris, G. (1990). Storytelling in the classroom: Crossing vexed chasms. *College English, 52*(2), 169–185.

Valenzuela, A. (1999). *Subtractive schooling: U.S. Mexican youth and the politics of caring.* New York: SUNY Press.

Villega, A. M., & Lucas, T. (2002). *Educating culturally responsive teachers: A coherent approach.* New York: SUNY Press.

Williams, P. J. (1998). *Seeing a color-blind future: The paradox of race* (1st American ed.). New York: Noonday Press.

Yosso, T. (2006). *Critical race counterstories along the Chicana/o pipeline.* New York: Routledge.

3

ACADEMIC ACTIVISM AND THE SOCIALLY JUST ACADEMY

Glen David Kuecker

I n August 2006 a young boy approached Carlos Zorrilla in the small Ecuadorian mountain town of Apuela. Carlos, an area resident, was in town for a meeting of the local environmental organization that has been at the center of a grassroots struggle against a proposed, but yet to be built, open-pit copper mine (Kuecker, 2007). As if acting from a B-rated espionage movie script, the boy gave Carlos a brown paper bag loaded with documents from Ascendant Copper, a Canadian mining company planning to develop the mining project. The bag contained copies of company documents detailing its strategy for defeating the local resistance to their development plans. Among the documents was a letter written by Ascendant Copper to the Canadian ambassador in Ecuador. The letter replied to a human rights denunciation made against the company by the Intag Solidarity Network. I was the principal compiler of the information presented in the denunciation, and I am a cofounder of the Intag Solidarity Network. Ascendant Copper's letter accuses me of making false charges against the company, and supporting the violent actions of locals against the company, including arson and kidnapping. Once Carlos read the letter, which I now possess, he notified me that the company was making accusations against me. The Canadian government never made an effort to contact me concerning the issue, and I would have never known of Ascendant Copper's rebuttal if the document had not mysteriously fallen into Carlos's hands.

At roughly the same time as the boy slipped Carlos the bag of documents, Ascendant Copper was mobilizing its social capital. The company contacted two apparent acquaintances, both members of the board of trustees at DePauw University, where I am a tenured professor. On September 6, 2006, the company authored a letter to the dean of the faculty. It began, "I am writing to request your help in addressing the very disturbing and unprofessional conduct of Dr. Glen Kuecker." After offering some brief context, the writer continued, "On behalf of Ascendant, and in light of the detrimental influence Dr. Kuecker is having on DePauw's students and the university's overall reputation, I respectfully urge you to investigate his activities, and take appropriate and expeditious action to address them." In the five-page letter the company accused me of "[having] embarked on a concerted and coordinated campaign with a few extremist non-governmental organizations ('NGOs') to discredit Ascendant's record in Ecuador. Our work has been stymied, in gross violation of the rule of law, as Dr. Kuecker and his associates have sought to bully, intimidate, and force us to abandon our legally held concessions in Ecuador." The company repeated accusations that I supported arson and kidnapping. When the university provided me a copy of this letter, I immediately thought that I was going to be fired. I wondered how my efforts at advocating for human rights had reached this rather absurd situation.

Since coming to DePauw University in 1998, I have gradually developed a pedagogy that integrates research, writing, and teaching with activism. I have come to call this pedagogy "academic activism." Praxis is the guiding principle for this pedagogy: My experiences in the field have shaped my research and writing, which has influenced the course topics I teach, their content, and how I teach them. An added element builds on this not-so-unique pedagogy, because these research, writing, and teaching projects frequently draw me into activist work, especially solidarity projects in those places where I have done fieldwork. Through this element of activism I contribute toward answering the challenge, How do we go about constructing a "socially just" academy?

Becoming an Academic Activist

This process of becoming an academic activist started somewhat modestly. As other academics have done, I helped organize a student trip to the School of the Americas vigil at Fort Benning, Georgia, in 1999. The following year, I brought a group of students to Chiapas and Guerrero, Mexico, as part of a

January term project about indigenous resistance to globalization. This trip was organized with the Mexico Solidarity Network, and was linked to a fall semester course on the topic of globalization and social movements in Latin America. Subsequently, I organized multiple alternative spring and fall break trips for students to Guerrero, Mexico, where we did a "reality tour" with a local human rights organization. In the summer of 2001 I joined a Witness for Peace delegation to Colombia, and on my return participated in an act of nonviolent protest with other delegation members at the School of the Americas, which resulted in my arrest for trespassing on a military base and destruction of federal property (we spilled red paint that represented blood on the road). In 2000, I began working in Ecuador, and a former student invited me to visit the communities resisting mining. Subsequently, I organized several alternative fall and spring break trips to these communities, and I taught a January term class that traveled to these communities, again within the topic of grassroots resistance to globalization. I also organized summer trips to Ecuador that involved several university alumni. Through organizing these teaching trips, I had become sufficiently knowledgeable about the struggle against mining and began doing research and writing about the resistance movement.

In the process of teaching, research, and writing, it became overwhelmingly apparent to me that conflict between the mining company and the communities was escalating to a dangerous point. In the summer of 2004, conversations began with community members about forming an international human rights observation team that would live in the community most threatened by the mining company's presence. In the spring of 2005 the first observers, two DePauw University alumni, arrived in Ecuador. In the summer of 2006, there was sufficient evidence to indicate that the company may have been preparing to use violence in order to eliminate the resistance and was paramilitarizing the region. It was at this point that Intag Solidarity Network, which oversees the human rights project, sent the human rights denunciation to the Canadian embassy.

The academic activist pedagogy, although undoubtedly causing headaches for administrators obligated to protect the financial and symbolic capital of the university, has been productive. The process led me to write about the resistance in Ecuador, and those publications resulted in my co-editing a volume on social movements in Latin America (i.e., Stahler-Sholk, Vanden, & Kuecker, 2008). Research and writing dovetailed nicely, in that liberal arts kind of way, with teaching. The research and solidarity work led to significant development of my courses on globalization and social movements, but also pushed me to teach a first-year seminar on the topic of academic activism. The solidarity work involved a very steep learning curve about the mining political economy and pushed me toward more formal considerations about the environment. All of these resulted in more effective communication with students, especially a growing cadre of DePauw University students seeking a socially just academy. The work in Ecuador also resulted in new projects, especially a collaboration with the Globalism Research Center at RMIT University, Melbourne University. I currently work with the Center on Field Research in Papua New Guinea, where indigenous communities are fighting against mining including a somewhat fantastical plan for sea-bed mining along the coast. One area of our work has been more methodically thinking about how the academy should interact with communities in resistance. This work has resulted in a deliberate process of unpacking the meaning of solidarity work in general, and academic activist work in particular.

Unpacking Solidarity

The process of producing scholarship derived from solidarity work and teaching about those experiences led me to understand that solidarity is a social relationship, a particular type of bonding between human actors. It happens when one joins into a collective responsibility by moving away from comfortable, known, and safe social practices and entering into less known, unpredictable, and potentially dangerous situations. The idea of collective responsibility is what inspires us to run the same risk as others because the collective ideal appeals to our humane capacity for empathy and a sense of shared belonging. Solidarity requires trust between the parties constituting the relationship. That trust constitutes an unwritten social contract premised on reciprocity and mutual understanding. Solidarity requires a level of consciousness and awareness between parties that is embedded in the interactive processes of structure and agency. Those in solidarity have undergone the transformation from the "I" narrative to the "we" narrative. Solidarity is a political form of social behavior, and is often aimed at addressing an injustice. It bridges between the local and global, and it is built on the experience of real face-to-face social interaction. However, it also requires its participants to engage in the abstraction of "imagined community." As a social reality, solidarity shares common ground with the practice and abstraction of community and radical forms of citizenship. Those things that make community sustainable are core components to solidarity, and an expanded understanding of citizenship—Carlos Vilas (1997) offers seven components of citizenship: democracy, accountability, equity, shared sense of belonging, empathy, equality, autonomy—is basic to solidarity. The commonality of core elements means effective solidarity is entwined with sustainable community and citizenship.

To be in solidarity is an exceptionally difficult proposition because of unequal power relationships between parties, which will be discussed in this chapter in a section on power. For now, let's establish that solidarity most often involves actions between persons or groups in unequal positions of power, in which the person or group enjoying a privileged position in the structural domains of power acts to support the project of a person or group in a less privileged position of power. The inherent inequalities in the solidarity relationship subvert, if not openly contradict, the basic definitions of solidarity.

The difficulty in solidarity projects resides in the challenge of mitigating the negative consequences of power differentials. Some argue that the only way to reduce the negative is by purging one's power, but others maintain that the best path is to leverage one's position of power. In either case, we find an act of solidarity. Although purging one's power may appear the purest, truest form of solidarity, it also carries the potential for limiting the ability of an actor to challenge the system of power, presumably a goal of solidarity. We almost always find that the person who purged power retains the artifacts of that power, especially in domains of formal education, cosmopolitan experience, and ability to maneuver within the structures of power. This retention often puts people in positions of leadership despite their efforts at not leading. The example of Subcomandante Marcos illustrates this point. He stripped himself of bourgeois life, leaving a professorial job in Mexico City to become a revolutionary in Chiapas. Marcos was forced to drop the top-down Guevarist *foco* strategy and dive deeper into equalizing power relations by subordinating himself to the indigenous communities he intended to revolutionize. Instead of transforming the indigenous, they transformed him. Despite the real and significant inversions of power relationships, the artifacts of his position of privilege remain. Although Marcos "leads by following," he retains the power of representation, as the movement's "spokesperson," something that makes him an irreplaceable character for indigenous/local articulations to the world as well as for the world's relationship with the Zapatistas (Gossen, 1995; Guillermoprieto, 2002; Henck, 2006).

The challenge is even steeper for the academic seeking to do scholarship driven by solidarity. It is exceptionally difficult for us scholars to accomplish solidarity with those we study. Higher education has become structured to prevent solidarity (I deliberately give this sentence the passive voice to emphasize the structural nature of the problem). The divide between objectivity and subjectivity, so nicely critiqued by bell hooks in her *Teaching to Transgress* (1994), provides one reason. Scholars are expected to leave their politics, emotions, and passion outside the university and enter it with only reason. The disembodied scholar serves as the dispenser of knowledge to society, which trusts our teachings to be nothing but the objective pursuit of truth. As Paulo Freire (1993) informs, production and dissemination of knowledge by means of the "banking system" of education carries exceedingly unequal relations of power between academics and society. Two realities are obscured in the process. First, the subjectivity of the scholar does not necessarily undermine pursuit of knowledge by reason. If anything, embracing subjectivity makes the pursuit more honest. Second, higher education serves the capitalist market, which is a highly subjective reality especially when it uncritically advances the ideological project of neoliberalism (McLaren, 2005).

In the "post-social" world of neoliberal higher education, community service and service-learning are presented as objective social goods, void of ideology, politics, and subjectivity. Activist scholarship, however, is seen as flawed by the prejudices of the scholar, a betrayal of the sanctity of reason. These lessons are taught throughout our learning careers but become professional norms in graduate school by making us "experts" in the field and socializing us to a set of discipline-specific norms. Academics learn quickly that being political can kill your chances at getting grants, finding a job, and securing tenure (Giroux, 1988). For example, I am often at a loss about where on my *curriculum vitae* to put the fact that my academic work contributed to the defense of one of the most biodiverse regions on earth and helped to defeat a transnational mining company, or that my research, writing, and teaching helped to defend the human rights of people in Ecuador. In the

United States, with the likes of David Horowitz (2006, 2007) fanatically pursuing a witch hunt of radical professors, even those with tenure can be fired for their politics. Additionally, academics are overwhelmingly bourgeois in outlook and action. Our bourgeois sentiments can lead to radical analysis but seldom lead to direct action, stepping beyond the comfort zone to undertake acts of solidarity, especially if those acts might threaten our material comforts and privileged positions of being paid to think.

Pedagogy of Academic Activism

Unpacking the meaning of solidarity in academic activism invites consideration of how solidarity and pedagogy are related. The radical pedagogy of Paulo Freire (1993) provides two key points for unpacking the meaning of solidarity. The first is a theory of education for marginalized people; the second is a theory of education for the privileged. For the marginalized, it is a system of education that recognizes the legitimacy of their life knowledge and uses that knowledge as the vehicle for advancing formal education. It emphasizes lived experience, which promotes a praxis model for educators. It also aims to equalize power relationships between student and teacher, in which the "banking model" of teaching is replaced with teacher as facilitator. The replacement subverts the traditional teacher–student power dynamic in which the teacher enjoys the privileged position of subjectivity and the student is subordinated in a passive, objective place. Freire's method equalizes the teacher–student relationship by decreasing the relative subjectivity of the teacher by transforming the passive student object into an active learning subject. On the second front—Freire's theory of education for the privileged—the focus is on critical self-reflection for those in positions of relative power. Freire challenges us to understand that the oppressor is perhaps in as much need of liberation as the oppressed. This approach opens vistas to power relationships, especially in terms of race, class, and gender privilege, as well as between the Global North and South, and can make solidarity a possibility by allowing for border crossings (McLaren, 1999).

Pedagogy and solidarity have clear connections in that a theory of teaching and learning, especially in its radical articulation, can inform our acts of solidarity, especially in the area of critical self-reflection and consciousness. Of special importance to the connection is the idea of "process" in solidarity work. It is one of the terms most frequently used by the grassroots and, to a more limited degree, by academics working with organizations. Process is the method of solidarity, the quotidian muddling through the dynamics of the relationship between academic and community. Process is the give-and-take of lived experience that defines Freire's radical pedagogy, the laboratory of knowledge production generated through solidarity work. It is the structure–agency interaction where the subjectivity of the academic meets the community-object and the subjectivity of community interacts with the academic-object, often in challenging ways, and provides the material of self-reflection demanded by solidarity. Process is the working through of complex power relationships at play between academic and community.

The idea of "process" highlights the fluidity and movement of solidarity, as well as its instability. Its movement suggests solidarity is a process of crossing borders. Henry Giroux (1991)—taking from writers like Gloria Anzaldúa (1999)—offers insights about the importance of border crossing for thinking about solidarity. He develops the idea of "border pedagogy" as a way to embrace the importance of "difference as part of a common struggle to extend the quality of public life" (Giroux, 1991, p. 51). In the interaction between solidarity partners, "the category of border signals in the metaphorical and literal sense how power is inscribed differently on the body, culture, history, space, land, and psyche. Borders elicit a recognition of those epistemological, political, cultural, and social boundaries" (p. 51). The recognition of borders allows a questioning of "the language of history, power, and difference. . . . It signals forms of transgression in which existing borders forged in domination can be challenged and redefined" (p. 51). Giroux explains, "border pedagogy serves to make visible the historically and socially constructed strengths and limitations of those places and borders we inherit and which frame our discourses and social relations. Moreover, as part of a broader politics of difference, border pedagogy makes primary the language of the political and ethical. It stresses the political by examining how institutions, knowledge, and social relations are inscribed in power differently; it highlights the ethical by examining how the shifting relations of knowing, acting, and subjectivity are constructed in spaces and social relationship[s]" (p. 52).

Giroux's "border pedagogy" illustrates that the work of academic solidarity subverts the closed, hierarchical, institutional places of academia, opening it up to a process of democratization by engaging in the fluid, contested, and unstable spaces of the public. When undertaking solidarity work academics "cross over into realms of meaning, maps of knowledge, social relations and values that are increasingly being negotiated and rewritten as the codes and regulations that organize them become destabilized and reshaped. Border pedagogy decenters as it remaps. The terrain of [research] becomes inextricably linked to the shifting parameters of place, identity, history, and power" (Giroux, 1991, p. 53).

The relationship between pedagogy and solidarity is also important because teaching is embedded in a place. The place of pedagogy is the university, a structure that allows the production and dissemination of knowledge. As a place of instruction, the university separates academics from the world, ostensibly generating a place of contemplation and safety from political agendas that would assault academic freedom. The removal from the world replicates what bell hooks identifies as the mind/body division of the classroom, where the university becomes a place where reason rules over emotion, but at the expense of effective teaching and thinking. The result is a remarkably artificial and often hypocritical place, one where professorial claims of objective positioning masquerade as thought but mask the highly subjective, political, and ideological nature of 21st century academia. The place of pedagogy becomes especially contorted when it transcends the university and engages the "real world" through projects like civic engagement and service-learning. The contortion happens because the mind/body, objective/subjective problematic is projected, but in an inverted fashion, onto the object of service and allows for the university's transcendence, making solidarity between academic and community nearly impossible. A possible solution to the problem is constructing autonomy within the structure of producing and disseminating knowledge, a situation in which the university is liberated from commands of capitalism. Metaphorically, autonomy would be a university without walls, where the separation between academia and community is eliminated. One example of this idea is Mexico Solidarity Network's autonomous university (www.mexicosolidarity.org/studyabroad). Barring autonomy, the only other path is to reduce the contortion by adopting a radical pedagogy.

Navigating Power Relationships

The interaction between pedagogy and solidarity, as suggested by the idea of autonomy, concerns power relationships. Power is the ability to influence circumstances toward desired outcomes. Power is positional and relational, making it a spatial human reality, one defined by the interaction between structure and agency. A given agent's power is defined by the ability to control, manipulate, or direct the matrix of social, political, economic, and cultural relationships—structures defining everyday life. As John Holloway (2002) makes clear in his analysis of Marx's notion of alienation, the central question of power is the distinction between "power over" and "power to." For Holloway, the central question is the objective of power, what the agent does with its positional and relational place within the structures. "Power over" finds agents seeking dominance and control over the structures and other agents, and the goal of domination and control is keeping or enhancing the existing position and relation of power. "Power to" finds agents seeking equity and equality between agents within the structures. The ideal state, one advocated by anarchists, is purely horizontal positions and relations of power in which all relations of power are distributed equally. "Power to" is the unity of collective action, the notion of community, and the commons that defines and animates the ideal state of solidarity (Holloway, 2002).

Power is deeply embedded in the relationship between solidarity's pedagogy of "process" and of "place." David Slater (2004), in exploring the postcolonial problem of how Western academia generates silences within third world academia by exclusion from knowledge production, raises the theme of "reflexivity and the geopolitics of knowledge" (pp. 28–29). He states,

> a key part of thinking critically involves the situatedness of knowledge, the geographies of reference and the positionality of the writer. . . . The geopolitics of knowledge can help us raise questions that go beyond the thematic and conceptual contours of writing and focus more on the spatial contextualizations of analysis itself. This contextualization has frequently been tied to a Euro-Americanist frame, and generalizations have been made which are rooted in the implicit universality of the West (Slater, 2004, pp. 28–29).

The process of breaking through colonial barriers and entering a condition of solidarity requires the Global North academic to be critically aware of the position of power that produces knowledge. This reflective mapping is central to Giroux's notion of border crossing, and it is central to the work of Chandra Talpade Mohanty (2003). She begins her book *Feminism Without Borders*, perhaps the best analysis of academic solidarity, by positioning her place in the world, geographically as well as in terms of race, class, and gender. She situates herself within Slater's "geopolitics of knowledge," although recognizing her place as a border crosser. As a female, South Asian, native of Mumbai, living and working in the United States, Mohanty takes on the positionality of a postcolonial academic, one with multiple identities embedded in multiple localities that force her to navigate multiple identity borders. The geography of solidarity, the ability to identify the differences of race, class, and gender borders in order to transcend the differences in acts of solidarity, requires a pedagogy of critical consciousness about where one is located as well as those one pretends to be in solidarity with. As Mohanty's book illustrates, navigating the borders is essential to a pedagogy of solidarity and postcolonial struggle.

Power also concerns the Gramscian proposition of cultural hegemony. In this formulation, power is an elite-generated consensus about the configuration of structural relationships. It is common sense, the unquestioning acceptance of positions and relations of power, that defines power's purest form (Lears, 1985). This ideological formation of power pertains directly to the problem of consciousness embedded in the pedagogy of solidarity. The process of solidarity questions hegemonic structures. To be in solidarity this pedagogy must be radical; the "process" of questioning power needs to be a mutual project of collective action. A pedagogy of solidarity constitutes a counterhegemonic project in that the consciousness required for a pedagogy of solidarity presumes a political and ideological project.

Praxis and the Socially Just University

The triangular relationship among pedagogy, power, and solidarity points us to the key concept of praxis. Discontent over the Enlightenment's mixed success with the project of human liberation and a perceived sluggishness in the progressive history of humanity's perfection led social theorists to the concept of praxis. It is at once inherent to the Enlightenment and a rejection of its historical product. Praxis carries with it the Enlightenment conviction that human agency can alter the structures that define the possibilities of that agency. We might consider the implications of praxis with Marx's passage in the *Eighteenth Brumaire of Louis Bonaparte* (1852/1999): "Men make their own history, but they do not make it as they please; they do not make it under self-selected circumstances, but under circumstances existing already, given and transmitted from the past." Praxis is the product of agency, the conscious and willed attempt by humans to transform the structures that conspire to undermine humanity's perfectibility. It is the transformation of theory through a deliberate application of theory to social reality, or what is termed "practice." Not only is praxis the transformation of theory, but it also causes societal change as well as the transformation of those who practice it. In London's Highgate Cemetery, the idea of praxis is inscribed on Marx's gravestone: "Philosophers have interpreted the world in various ways, the point however is to change it."

The transformative idea of praxis is where the tensions between solidarity and academic generate conflict. As we use knowledge derived from solidarity work to produce a deliberate pedagogy, a consequence can be substantive challenges to the relations of power within the university, especially if the pedagogy of academic activism calls on the university to take political positions. When praxis prompts institutional transformation, the university's need to protect financial and symbolic capital may trump solidarity and compromise claims to a socially just academy.

In the final analysis, where does the proposition of academic activism stand in relation to the proposition of a socially just university? On one level it illustrates the importance of pushing the boundaries of higher education, especially into controversial areas of the public. For many academics, such as Stanley Fish (2008), this pushing is an inappropriate political intervention that corrupts the objective production and dissemination of knowledge, yet evidence presented here shows how academic activism advances the frontier's knowledge. There is, however, the not-so-subtle problem of the limitations of activist work conducted within the confines of the university. Thankfully, I was not fired. However, often this may not be the case, especially if a university's financial and symbolic capital is risked by academic activism. When institutional interest, driven by a threat of a lawsuit, trumps academic activism, has the socially just institution been irreparably compromised? Sorting out these questions will become increasingly important as liberal arts colleges increasingly move toward teaching social justice issues that are directly engaged with communities experiencing inequity and injustice. As we move in this direction, it is well possible that more Ascendant Coppers will write letters to DePauw Universities, and the thorny issues surrounding the relationships among research, writing, teaching, and activism will increase in number and complexity.

As we wrestle with the challenges of building a socially just academy, academics, students, administrators, and the public will confront two interconnected issues. First, the administrative problem of risk management needs to be explored critically from the perspective of what we mean by "socially just academy." On this point, we might take from those who have explored Michel Foucault's "governmentality," especially the ways neoliberal capitalism places university within a political economy of the "post-social," and how this placement generates an administrative pedagogy of "prudentialism" that frames a rubric of power defining permissible forms of teaching, research, and writing (Berry, Osborne, & Rose, 1996; Dean, 1999). Second, we need to critically examine how this postsocial "governmentality" defines faculty development programs, and how faculty internalize the imperative of administrative prudentialism. In particular, we need to explore the tension, if not contradiction, between the critical pedagogy inherent to the proposition of a socially just academy and the realities of education in a capitalist society.

References

Anzaldúa, G. (1999). *Borderlands/la frontera: The new mestiza* (2nd ed.). San Francisco: Aunt Lute Books.

Berry, A., Osborne, T., & Rose, N. (Eds.). (1996). *Foucault and political reason: Liberalism, neo-liberalism, and rationalities of government.* Chicago: University of Chicago Press.

Dean, M. (1999). *Governmentality: Power and rule in modern society.* Thousand Oaks, CA: Sage.

Fish, S. (2008). *Save the world on your own time.* New York: Oxford University Press.

Freire, P. (1993). *Pedagogy of the oppressed.* New York: Continuum.

Giroux, H. (1988). *Teachers as intellectuals: Towards a critical pedagogy of learning.* South Hadley, MA: Bergin & Garvey.

Giroux, H. (1991). Border pedagogy and the politics of postmodernism. *Social Text, 28,* 51–61.

Gossen, G. (1995). Who is the comandante of subcomandante Marcos? In K. Gosner & A. Ouwenell (Eds.), *Indigenous revolts in Chiapas and the Andean highlands* (pp. 107–119). Amsterdam: CEDLA.

Guillermoprieto, A. (2002). The unmasking. In T. Hayden (Ed.), *The Zapatista reader* (pp. 33–45). New York: Thunder's Mouth Press/Nation Books.

Henck, N. (2006). *Subcommander Marcos: The man and the mask.* Durham, NC: Duke University Press.

Holloway, J. (2002). *Change the world without taking power: The meaning of revolution today.* London: Pluto Press.

hooks, b. (1994). *Teaching to transgress: Education as the practice of freedom.* New York: Routledge.

Horowitz, D. (2006). *The professors: The 101 most dangerous academics in America.* Washington, DC: Regnery.

Horowitz, D. (2007). *Indoctrination U: The left's war against academic freedom.* New York: Encounter Books.

Kuecker, G. (2007, March). Fighting for the forests: Grassroots resistance to mining in northern Ecuador. *Latin American Perspectives, 34*(2), 94–107.

Lears, T. J. J. (1985, June). The concept of cultural hegemony: Problems and possibilities. *American Historical Review, 90*(3), 567–593.

Marx, K. (1999). The eighteenth brumaire of Louis Bonaparte (S. K. Padover & Progress Publishers, Trans.). Retrieved October 4, 2008, from http://www.marxists .org/archive/marx/works/1852/18th-brumaire/index.htm (Original work published 1852)

McLaren, P. (1999). *Che Guevara, Paulo Freire, and the pedagogy of revolution.* Lanham, MD: Rowman & Littlefield.

McLaren, P. (2005). *Capitalists and conquerors: A critical pedagogy against empire.* New York: Rowman and Littlefield.

Mohanty, C. (2003). *Feminism without borders: Decolonizing theory, practicing solidarity.* Durham, NC: Duke University Press.

Slater, D. (2004). *Geopolitics and the post-colonial: Rethinking north-south relations.* Oxford: Blackwell.

Stahler-Sholk, R., Vanden, H., & Kuecker, G. (Eds.). (2008). *Latin American social movements in the twenty-first century: Resistance, power, and democracy.* Lanham, MD: Rowman and Littlefield.

Vilas, C. (1997, July/August). Inequality and the dismantling of citizenship in Latin America. *NACLA Report on the Americas, 31*, 57–63.

4

FROM SCIENTIFIC IMAGINATION TO ETHICAL INSIGHT

The Necessity of Personal Experience in Moral Agency

Arthur Zajonc

I am not a professional philosopher or ethicist, and so will approach the subject of social justice through my experience with the sciences but also as a teacher interested in exploring the relationship among science, the humanities, and the contemplative traditions.

From my work in physics, I have come to appreciate the several factors that are part of scientific progress. Although experimentation and mathematical analysis are key components of my discipline, the use of these alone would only result in a sterile method of inquiry. Every scientific insight or discovery must also make use of highly synthetic and creative faculties called variously *imagination* and *intuition* and *insight*. Although much cannot be carried over from science to the area of social justice, I believe that considerations concerning these creative faculties are transferable. In particular, although I appreciate the roles of biology and society in the formation and support of our life of values, I will argue that these are not the ultimate sources of values. Rather, true moral agency is enabled through moral imagination and compassion and is actualized in stages following the direct experience of moral insight.

Given originally as a lecture at the Yale University Interdisciplinary Center for Bioethics, January 24, 2007.

I would like to begin with the story of a beguine, or lay religious woman, by the name of Marguerite Porete, who lived around the year 1300 in what is now Belgium. Little is known about her aside from her book, *Mirror of Simple Annihilated Souls,* and the trouble it caused her (Spearing, 2002, pp. 120ff.). The book is a kind of spiritual love story told in several voices; primary among them are the voices of the Soul, Love, and Reason. Porete's book opens with the story of a noble and gracious princess who hears of the great courtesy and generosity of a far-off king, Alexander. Without ever meeting him, the princess forms a deep and abiding love for the distant king that endures all trials. It is, in the tradition of the troubadours, a true *amour de loin,* or "love from afar." Marguerite Porete's beloved was, of course, no earthly king but her God. The intensity of her love for this distant universal king would get her in deep trouble with Church authorities. How, you might ask, could the devout love of God in 14th-century Europe land a well-behaved woman in profound difficulties? The answer concerns the ultimate source of moral authority or agency, and whether a devout laywoman could have direct access to that source of morality without the mediation of the Church.

Let me quote a few passages from the *Mirror of Simple Annihilated Souls* so you can gain a sense of Porete's (and the Church's) dilemma. Remember that this is an *interior* conversation among the Soul, Love, and Reason, with Porete, of course, writing all three parts. After speaking of the spiritual attributes of her divine lover—God—Porete opens with an exchange between the Soul and Love:

> "Such is the beloved of our souls," says the Soul.
> "Through such love," says Love himself, "the Soul may say to the Virtues, 'I take leave of you'—and the Soul has been a servant to those Virtues for many a day."
> "I agree, Lady Love," says the Soul, "that is how it was then; but now it is like this; your courtesy has removed me from their dominion. Therefore I say; Virtues, I take leave of you for evermore. Now my heart will be freer and more at peace than it has been." (Spearing, 2002, p. 123)

Porete's soul had been, we learn, a servant to the Virtues for many years, but now everything has changed and the Virtues are set aside in favor of a direct relationship to Love.

"Well, Love," says Reason, "when was she a servant?"
"When she dwelt in Love and was under obedience to you and to the other
Virtues," says Love. "The souls that are of this kind have dwelt so long
in Love and under obedience to the Virtues that they have become free."
(Spearing, 2002, p. 123)

Porete saw herself as having begun under obedience to the Virtues in
what she termed "Holy Church of the Little," which was governed by Reason, but she had graduated to Holy Church the Great, in which Love's
favored servants (the annihilated souls of the book's title) worshiped. In
moving from the Church of the Little to the Church of the Great she had
become free. If Porete considered herself free of the Virtues (i.e., the precepts
and power of institutionalized religion) and was no longer under Reason's
authority, what would guide her? Here Porete has Reason provide the
answer, paraphrasing St. Augustine, saying, "Love, Love, and do what you
will." Her love for Love itself was to guide Porete's life. She was a lover, and
her beloved—who was Love—would guide her speech and actions.

Porete's book was sufficiently heterodox to effect its denunciation by
certain bishops. In 1308 Porete was arrested by the Dominican Inquisitor
William of Paris, confessor to the King of France. Marguerite would neither
defend herself nor retract her teachings, simply refusing to respond to her
interrogators. She remained in prison and was ultimately convicted for what
would become a few years later an official heresy, "The Heresy of the Free
Spirit," named after the passage from St. Paul's second letter to the Corinthi-
ans, 2 Cor 3:17, "where the spirit of the Lord is, there is liberty." So it came
to pass in 1310 that Marguerite Porete was condemned as a relapsed heretic
and was sentenced to death in the Place de Grève, the first heretic to be
burned at the stake in the Paris Inquisition. The crowds, it was reported,
wept on seeing the noble bearing she maintained as she was led to the fagot
and there set ablaze.

My point in telling this story is that, already in 1300, Marguerite Porete,
at least, understood that the source of moral authority and agency ultimately
does not reside with civil or religious institutions. (Thoreau, Gandhi, and
Martin Luther King Jr., in his "Letter from Birmingham Jail," remind us of
this point.) Instead, Porete maintained that the free individual could seek
and find moral inspiration through a personal (loving) relationship to a
higher spiritual authority or source—which she called Love. Although hers

is the language of the 14th century, the issues she raises are perennial, and in my view, they have never been more pressing than today, when we are called on to assess the powers of political and legal institutions to make war. Where is the true source of moral authority? On what faculty do we rely for moral judgment? What moral voice do we obey? How do we know to trust it?

In Kohlberg's Theory of Moral Stages (see Crain, 1985), Marguerite is far beyond the "Level II Conventional stages" of morality, in which one's moral values require one to maintain the conventional order as prescribed by moral authorities outside oneself. Indeed, Porete qualifies as Kohlberg's highest level, Level III Post-conventional, stage 6, in which all moral authority is derived from personal judgments guided by one's conscience and an appreciation for universality. Her personal evaluation of her moral conduct superseded all comparable evaluations by juridical or ecclesiastical bodies no matter how learned or powerful. Unfortunately, she was centuries ahead of her time, a time collectively committed to an ethics based on Kohlberg's Level II conventions.

And here we come to the nub of the question: What did Marguerite Porete *experience* that trumped all outer conventional institutions of moral authority so that she was willing to burn at the stake for her convictions? Hers was no dry abstract moral stance born of a utilitarian calculus; neither were the ethical positions of King, Gandhi, or Thoreau. No, something powerful moves into the human heart when one loves Love, to use Marguerite and Augustine's expression. But is there any reason at all to heed the call of Love?

Science—The Central Role of Insight

In attempting to understand the ultimate foundations of ethics and what to make of Marguerite Porete's moral stance, I would like to turn to science and inquire into its methods, goals, and the standing of its insights. How does science achieve its insights? Although reason concerning facts plays a role, it is clear that brute empiricism alone is not enough, nor can one simply reason one's way to original insight. Science is not a mere collection or assemblage of facts. Indeed, early science may well display something of this character, in which a group such as the newly founded Royal Society appears to be occupied chiefly with the recording of curiosities and interesting natural phenomena, but the scientific poverty of such an approach is quickly apparent. Likewise, reason alone can only elaborate what it already knows; it is at its root tautologous.

In the so-called context of discovery, a third form of reasoning must be added to induction and deduction, one that Charles Pierce termed *abduction*, that David Bohm termed *Insight*, and Coleridge termed *Imagination* (primary and secondary). In his *Biographia Literaria*, Coleridge (1852) calls primary imagination ". . . the living Power and prime Agent of all human Perception, and [as] a repetition in the finite mind of the eternal act of creation in the infinite I AM" (p. 378). This is the flash of knowing by which human beings gain a sudden understanding of circumstances, situations, society, or nature. Coleridge believed this knowing to be a reflection of God's own creative process. He goes on to describe secondary imagination as the same in "kind of its agency" with relation to primary imagination but differing only "in degree and in the mode of its operation" (p. 378). Although it is also reflective of God's creative process, those in artistic fields utilize or experience secondary Imagination often. Coleridge claims of secondary Imagination, "It dissolves, diffuses, dissipates, in order to re-create . . . it struggles to idealize and unify" (p. 378). Are these not also the faculties on which scientists draw in their creative moments? Einstein (1929) famously said, "Imagination is more important than knowledge. Knowledge is limited. Imagination encircles the world. For although knowledge defines what we currently know and understand, imagination points to all we might yet discover and create" (p. 117). I would hold that the "new" enters science by the door of imagination. It may be validated or falsified by ratiocination or experimental results, but it first appears to Insight-Imagination (Sloan, 1983).

What is science seeking? Early science subscribed to a mechanical and materialistic philosophy that persists even today, especially in the life sciences. All phenomena were to be reduced to a mechanical, causal account of objects conceived in terms of enduring primary qualities such as extension, mass, velocity, position, and so on. Such accounts have long been considered "explanatory," and it was such accounts that scientists of that era sought. Since the 17th century, pride of place has been given to mechanism, and something has been considered explained when the mechanism by which the effect is brought about has been sufficiently described. This is what Aristotle termed *efficient cause*. In 1884 Lord Kelvin famously declared, "I never satisfy myself until I can make a mechanical model of a thing." Bernard de Fontenelle, secretary to the French Academy of Science, wrote in 1686 in his *Plurality of Worlds* that nature is like the grand spectacle at the opera. Most viewers are concerned only with the drama, but "he who would see nature as she truly is, must stand behind the scenes." Or, as Helmholtz put it in 1853, the true natural philosopher "tries to discover the levers, the chords, and the pulleys which work behind and shift the scenes" (1853/1897, p. 58).

By contrast, modern science is less concerned with mechanistic accounts (which often prove of limited utility) and seeks instead the formal regularities and patterns that nature displays, often seeking purely mathematical accounts of a phenomenal domain. The great symmetry principles of physics come to mind: charge conjugation, parity, time reversal invariance, and Noether's theorem, which relates spatial isotropy and homogeneity to the conservation laws of angular momentum and energy, respectively. Or the principle of least action, from which so many of the laws of physics can be derived, including the Euler-Lagrange equations of dynamics and the path integral formulation of quantum mechanics of Richard Feynman. Or Einstein's principle of special relativity, which declares that all the laws of physics are identical no matter what the uniform motion of the observer may be. Such principles take precedence over material properties (including the primary qualities of extension, temporal interval, and dynamic quantities of force and mass) and thus over even mechanism. Our very concepts of space, time, and simultaneity must be more flexible as a consequence of the principle of relativity.

Notice that there is nothing of mechanism about these laws. Hendrik Lorentz complained that Einstein took the principle of relativity as a postulate; however, he (Lorentz) had labored long and hard (and unsuccessfully) to find the physical basis for the so-called Lorentz contraction, which is described formally by the mathematical transformations that bear Lorentz's name. No mechanical account exists for length contraction and time dilation (moving clocks slowing down); rather, our very conception of space and time has changed fundamentally. Modern physics really is based not on mechanism but on *principles* or *formal* causes such as those already mentioned. In contrast to Aristotle's four causes, today's physics has largely abandoned the search for efficient causes so dear even to the 19th century in favor of formal mathematical understanding.

As a consequence of the changes in our understanding of space, time, and energy, the worldview of philosophically minded physicists (and there are not so many) changed considerably during the 20th century. Anton Zeilinger, the Schroedinger professor in Vienna, puts it this way:

. . . one may be tempted to assume that whenever we ask questions of nature, of the world there outside, there is reality existing independently of what can be said about it. We will now claim that such a position is void of any meaning. It is obvious that any property or feature of reality out there can only be based on information we receive. There cannot be any statement whatsoever about the world or about reality that is not based on such information. It therefore follows that the concept of a reality without at least the ability in principle to make statements about it to obtain information about its features is devoid of any possibility of confirmation or proof. This implies that the distinction between information, that is knowledge, and reality is devoid of any meaning. (2004, pp. 218–219).

That is, modern physics demands that we turn sharply away from an ontology of conventional matter and mechanism and turn toward an ontology of information. Knowledge and reality, in this view, arise together. Moreover, it is a knowing that is constituted through relationship. There is no "knowing" in physics separate from an observer, real or imagined, no "true" state of affairs accessible only to a privileged observer. That is, there is no view from nowhere. Reality is always *relational,* as relativity and quantum mechanics demonstrate.

As an aside, let me remark that molecular biology remains infatuated with mechanism but will, I believe, at some point make the transition to formal analysis once mechanism proves truly elusive. The field has yet to go through the equivalent of the quantum and relativity revolutions of physics.

The Question of Moral Agency

I have belabored physics, its history and philosophy, because I hope to learn what it can teach us concerning how to proceed with social justice. Certainly many things will not carry over, but I would like to suggest that some central features will.

First, we need to consider the efforts by evolutionary biologists to seek a material and mechanistic account for ethics. E. O. Wilson and Richard Dawkins are the best-known spokesmen for this view, but their number is legion. From the experience of physics, we should be cautious about such accounts. They have proven of limited validity and offer, in my view, no fundamental account. That social behavior is allowed for and supported by our biology is obviously required if we humans are going to display it. The biological capacity for social or even altruistic behavior is totally different from its intentional display. That is surely evident from the lack of altruism we often witness. Biology here is *not* causal, not deterministic; it does not work to a given end (which would falsely bring back final causes into biology). That I can write with a pen is enabled by the biology of my hand, but my hand did not cause writing in any meaningful sense. Likewise, my biology must of necessity be consistent with and supportive of moral conduct, but what is necessary for morality is not sufficient.

Are values merely social constructs? Marguerite Porete did not experience the Virtues that way. Yes, for a parishioner in the Church of the Little, the precepts of the faith community are supported and even enforced by the church. But social institutions are not the true source of ethical values either. Conventional morality is indeed organized by religious, political, and legal institutions, but even they themselves do not believe in or experience the institution as the source of moral authority but merely as its arm. Where then is the source to be found, and what capacity is available to us to tap that source in order to make moral judgments?

In a recent paper on "Feynman's Unanswered Question," Herman Daly (2006) likened the moral sensibility in the human being to a compass needle aligning itself with the moral magnetic field of the universe. He conceived the moral order as outside us and pre-existent. This is not unlike the ethical equivalent of the sort of conventional scientific realism Lord Kelvin embraced. The Ten Commandments are, in essence, "out there" as metaphysical realities. The magnetic field, by the way, is not a Lorentz invariant; that is, in some reference frames it is zero. In such analogous moral frames is there then no moral order? This suggests that we look more carefully at the basis for moral order. If there is no neat moral code "out there" to be read off and carved into stone, then how might real-life morality arise? Are there high-level principles (as there are in physics) that may be implemented in specific ways in specific contexts but that are themselves invariant across frames of reference? (Remember, the laws of physics are true in all inertial frames; that is the principle of relativity.)

As an aside, I would like to state that, although our particular ethical judgments must be made in terms of our own frame, I am not advocating moral relativism of the conventional sort. Einstein's theory is not one that spawns a lawless universe. In fact, it shows the profound ways in which the universe is ordered—indeed, must be ordered—in accord with the principle of relativity in order to be coherent. It is likewise for the moral universe. I suspect that we are better off thinking in similar terms about moral principles. What might be the high principles that work across reference frames? Principles such as "Do unto others as you would have them do unto you" and Rawls's related principles of justice (behind a veil of ignorance) (1971/ 1999).

What of the human faculty for moral insight? I believe that here, as in science, reasoning can be an important aid to moral reflection, clarifying circumstances and anticipated consequences, but left to itself reason alone is not competent to judge. No, here also, like Porete, I would maintain that, independent of social institutions and the Virtues they espouse, the individual possesses sensibilities sufficient to allow for genuine moral insight. These sensibilities include moral imagination, compassion, and intuition. Moral imagination allows us to enact imaginatively the situation of the other, that is, to exchange places with them. In addition, compassion is needed; not only must we imagine the other's circumstances but we need to feel the impact of those circumstances, in some measure, as the other would feel them. The capacity for compassion permits such "feeling with." Imagination and compassion become then the basis for our moral intuition. *Love* is the word that we use to describe this combination of participation and compassion. Love in this way becomes a power of knowing that is not a distant objectifying act of ratiocination but a living *into* and *with* that can yield moral insight. This moral insight fuels our concern for and understanding of social justice. Without moral insight we are not genuinely sensitive and responsive to inequity and injustice.

Toward an Epistemology of Love

We are unaccustomed to thinking of love as more that an emotion or mere sentiment. Yet the stages of love as a means of knowing can be elaborated more fully (Zajonc, 2006). They include the following:

- Respect—When approaching the object of our contemplative attention, we do so with respect and restraint. Concerning the relationship to the beloved, Rilke (1901/2007) maintained that "a togetherness between two people is an impossibility" (p. 57). Instead of an easy fusion with the beloved, Rilke recommended that we "stand guard over the solitude of the other" (cited in Zajonc, 2002). Likewise, I feel that the first stage of contemplative inquiry is to respect the integrity of the other, to stand guard over its nature, over its "solitude," whether the *other* is a poem, a novel, a phenomenon of nature, or the person sitting before us. We need to allow it to speak its truth without our projection or correction.

- Gentleness—Contemplative inquiry is gentle, or delicate. In his own scientific investigations, Goethe sought to practice what he called a "gentle empiricism" (*zarte Empirie*) (1988, p. 307). If we wish to approach the object of our attention without distorting it, then we must be gentle. By contrast, the empiricism of Francis Bacon spoke of extracting nature's secrets under extreme conditions, putting "her" to the rack.

- Intimacy—Conventional science distances itself from nature and, to use Erwin Schrödinger's (1967) term, *objectifies* nature. Ideally, science disengages itself from phenomena for the sake of objectivity. Contemplative inquiry, by contrast, approaches the phenomenon, delicately and respectfully, but it does nonetheless seek to become intimate with that to which it attends. One can still retain clarity and balanced judgment close-up, if we remember to exercise restraint and gentleness.

- Participation—Gentle intimacy leads to participation by the contemplative inquirer in the unfolding phenomenon before one. Outer characteristics invite us to go deeper. We move and feel with the natural phenomenon, text, painting, or person before us, living "out of" ourselves and "into" the other. Respectfully and delicately, in meditation we join with the other, while maintaining full awareness and clarity of mind. In other words, contemplative inquiry is experientially centered in the other, not in ourselves. Our usual preoccupations, fears, and cravings work against authentic participation.

- Vulnerability—In order to move with the other, in order to be gentle in the sense meant here, in order to participate with the other truly, we must be confident enough to be vulnerable, secure enough to resign ourselves to the course of things. A dominating arrogance will not serve. We must learn to be comfortable with not knowing, with ambiguity and uncertainty. Only from what may appear to be weakness and ignorance can the new and unknown arise.

- Transformation—These last two, participation and vulnerability, lead to a patterning of ourselves on the other. What was outside of us is internalized. Inwardly, we assume the shape, dynamic, and meaning of the contemplative object. We are, in a word, transformed by contemplative experience in accord with the object of contemplation.
- *Bildung*—This is education as formation. The individual develops, or, we could say, is sculpted, through contemplative practice. In German, education is both *Erziehung* and *Bildung*. The later word stems from the root meaning "to form." The lineage of education as formation dates back at least as far as the Greeks. In his book *What Is Ancient Philosophy*, French philosopher Pierre Hadot (2002) writes of the ancient philosopher, "the goal was to develop a *habitus*, or new capacity to judge or criticize, and to transform—that is, to change people's way of living and seeing the world" (p. 274). Simplicius asked, "What place shall the philosopher occupy in the city? That of a sculptor of men" (in Hadot, 2002, p. xiii). Hadot paraphrases Merleau-Ponty (1962) declaring that we need to "relearn how to see the world" (in Hadot, 2002, p. 276). In an essay on science, Goethe (1988) declared, "every object well-contemplated creates an organ of perception in us" (p. 39). Parker Palmer's important work (2007) also centers on education as formation.
- Insight—The ultimate result of contemplative engagement as outlined here is organ formation, which leads to insight born of an intimate participation in the course of things. In the Buddhist epistemology this is called "direct perception"; among the Greeks it was called *episteme* and was contrasted to inferential reasoning, or *dianoia*. Knowing of this type is experienced as a kind of seeing or direct apprehension rather than an intellectual reasoning to a result (Sloan, 1983; Sternberg & Davidson, 1995).

Many are the sources of deception, but that does not mean that moral insight is impossible. For example, a three-dimensional object such as a wire square may look deceptively like a line when viewed edge-on or rhomboid from another angle, but by completely rotating the object we can intuit its real shape. So it is in this case. Patience, variation, and so on, often can clarify morally complex situations, opening them to moral intuition. In fact, in my view, genuine moral agency arises only in those cases in which we are free of all such deception, whether it stems from the external compulsions of society and family or internal biological and psychological forces. But once free of them all, how do we act? Whence come the moral insights that guide free human action? Here we come back to Porete and to her love of Love, which becomes a firm and reliable faculty of moral knowing. One worth dying for.

Contemplative Traditions and the Cultivation of Contemplative Insight

Porete was a beguine, which means she was a contemplative. She had grown up in the "Church of the Little," practicing the conventional Virtues as prescribed by the Church. But gradually she matured and fell in love: in her case, with Love itself. In other words, she practiced love. In many spiritual traditions one practices love, deepening it, extending to larger and larger "circles of affection," as the Stoics called them. I see the contemplative traditions as very important sources for practices that aid us in the refinement and strengthening of our moral sensibilities of imaginative participation, compassion, and moral intuition/insight. These practices are valuable resources for academics, whose training does not emphasize such sensibilities. Goethe (1988), once remarked, "every object well-contemplated opens an organ within us" (p. 39). By practicing love, by contemplating the Virtues well, we become free and are possessed of the high faculty of moral intuition and insight. Don't we recognize exactly this faculty in those we most admire; don't we, in the end, rely on this capacity ourselves? Experience, in this high sense, is the ground of moral agency for the free human being.

Science is as much a matter of the heart and of sympathetic feeling as it is of reason and experiment. Concerning scientific intuition and the heart, Einstein (1918/1954) wrote, "only intuition, resting on sympathetic understanding, can lead to [these laws]. . . . the daily effort comes from no deliberate intention or program, but from the heart" (p. 226). In one's classrooms, one's research, one's communities, one must return again and again with respect and delicacy to the subject at hand. Only then are the capacities of understanding and insight formed. The image I have of this process is depicted in Figure 4.1: By attending to the object of research (i.e., the candle in the figure), the organ of perception is formed. The process repeats: attention—formation, attention—formation . . .

FIGURE 4.1

Attention-Formation

Attention

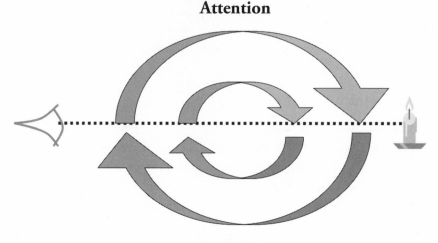

Formation

In her remarkable biography of the Nobel laureate Barbara McClintock, Evelyn Fox Keller (1983) describes McClintock's knowing as "a kind of seeing." Concerning insight, McClintock urged that one must "let it come to you . . . hear what the material has to say to you; get a 'feeling for the organism" (cited in Keller, 1983, p. 198). Keller called this a learning by "identification," that requires one to "dwell patiently in the variety and complexity of organism" (p. 207). In a lecture near the end of her life, McClintock urged a group of Harvard graduate students "to take the time and look." As Keller commented, "The pace of current research seems to preclude such a contemplative stance" (p. 206). However, it is my conviction that, whether in the research laboratory or in matters of ethical conduct, our most creative and inspired insights come from exactly such a contemplative stance. Those of us in the academy who are concerned with ethics and social justice should take the time to look, to attend fully and patiently, to allow the world to work itself into us and shape us. Then might the high principles we seek—with the heart as well as the mind—gradually become apparent to us, and they will permit us to both understand through identification and to act out of compassionate moral intuition (Zajonc, 2009).

References

Coleridge, S. T. (1852). *Biographia literaria* (Vol. 1, p. 378). New York: W. Gowans.

Crain, W. C. (1985). *Theories of development* (pp. 118–136). Prentice-Hall.

Daly, H. (2006). Feynman's unanswered question. *Philosophy and Public Policy Quarterly, 26*(1/2), 13–17.

Einstein, A. (1929, October 26). What life means to Einstein: An interview by George Sylvester Viereck. *The Saturday Evening Post.*

Einstein, A. (1954). Principles of research. In *Ideas and Opinions* (S. Bargmann, Trans). New York: Wings Books. (Original work published 1918)

Goethe, J. W. von. (1988). *Scientific studies* (D. Miller, Ed. & Trans.). New York: Suhrkamp.

Hadot, P. (2002). *What is ancient philosophy?* Cambridge, MA: Harvard University Press.

Helmholtz, H. (1897). *Popular lectures on scientific subjects* (E. Atkinson, Trans.) (2nd ed.). New York: D. Appleton. (Original work published 1853)

Keller, E. F. (1983). *A feeling for the organism.* New York: W.H. Freeman.

Merleau-Ponty, M. (1962). *Phenomenology of perception.* London: Routledge.

Palmer, P. (2007). *The courage to teach: Exploring the inner landscape of a teacher's life.* San Francisco: Jossey-Bass.

Rawls, J. (1999). *A theory of justice.* Cambridge, MA: Harvard University Press. (Original work published 1971).

Rilke, R. M. (1945). *Letters of Rainer Maria Rilke.* W. W. Norton. (Original work published 1901).

Schrödinger, E. (1967). *Mind and matter.* Cambridge: Cambridge University Press.

Sloan, D. (1983). *Insight-imagination: The emancipation of thought and the modern world.* Westport, CT: Greenwood Press.

Spearing, E. (Ed.). (2002). *Medieval writings on female spirituality.* New York: Penguin Classics.

Sternberg, R. J., & Davidson, J. E. (1995). *The nature of insight.* Cambridge, MA: MIT Press.

Zajonc, A. (2002). *Dawning of free communities for collective wisdom.* Retrieved January 15, 2009, from http://www.collectivewisdominitiative.org/papers/zajonc _dawning.htm#love

Zajonc, A. (2006). Love and knowledge: Recovering the heart of learning through contemplation. *Teachers College Record, 108*(9), 1742–1759.

Zajonc, A. (2009). *Meditation as contemplative inquiry: When knowing becomes love.* Great Barrington, MA: Lindisfarne Press.

Zeilinger, A. (2004). *Science and ultimate reality* (J. D. Barrow, C.W. Davies, & C. L. Harper Jr., Eds.). Cambridge: Cambridge University Press.

5

CHANGE TO SOCIAL JUSTICE EDUCATION

Higher Education Strategy

Karen L. St. Clair and James E. Groccia

T he social justice education advances described in this book came about through collaborations among offices of diversity and multicultural affairs, and centers for teaching and learning. These kinds of collaborations do not develop spontaneously. Leaders who are knowledgeable about organizational change and skilled at instituting it make the collaborations and changes happen. This chapter examines higher education institutions and changes within them and proposes a strategy for facilitating change to social justice education. The strategy involves a teaching and learning model for practicing social justice education and collaborations fostered by the institution's academic development leadership.

Social Justice Education

Bell (2007) defines social justice as a goal and a process:

> The goal of social justice is full and equal participation of all groups in a society that is mutually shaped to meet their needs. Social justice includes a vision of society in which the distribution of resources is equitable and all members are physically and psychologically safe and secure. . . . The process for attaining the goal of social justice . . . should also be democratic

and participatory, inclusive and affirming of human agency and human capacities for working collaboratively to create change. (pp. 1–2)

It follows from Bell's definition that social justice education involves leading learners toward the social justice vision by a similarly participatory and collaborative educational process. Such efforts to change to social justice education could result in broad, far-reaching, and positive implications for society and for pedagogy in higher education, but change can involve struggle. To understand the struggle, it is helpful to be informed about higher education institutions and change within them.

Higher Education Institutions

In 1988 Birnbaum published his now oft-quoted book, *How Colleges Work: The Cybernetics of Academic Organization and Leadership*. In it he presents four models of higher education governance, organization, and leadership: the collegial, the bureaucratic, the political, and the anarchical. To illustrate the four models, he describes the fictitious Heritage College in terms of each. As an example, here is a summary of Heritage College as a collegial system: The faculty and administrators have advanced academic or professional degrees, hence hierarchy is not very important. Informal interactions are the norm. Although there appears to be an interest in the opinions and concerns of staff and students, they are not given equal participation in conversations. Those who have the most influence in discussions toward consensus (which is ideal) have that influence because of norms and personal qualities. Discussions take time, and some contributors become frustrated; participants may change their minds on issues. Faculty members serve as administrators for a period of time; their service is typically without training. They also expect the president to be an equal who can make decisions for Heritage. Board members are usually alumni. The collegial culture is supported easily for most people on campus through constant communications, similarities in individuals' backgrounds, and local connections. Deliberation and thoroughness are emphasized, and decision-making can be slow.

It is evident that there are a variety of characteristics within this model. Because this is true of each model, we contend that there is no valid or reliable way to categorize higher education institutions in order to simplify selecting a change process. Studying change in higher education is a more informative endeavor.

Change in Higher Education

Definitions of Change

Scott (1999) differentiates between two major types of educational change: those in learning programs and those in the milieu. A few examples of changes in learning programs include changes in the learning objectives and content, teaching and learning strategy, learning resources, learning sequencing, and approaches to evaluation and enhancement. A few examples of changes in the milieu include changes in the culture and climate, staff selection and support, leadership, communication systems, planning and decision-making, and approaches to identifying and disseminating good practice. Changes in learning programs and milieu affect each other. And the context consists of multiple factors that interact to affect the change process. There are conditions, procedures, and key players at each educational institution, and at each level. The levels are the external, administrative, and local.

Adrianna Kezar (2001) distinguishes among several other terms frequently used for change: *diffusion, institutionalization, innovation,* and *reform*. In Kezar's terms, change may be considered to be an innovation institutionalized by diffusion or through reform.

In his analysis of educational change, Fullan (2007) further qualifies the definition of change by suggesting that "[t]he implementation of educational change involves 'change in practice'" (p. 30). Practice is multidimensional, involving new or revised materials, new teaching approaches or strategies, and altered beliefs (i.e., theories or assumptions). One, two, or all three could be implemented by any one individual or group. Although Fullan does not focus on higher education, his points are intuitively applicable at that level. His analysis is analogous to viewing change as a noun and as a verb: the meaning and process of change. As we continue to explore change in higher education, we accept Fullan's qualified definition because change to social justice education is a change in practice.

Theories and Models for Change

Beyond defining change in higher education, Kezar (2001) discusses change through theoretical frameworks that address why change occurs, how it occurs, and what will occur. To consider why change is occurring, for example, one can ask if the source is internal or external to the institution. To consider how it will occur, one might ask if it will be planned or unplanned. To consider what will change, one can ask if the outcome will be new structures or a new mission. Identifying the answers to these questions and identifying and considering the characteristics of a particular higher education institution will provide an initial understanding about the potential for change at that institution. Kezar (2001) also identifies six types of change theories and models in higher education. Each type differs with regard to underlying assumptions, key activities, benefits, and weaknesses. The types are *evolutionary, teleological, life cycle, political, social cognition,* and *cultural.*

The cultural models and theories seem most relevant for change to social justice education. They emphasize a participatory and collaborative process for change, which focuses on the leaders' abilities to shape the institutional culture. In addition, key activities for creating change "include modifying the mission and vision, creating new myths and rituals, leaders performing symbolic actions, using metaphors, assessing the institutional culture, tapping into energy, developing enthusiasm, altering motivations of people through spirituality, and communicating values and beliefs" (Kezar, 2001, p. 52). These characteristics align with Bell's (2007) definition quoted at the start of this chapter. Recall that Bell's definition includes a vision of equitable resources, physical and psychological safety and security for all, and a participatory and collaborative process. When social justice education is in place, learners are led toward the vision through a similarly participatory and collaborative change process. Thus, the cultural model most closely aligns with the goals of social justice educators.

Models and theories add to our background knowledge about institutional change, but they lack instructions for implementation. In addition, what is especially telling in Kezar's (2001) work is her caution that the "problem with any model is the temptation to apply it within all situations. . . ." (p. 114). Yet creating new change models is not practical. What is appropriate is to target the factors that influence change implementation in order to guide the change process.

Factors for Change Implementation

Each institution can be viewed as having its own implications for change process implementation. Kezar (2001) notes that higher education institutions are interdependent organizations: They have connections with other institutions, professional organizations, and the community. All are potential sources of change. When more than one exists, the likelihood of change is increased. However, many other characteristics of higher education institutions can impede success. Institutions are driven by multiple values: Each discipline has its own values set; administrators' values differ from faculty's. Change toward a new set of values, such as those inherent in social justice education, could be a slow and difficult process. Another characteristic of higher education that could prevent swift and easy change is the power structure. In higher education institutions there are multiple levels of power: Faculty members have power over curricula; trustees have power over resources. It may be unclear who has authority over which decisions.

Fullan (2007) summarizes the key factors that influence change and makes an important point about commitment and vision:

> One of the initial sources of the problem is the commitment of reformers to see a particular desired change implemented. Commitment to what should be changed often varies inversely with knowledge about how to work through a process of change. In fact, strong commitment to a particular change may be a barrier to setting up an effective process of change. . . . The adage, "Where there's a will there's a way," is not always an apt one for the planning of educational change. There is an abundance of wills, but they are in the way rather than pointing the way. A certain amount of vision is required to provide the clarity and energy for promoting specific changes, but vision by itself may get in the way if it results in impatience, failure to listen, and so on. Stated in a more balanced way, promoters of change need to be committed to and skilled in the change process as well as in the change itself. (p. 108)

Commitment and vision alone will not prevail, according to Fullan; change agents must also be skilled in the change process.

Finally, mission and vision should not be overlooked (Kezar, 2001). The institution's mission is typically long-standing; thus any proposed change must align with it. An institution's mission typically reflects what the institution does to work toward its vision. Institutional visions are, by their very nature, not yet realized. They are statements about what the institution wants to be like in the future; they are statements of a desired culture or position. Periodically, visions can be changed to align with trends, new values, or governing bodies' interests. Consequently, the mission can be adjusted to accommodate new and different actions that would be necessary to reach the vision. When social justice becomes part of an institution's vision, the mission can then incorporate strategies to change to that focus.

It makes intuitive sense that the role the factors play is important. However, Kezar's (2001) and Fullan's (2007) factors do not specify strategies for change. When it comes to action, we highly recommend Clark's (2007) advice to engage in an "integrated pursuit of things that work" (p. 323):

> The disconnect between researchers and practitioners in understanding universities remains acute. . . . When questions of how change comes about in universities take the stage, the gap widens. . . . A new approach . . . centers on use-inspired, practice-driven research that can serve also as research for basic understanding. . . . In the complex realities of practice, we can pursue what works. We find out what significant organizational changes Stanford made in the last half of the twentieth century to become an outstanding university. . . . We find out how Michigan and Wisconsin continue to prosper in research *and* in teaching *and* in service as public U.S. universities, even as they extend themselves to include new populations and outside business and professional groups. . . . A more integrated pursuit of things that work should also bolster optimism and hope for the future of universities and colleges in the twenty-first century. (pp. 319–323)

Vision and process consistently emerge from the advice: Be mindful of institutional mission and vision; lead by creating collaborations. In line with Fullan's (2007) advice about commitment and process, we believe that having a focused vision suggests commitment to change; leading through collaborations suggests the change process. In line with Clark (2007), we propose considering what has worked.

Strategy for Change to Social Justice Education

Knowledge about higher education institutions and change within them provides a foundation for selectively following the experts' advice (see Civian, Arnold, Gamson, Kanter, & London, 1997; Clark, 2007; Fullan, 2007; Kezar, 2001; Lindquist, 1997; and Scott, 2003): Commit to a vision for social justice education that is likely to fit within the institution's culture, select a change process that is participatory and collaborative, and ensure that leadership is powerful enough to establish the collaborations and realize the vision.

Also, consider what has worked. Roper (2007) presents an illustrative case example: At Oregon State University student activists had concerns about "negative conditions and the chilly climate for diversity" (p. 228). In addition to asking for a diversity course, the students asked the president to endorse several values. Roper attributes to the leadership the successful evolution of Oregon State University's Difference, Power, and Discrimination Program from a course into a program. Besides students, faculty from a range of disciplines, advisory board members, and program workshop participants advocated for program funding when its future was threatened. The course eventually became part of the core curriculum, and the program became a concept (i.e., difference, power, and discrimination) and a process (i.e., social justice pedagogy). Roper (2007) acknowledges that the leadership must not only be committed, it needs to be supported. He explains, "This effort will involve significant struggle and must be approached using the leaders' knowledge of personalities, systems and structures" (p. 230).

Oregon State University's program emphasized context, leadership, and teaching. Any change for social justice education would involve a change in teaching and learning as a change in practice. Consequently, a change to social justice education must address how teaching and learning will be different and how the change process can be facilitated. If the institution can first commit to a vision of change in teaching and learning, the process for change can then unfold.

Haverford College is another successful change example ("Advancing a Tradition," n.d.). Having Quaker traditions, it was able to reach consensus on its commitment to diversity. Its diversity course requirement began in 1984, but in 1990 Haverford faculty noticed a dearth of courses on prejudice. They then adopted a specific requirement for social justice. Leaders addressed the need for campus-wide professional development, interdisciplinarity, and communication about goals and values in academics and student life. Collaborative leadership promoted commitment to the vision.

The Oregon State University and Haverford College examples are about institutions that were successful in committing to a vision and engaging leaders to support collaborations. The nature of a change to social justice education is, as Fullan (2007) states, change in practice. Specifically, the practice is teaching. The change process focuses on leadership for and through collaboration. Therefore, teaching and learning are at the core of a committed vision to social justice education that requires a collaborative change process with regard to the specific context.

Change as a Noun

Marchesani and Adams (1992) acknowledge the "large-scale, complex, sustained organizational and cultural transformation" (p. 10) that is required to achieve a multicultural higher education environment (see also Jackson & Holvino, 1986; and Smith, 1989). In addition, Marchesani and Adams stress that at the center of such a transformation is teaching and learning—elusive dimensions within the vision for a multicultural environment. They propose a model focused on four dimensions: the students, the instructor, what is taught, and the teaching methods. We believe there are other teaching and learning elements to consider. In the late 1990s, one of us (Groccia, 2007) conceived a model of seven interrelated variables that influence teaching and learning. It extended and built on Dunkin and Biddle's (1974) model for studying classroom teaching and Shulman's (1986) synoptic map of research on teaching. Considering each variable in this model can facilitate change to social justice education by revealing what is involved in teaching and learning; they are at the core of the institution's vision for social justice education.

The seven interrelated variables are not new to faculty in higher education. However, for myriad reasons, faculty members tend to focus on one or two of them and overlook the others. The model is similar to Marchesani and Adams's (1992) model in that it emphasizes that teachers need to understand who they are and what they bring to the learning situation. Socioeconomic, race, gender, age, and cultural background; academic preparation; and personal characteristics, such as thinking and learning styles, attitudes, and values, affect teaching, curricular development, and relationships with students. Our review of institutional change reveals the importance of knowing about the institution's mission, vision, and culture in order to facilitate change to social justice education. This model extends that knowledge to the micro level. Knowledge of where the teaching will take place is equally important. In our model, the variable that draws teacher, learner, learning process, learning context, and content together is instructional processes, or pedagogy. Teaching and learning are at the core of social justice education, and change to it is a change in practice. Commitment to social justice education is a commitment about teaching and learning and its multiple variables.

The change process follows full analysis of an institution and its intended social justice educational outcomes.

Change as a Verb

Ignoring the institution's mission and vision when attempting to institute change of any kind is tantamount to failure. Roper (2007) states, "Institutional change, minor or major, is more easily implemented and sustained when it is tied to the core mission or espoused educational outcomes of the institution" (p. 231). Once it is clear that the institution's mission and vision embrace change to social justice education, the change process can be undertaken through leadership actions.

No matter which group on campus raises concerns about social justice, if the desired outcome will fit within the institution's vision and mission, leadership must be approached, and that leadership must respond. To change an institution to social justice education, leadership must promote the social justice vision by establishing collaborations that will support all the teaching and learning variables shown in Figure 5.1. Leadership for change should reside within the campus' faculty teaching and learning center. Because of its central location and mission to enhance teaching and learning, the center can promote the social justice vision and establish collaborations that will support it.

In higher education, *academic development* is often used interchangeably with *educational development*. In the United States, academic development in higher education has a relatively short history. It was not until the 1970s that attention was paid to development efforts around teaching (Fletcher & Patrick, 1998). Now, academic development is conducted in countless institutions at varying degrees of intensity, and the actions have expanded well beyond merely assisting faculty with teaching (Sorcinelli, Austin, Eddy, & Beach, 2006).

The Professional and Organizational Development (POD) in Higher Education Network (POD) (n.d.), the leading association for academic developers in the United States, defined three types of actions: *Faculty development* includes programs that assist faculty in teaching, scholarly and professional work, and personal issues related to well-being. *Instructional development* focuses on course and curricular design and student learning. *Organizational development* involves activities to maximize institutional effectiveness. Instructing about and assisting with tasks related to institutional structures and

FIGURE 5.1
Model of Seven Interrelated Variables That Influence Teaching and Learning
A Model for Understanding Teaching and Learning

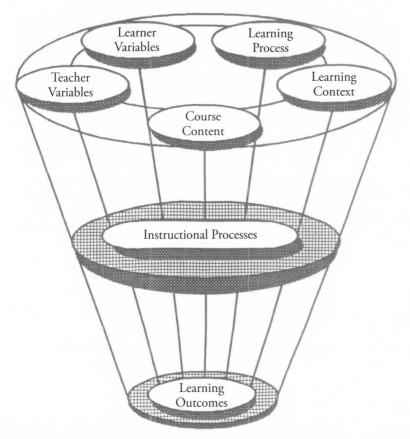

From "Planning Faculty Development Activities: Using a Holistic Teaching and Learning Model," by J. E. Groccia, Winter 2007, *POD Network News*, pp. 1, 3. Copyright 2007 by J. E. Groccia. Reprinted with permission.

functions are primary functions in the organizational development category. The typical mechanisms by which academic developers work in all three categories include workshops, seminars, retreats, consultations, evaluations, instruction, research, and communications.

The academic developer's work in faculty, instructional, and organizational development can be integrated into our model for understanding teaching and learning. Besides assisting in conducting assessments throughout the model, the academic developer's work with each variable can facilitate change to social justice education.

1. Teacher variables are addressed by faculty development actions because they can help teachers become self-aware about their views on social justice.
2. The learning process variable is addressed through faculty and instructional development functions because they can inform teachers about how people learn, and how teachers can best learn about social justice.
3. The learning context variables are addressed by faculty, instructional, and organizational development functions, because they can help identify elements of the learning context that would facilitate or hinder the social justice educational process.
4. Instructional processes are addressed by instructional development functions because they can promote effective teaching about social justice.
5. Learning outcomes variables are addressed by instructional and organizational development functions because they can help identify broad and narrow outcomes for social justice education.
6. Course content variables are addressed through collaborations that academic developers can arrange in order to identify specific social justice content. The content work is within the instructional development category.
7. Learner variables are addressed through collaborations that academic developers can arrange in order to identify students' beliefs about social justice. Work about student learning is within the instructional development category.

The academic developer is also a leader on campus. Taylor (2005) conducted a study to better understand the leadership functions of an academic developer. Thirty academic developers were interviewed. Taylor reports on these individuals' conceptualizations of their own leadership roles and on their beliefs about the characteristics of an academic developer's leadership and leadership strategies. Not surprisingly, the primary leadership role they named was "facilitating learning." "Context" was the strongest theme reported. Knowing the context was considered to be relevant to helping "shape the agenda" (Taylor, 2005, p. 38) of the institution. The academic developer's leadership strategies revealed by Taylor align with the three academic development functions:

1. Organizational development actions can enable participation in the university's strategic plan.
2. Organizational development can enable leadership expression and modeling in order to change an institutional vision or mission.
3. Organizational development can enable networking and connections for information gathering.
4. Faculty and instructional development actions can facilitate learning.
5. Faculty and instructional development actions can keep discussions grounded in teaching and learning.
6. Faculty, instructional, and organizational development actions can help evaluate change by arranging opportunities for scholarship.

The academic developer's primary functions and his or her leadership position operate through networking and collaborations to gain the necessary resources for social justice education content, and for knowledge about the student body. Sell and Lounsberry (1997) and Fletcher and Patrick (1998) were early endorsers of collaborative work for curricular change and for academic development, respectively. In a survey of academic developers about the past, present, and future of academic development, Sorcinelli et al. (2006) report that academic developers have been "slow to incorporate multiculturalism into their . . . programs" (p. 84). They speculate that academic developers believe multicultural issues are student related rather than curricular; that developers do not have enough knowledge about the issues; and that previous, unsuccessful efforts on campus have turned multiculturalism into a risky issue to tackle. To have a fully functioning model for change to social justice education, academic developers can collaborate with offices of diversity and multicultural affairs to fill gaps related to the learner variables and course content elements of our teaching and learning model.

Kuh (1996) writes about collaborations between student affairs and academic affairs when involved in a change process, and he provides strategies for establishing those collaborations. These strategies can be applied to collaborations between offices of diversity or multicultural affairs and academic affairs. Kuh (1996) proposes that, to begin the change process, "[o]ne or more champions must emerge to create a sense of anticipation and to establish the momentum for change" (p. 137). Academic developers can easily emerge as champions because they are centrally located on campus. They have their ears to the ground, are networked across campus, and their mission is to lead efforts to facilitate learning and promote excellent teaching. Kuh recommend that those in student affairs and academic affairs seek a common vision or mission about the change desired. To encourage a shared vision, individuals must examine their personal beliefs, values, and visions. Student cultures must be examined in order to understand their connection to learning.

Kuh recommends a common learning and teaching language. Avoid jargon and specific language that can interfere with communications. Speaking the same language reflects a collaborative relationship. Also, Kuh recommends that offices invite people from campus groups to participate in the activities and events of their offices. Besides conducting the academic development functions and actions to maintain the highest level of effectiveness with the model, academic developers can invite staff from the office of diversity and multicultural affairs to participate in teaching and learning activities. It is through the academic developer's office that collaborative leadership for change to social justice education, which is a change in teaching and learning practice, can be realized.

Conclusion

Because social justice education advances a culture of social justice in higher education, teaching and learning would necessarily be at the heart of a change. Grounded in theories and models, academic developers have the resources required to understand higher education institutions and change within them. Skilled in faculty, instructional, and organizational developments, they can facilitate the change process through their programs and services. Through leading and collaborating, academic developers can ensure that the institution's mission and vision are aligned with the proposed change to social justice education, and facilitate the change.

References

Advancing a tradition of social justice (n.d.). *Diversity Digest.* Retrieved July 15, 2008, from http://www.diversityweb.org/Digest/F96/haverford.html

Bell, L. A. (2007). Theoretical foundations for social justice education. In M. Adams, L. A. Bell, & P. Griffin (Eds.), *Teaching for diversity and social justice* (2nd ed., pp. 1–14). New York: Routledge.

Birnbaum, R. (1988). *How colleges work: The cybernetics of academic organization and leadership.* San Francisco: Jossey-Bass.

Civian, J. T., Arnold, G., Gamson, Z. F., Kanter, S., & London, H. B. (1997). Implementing change. In J. G. Gaff & J. L. Ratcliff (Eds.), *Handbook of the undergraduate curriculum: A comprehensive guide to purposes, structures, practices, and change* (pp. 647–660). San Francisco: Jossey-Bass.

Clark, B. R. (2007). A note on pursuing things that work. In P. J. Gumport (Ed.), *Sociology of higher education: Contributions and their contexts* (pp. 319–324). Baltimore: Johns Hopkins Press.

Dunkin, M. J., & Biddle, B. J. (1974). *The study of teaching.* New York: Holt, Rinehart, and Winston.

Fletcher, J. J., & Patrick, S. K. (1998). Not just workshops anymore: The role of faculty development in reframing academic priorities. *International Journal for Academic Development, 3*(1), 39–46.

Fullan, M. (2007). *The new meaning of educational change* (4th ed.). New York: Teachers College Press.

Groccia, J. E. (2007, Winter). Planning faculty development activities: Using a holistic teaching and learning model. *POD Network News,* pp. 1, 3.

Jackson, B. W., & Holvino, E. (1986, October). *Working with multicultural organizations: Matching theory and practice.* Paper presented at the Organizational Development Network Conference, New York.

Kezar, A. J. (2001). *Understanding and facilitating organizational change in the 21st century: Recent research and conceptualizations* (ASHE-ERIC Higher Education Report Vol. 28, No. 4). San Francisco: Jossey-Bass.

Kuh, G. D. (1996). Guiding principles for creating seamless learning environments for undergraduates. *Journal of College Student Development, 37*(2), 135–148.

Lindquist, J. (1997). Strategies for change. In J. G. Gaff & J. L. Ratcliff (Eds.), *Handbook of the undergraduate curriculum: A comprehensive guide to purposes, structures, practices, and change* (pp. 633–646). San Francisco: Jossey-Bass.

Marchesani, L. S., & Adams, M. (1992). Dynamics of diversity in the teaching-learning process: A faculty development model for analysis and action. In M. Adams (Ed.), *Promoting diversity in college classrooms: Innovative responses for the curriculum, faculty, and institutions. New Directions for Teaching and Learning, No. 52* (pp. 9–20). San Francisco: Jossey-Bass.

Professional and Organizational Development in Higher Education Network (POD). (n.d.). What is faculty development? Retrieved July 17, 2008, from http://www.podnetwork.org/development/definitions.htm

Roper, L. D. (2007). Creating, sustaining, and transforming difference, power, and discrimination programs. In J. Xing, J. Li, L. Roper, & S. Shaw (Eds.), *Teaching for change: The difference, power, and discrimination model* (pp. 227–234). Lanham, MD: Lexington Books.

Scott, G. (1999). *Change matters: Making a difference in education and training.* St. Leonards, Australia: Allen & Unwin.

Scott, G. (2003, November/December). Effective change management in higher education. *Educause Review, 38*(6), 64–80.

Sell, G. R., & Lounsberry, B. (1997). Supporting curriculum development. In J. G. Gaff & J. L. Ratcliff (Eds.), *Handbook of the undergraduate curriculum: A comprehensive guide to purposes, structures, practices, and change* (pp. 661–683). San Francisco: Jossey-Bass.

Shulman, L. S. (1986). Paradigms and research programs in the study of teaching: A contemporary perspective. In M. C. Wittrock (Ed.), *Handbook of research on teaching* (3rd ed., pp. 6–9). New York: Macmillan.

Smith, D. G. (1989). *The challenge of diversity: Involvement or alienation in the academy?* (ASHE-ERIC Higher Education Report No. 5). Washington DC: George Washington University.

Sorcinelli, M. D., Austin, A. E., Eddy, P. L., & Beach, A. L. (2006). *Creating the future of faculty development: Learning from the past, understanding the present.* Bolton, MA: Anker.

Taylor, K. L. (2005). Academic development as institutional leadership: An interplay of person, role, strategy, and institution. *International Journal for Academic Development, 10*(1), 31–46.

PART TWO

COLLABORATIONS

6

BEYOND DIVERSITY

Social Justice Education Across the Curriculum

Kathleen Skubikowski

On March 2, 2007, speaking from the pulpit of Middlebury College's Mead Chapel, gazing over the thousand faces of students, faculty, staff, and townspeople seated in rows of polished wooden pews, environmental activist Terry Tempest Williams linked for her audience the work of environmental activism with the work of social justice. "Clear Cut," an exhibition of Robert Adams's photographs of dead tree trunks and broken limbs on display in the college museum just steps away, bears witness, she told us, to the same attitude toward the sanctity of life as do the hacked limbs and broken bodies left on the roadsides of Rwanda by machete-wielding Hutu gangs: "Just cut it."

"What can we do?" asked a student when Tempest had finished her talk. "Speak out," she said. "Stand together" (Williams, 2007).

The next evening, from the same pulpit, Paul Rusesabagina, the Rwandan Hutu who saved hundreds of Tutsis from massacre in a Kigali hotel, the subject of the 2004 film *Hotel Rwanda,* answered the same question:

What can we do?

Stand together. Speak out. "With words you can kill, but with words you can also civilize" (Rusesabagina, 2007).

As 21st century American academics we find ourselves in a time of challenge and change, well articulated in a 1998 pamphlet entitled "Encouraging Students in a Socially Diverse Classroom," collaboratively produced by the Bok Center for Teaching and Learning at Harvard University and the Harvard Office for Race Relations and Minority Affairs:

Colleges and universities are at a turning point. . . . Teachers of many years are being asked to acknowledge and accept students with perspectives other than their own and to include in their syllabi material that may be unfamiliar and uncomfortable. . . . All of us are asked to reexamine our own assumptions—about our students, our course contents, our universities, and even ourselves. Our collective ability to respond to and be enriched by these challenges will determine the success of our institutions in the next century.

What strikes me strongly about the Harvard call to embrace the challenge of change is that, although as faculty we are often colleagues and friends, both within and across institutions, our "collective ability" is not often engaged: We are rarely called to stand together as change agents. "Activist agent of institutional change" is not a familiar faculty role, nor is collaboration a familiar methodology in many of our disciplines. At our home institutions we are most often to be found speaking out to shape and change minds solely within the confines of our individual classrooms. And we rely on our colleagues to do similar work in classrooms we will never enter, as we exert our stewardship over four years of our students' learning lives. Autonomy is a time-honored faculty tradition. Yet the Williams and Rusesabagina messages of interdependence and voice, calling for something of a choir of activists, are as necessary to the microcosms of college and university campuses as they are to the global challenges relating to the environment and race.

Our institutions have been challenged before and have responded well. In the 1970s, in response to the "Johnny can't write" educational challenge, Writing Across the Curriculum (WAC) was implemented, and faculty development programs grew to support it. Now more than half our institutions embrace WAC. And we similarly responded to the digital technology challenge, which has, over the last two decades, transformed our classrooms, our campuses, and our institutional budgeting priorities. We have committed ourselves to spreading educational technology across our academic departments and have instituted faculty development programs in support. Indeed, many of our institutions' centers for teaching and learning were founded in response to the new possibilities of writing across the curriculum and of teaching in a digital age.

However, we have yet to embrace social justice across the curriculum or to commit resources to faculty development in social justice education. This chapter offers insights from a yearlong, intra- and interinstitutional collaboration in response to the social justice challenge to speak out, to act, and to change: the Mellon Foundation–funded "model institutes" at six liberal arts colleges, for developing faculty in social justice education. Based on our experiences with the model institute at Middlebury during the 2005–2006 grant year and now three years beyond, I suggest adopting social justice across the curriculum (SJAC) and faculty development programs in support. And we suggest that the two greatest challenges of faculty development in SJAC are the pedagogical practices of personal reflection and collaboration.

The Mellon Model Institutes

At Middlebury our first social justice collaboration during the 2005–2006 grant year was inter-institutional. With the aid of the Mellon Foundation, and inspired by the work of the Bok Center and of Maurianne Adams and Barbara Love at the University of Massachusetts, our first collaboration brought together for a weekend retreat at Middlebury the directors of centers for teaching and learning and the deans of diversity from Middlebury, Vassar, Denison, DePauw, and Furman. Working as institute local organizers, these directors and deans were challenged to identify, at their home institutions, a core group of faculty across a range of disciplines who wanted to address in either their pedagogy or their course content such issues as cultural diversity, race and ethnicity, religious difference, class, color, gender, sexual preference, privilege, global awareness, or civic engagement.

At the retreat, organizers exchanged information about their campus cultures and about what brought them personally and professionally to the topic of social justice education. Then they learned from Adams and Love to design faculty development venues, called "Mellon Institutes for Faculty on Social Justice Education," that would support the core faculty on their campuses. They were introduced to the four-quadrant model for analysis of social justice teaching and learning, and they practiced the tools from the "Know Yourself as Instructor" quadrant (Adams & Love, 2005). Through self-reflection and the reevaluation of their own pedagogical habits, organizers addressed the political nature of the educational process and began to see themselves as change agents. Adams and Love emphasize that beyond diversity or multiculturalism, the concept of social justice has emerged to address the interplay between difference and power within institutions with the aim of transforming them (Adams & Love, 2005, p. 12). In a retreat atmosphere that fostered introspection, personal interaction, and assessment, organizers established goals for the year ahead and decided to work with their core faculty to give a social justice emphasis to already scheduled events and already existing curricular and institutional structures on their individual campuses.

On each of the campuses, the Model Institute would emanate from a center for teaching and learning (CTL). CTL directors are often either senior faculty at their institutions or education professionals informed by the scholarship of teaching and learning (SOTL). The pedagogies of engagement these CTLs encourage help put student learning at the top of an institution's agenda. On a national level, SOTL encourages interactive, student-centered learning and makes faculty praxis, both inside and outside the four walls of the classroom, visible and available to inquiry, encouraging the analysis and discussion of student learning. SOTL studies of teaching praxis and student learning impacts are increasingly collaborative, encouraging, for example, projects like the reading of student portfolios by faculty across disciplines and across institutions. It was a premise of the grant year's work that, as an intellectual focus and motivator for CTL efforts in faculty development, social justice education could respond well to the changing demographics of both student and junior colleague populations, and put faculty in fruitful dialogue with their institution's mission statements and priorities.

Self-Reflection

Social justice education's principle method is self-reflection; thus, the first challenge it presents to faculty, and to faculty developers, is to make oneself an object of inquiry. Perhaps most controversial at the faculty development level, social justice education challenges faculty to balance the emotional and cognitive components of learning and the personal and the professional components of teaching. It draws faculty out of the classroom and into the community to engage in both research and service. Faculty who engage social justice education ideally begin by reassessing their own personal and institutional allocations of resources, their own conscious and unconscious biases; they then reengage the subject matter of their disciplines, conscious of power and privilege, and they reexamine their pedagogical practices with an eye toward inclusiveness (Adams, Bell, & Griffin, 1997). The supposition is that sharing personal and intellectual history as well as pedagogic choices will bring faculty to the edges of their academic disciplines, deeper into the meaning and purpose of their work as intellectuals and educators, and potentially into conflict with their institutions and their professions. The aim is to evolve classroom environments that are active and engaged within institutions that are also open to controversy and safe for disagreement.

At Middlebury, during the grant year the organizers began the Model Institute at what seemed to be the beginning: "Knowing Ourselves as Instructors." We planned two fall workshops, the first focusing on faculty's initiating the work of knowing themselves and the second focusing on knowing their students. It made sense to us as developers to consider initially what self-awareness we as faculty bring to the classroom, before considering our students, our disciplinary content and pedagogical choices, and finally, our institution's choices. In retrospect, however, it strikes us that we attempted to do the most difficult work first.

We began in October 2005 with the Social Justice Education Workshop for 20 interested colleagues at our Center for Teaching, Learning, and Research (CTLR). We knew that an invitation to such a workshop would attract faculty with previous interest in the subject and, in fact, hoped to begin consolidating a core group on campus, "the choir." We began the workshop by examining the critical terminology of any social justice discussion: "diversity," "multicultural," "social justice," "equality," "equity," "discrimination," "prejudice," "racism," and "white privilege" (Kendall, 2006, pp. 21–22). As longtime social justice educator and author of *Understanding White Privilege* Frances Kendall notes, even a *Random House Dictionary* definition of such potentially off-putting terms can lower anxiety and resistance levels and clarify the issues, both in workshops and in the classroom (Kendall, 2006). Then we introduced faculty to the Adams/Love four-quadrant model, asking each participant to produce a personal inventory of group affiliations. Each colleague entered her or his name into a circle in the middle of a handout; then in concentric circles each identified five peer groups to which she or he belonged. Next, each participant chose one group membership and wrote about the positive connotations this group elicited, then chose another group membership and wrote on its negative connotations. The aim of the exercise, one that Diane Goodman and Steven Schapiro used in examining sexism with their students, was to identify and examine spheres of influence in our lives (Adams et al., 1997), consider their roles in the privileges and oppressions we experience, and eventually identify ways to interrupt negative influences.

In the ensuing discussion, some of our colleagues exhibited a good deal of anxiety. Some of them viewed personal information, concerns, and problems as nonacademic and thus as not pertinent to their roles as college educators. One participant announced, "This is too touchy–feely." Others admitted, perhaps reflecting our graduate training, that it was extremely difficult to include their personal histories and feelings into their understanding of themselves as faculty. Bell, Washington, Weinstein, and Love (1997) explain, "For most faculty, our professional training has not prepared us to address emotionally and socially charged issues in the classroom. Social justice education is not simply new content but often a radical change in process as well" (p. 299).

Perhaps we should have expected that it would take time to access participants' faculty identities as objects of inquiry. Although self-reflection and personal change lie at the center of social justice pedagogy, by the end of the first workshop we were unsure whether a core faculty, let alone our colleagues at large, were ready to engage in questions of self-analysis, and whether we as faculty developers were entirely ready to lead such discussions. On some of the Mellon Model Institute campuses, prior conversations on diversity and multiculturalism had faculty well prepared to participate in the institutes' next steps forward. On others, faculty had been less involved in their institution's responses to diversity. Were our Middlebury colleagues ready to participate actively in social justice teaching? Was our campus ready to move from discussion to evaluation and, ultimately, to action? What exactly is the role of a change agent? This work demanded a new expertise, proficiency, and competence, even from those experienced in faculty development.

Our questions lingered to some extent for the rest of the year, and were certainly with us when we organized our second fall event, "Knowing Our Students," at a well-attended brunch at CTLR. We first viewed a student project from a psychology course, a digital story on racial segregation on our campus entitled "Why Are All the Black Kids Sitting Together in the Cafeteria?"—its title taken from Beverly Tatum's (1997) book, and its aim to test her findings on the Middlebury campus. Instead of focusing the ensuing discussion on an evaluation of the student's project, we asked participants for their personal reactions. One colleague shared his experience of learning, not entirely successfully, to use digital media alongside his students. He had felt "unprepared" for his venture into collaborative and "creative" work. Another noted that she felt pressure to maintain her distance and authority as a teacher, or else she would be seen as "soft." She described frustration with the "teacher" roles available to her. A third expressed gratitude simply for being invited to the discussion and wondered how we knew that she made efforts to address social justice in her classes. With a student's work at the center of the discussion, faculty apparently could talk, albeit hesitantly at first, about personal and professional choices. These and other contributions helped us rethink our approach to guiding our colleagues' reflections, and to identify the need for concrete teaching support as a focus for our CTLR work during the grant year and beyond.

We decided that at CTLR we could continue the work of change beyond the grant year by refocusing our annual summer pedagogy series for faculty, "Pedagogies and Tools," originally about technological tools, to include the pedagogical tools of social justice across the curriculum. The next summer we included a panel, "The Position of the Teacher," at which participants, including colleagues from our brunch workshop, were able to discuss their presence in the classroom vis-à-vis their gender, sexuality, and ethnicity. By summer 2008 we had changed the series to a "Pedagogy Roundtable" and included alongside the traditionally popular sessions like "Teaching With Multimedia" new, cross-curricular sessions on "Contemplative Pedagogy," "Feminist Pedagogy," and "Social Justice Pedagogy." This Roundtable series gave us an opportunity to institutionally support cross-curricular discussion regarding the position of the teacher, and the possibilities and challenges of emerging pedagogies. We had learned as faculty developers to take conversations about social justice education out of the margins and place them within an existing structure, aiming to transform that structure. And it did. At all the Roundtables we now begin by asking faculty what brought them to the topic, and we find that, once a few colleagues respond to the invitation to bring personal and intellectual histories to the table, the conversations move animatedly and sometimes even heatedly among the topics of our roles in our classrooms, within our disciplines, within our institution, and within our communities. At the ends of all the 2008 Roundtable sessions, engaged faculty asked the CTLR to help design venues for further conversations during the academic year. And at the end of the "Social Justice Pedagogy" Roundtable, the newly formed Diversity Curriculum Committee met to draft guidelines for department chairs to help them assess their curricula from a social justice perspective.

Collaboration

In her workshops on campuses like Middlebury and in workplaces across the country, Frances Kendall informally cites such systems analysts as Elizabeth Cooney and Peter Senge to remind her audiences of would-be change agents that any sustained change, beyond engaged conversation, must be systemic. Institutions are exquisitely designed, she reminds her audiences, to produce the outcomes they produce. If you want to change the outcome, you have to change the institution. And, according to Kendall, the "you" in social justice work is necessarily plural: On the shoulders of one person the work of systemic change is suicide; on the shoulders of two, a lovers' leap; on the shoulders of three or more, collaboration begins (Kendall, 2005).

A second challenge of social justice education for faculty is to collaborate. Among the lessons learned from the James Irvine Foundation–funded 2000–2005 Campus Diversity Initiative across the colleges and universities of the California state higher education system is that "Conceptually, diversity must move from being thought of as the responsibility of a few designated individuals to being understood as a *shared endeavor across campus constituents*" (Clayton-Pedersen, Smith, Moreno, & Teraguchi, 2007, p. 3). On a practical level, social justice change cannot end with the work of the office of admissions' bringing students of color to our campuses and our classrooms, nor can the office of institutional diversity be isolated in its responsibilities. On campuses like ours, however, it was rare in 2005–2006, our grant year, for diversity officers to engage faculty in discussions of pedagogic choices in any systematic way, or for colleagues affiliated with CTLs and diversity offices to collaborate with or learn from each other.

At Middlebury we decided that sustained, systemic change should begin with the curriculum, and in January of the grant year CTLR organized a cluster of courses under the theme of social justice during Middlebury College's monthlong Winter Term, a term in which students take only one course and faculty teach only one. It was a space, albeit on the margins of the academic calendar, to put social justice across the curriculum into practice. And although theorists of systemic change warn against "piecemeal reactions" and favor "actions that foster both organizational and individual learning" (Clayton-Pedersen et al., 2007, p. 7), for us Winter Term has long been a locus for pedagogical and curricular experimentation. Thus Winter Term is an institutionally sanctioned space for risk taking, and in it Middlebury students have come to expect teaching and learning to be different. In addition, the cluster took advantage of preexisting support from the dean of faculty's academic enrichment fund, which had not been tapped to support enrichment activities for a cluster of Winter Term courses in at least 10 years.

CTLR invited faculty teaching during this term to join a "Winter Term Social Justice Cluster." Seven faculty signed up from five different disciplines: art history, French, music, English, and sociology, to teach the following courses: African American Art, Existentialism and the Absurd, Global Popular Music, History of American Negro Spiritual and Its Influence on Western Civilization, Writing for Social Change, The Art of the Personal: James Baldwin's Non-Fiction, and the 1960s. As instructors they represented a range of social identities: African American, White, gay, straight, male, female.

In a series of meetings, cluster faculty discussed options for collaboration and decided to share guest speakers and to engage in a common, central activity. They scheduled Tuesday lunches for the entire cluster—seven faculty and 120 students—at each of which they shared an event, a guest speaker, and a discussion pertaining to social justice. Over the course of the term, participants responded collectively to texts by Martha Nussbaum and James Baldwin, learned about and learned to sing Negro spirituals, engaged in deliberative dialogue on gender issues nationally and on campus, and heard guest lectures. Throughout the January term, CTLR also organized a weekly film series around the theme of social justice, which included a documentary on Howard Zinn, *You Can't be Neutral on a Moving Train; Refugee All Stars; La Haine;* and *Darwin's Nightmare.* Each film was selected by a faculty member interested in, but unable to teach in, the cluster, who participated by introducing the film.

During the final cluster lunch session, selected students presented their term's work, providing all participants with windows into one another's classes and offering faculty glimpses into each other's pedagogies. Students from the writing classes shared digital stories on James Baldwin and on aspects of identity, such as national identity as understood by a young Afghan woman, and ethnic identity, or the issue of "passing," as seen through the eyes of a Puerto Rican American male. The 1960s class described their research on the Civil Rights Movement. A service-learning class that spent winter term rebuilding homes in New Orleans after the devastation of Hurricane Katrina joined the cluster that day to share stories of their experience.

In the end, we viewed the social justice course cluster as a positive event having produced both individual and organizational learning. The coming together of student voices at the final lunch generated a sense of activism. Following the presentations, for example, connections were made between a student organization, Women and Global Peace, and the teacher of a future first-year seminar that would support the organization and engage service-learning. A connection was also forged between CTLR and an artist in residence that resulted in his participation in a joint CTLR and Office of Institutional Diversity weblog project. We were successful, too, in creating visibility on campus around the theme of social justice. The cluster appeared in the course catalog, and its success was reported in the student newspaper. Its dialogues helped create better prepared faculty and student audiences for campus visits in the spring by Frances Kendall and Tim Wise, who spoke on White privilege. And in a white paper to the college's president, the *Report of the 2006 Human Relations Committee,* it was described as a "curricular innovation" and listed as a constructive example under their recommendation for the college "to develop the curriculum to increase student exposure to topics related to diversity" (Report, 2006, pp. 17–18).

Conclusions and Beginnings

In June of 2006, the end of the grant year, the organizers from the six Mellon campuses met again, at the National Conference on Race & Ethnicity in Higher Education (NCORE) in Chicago, to share local experiences and extrapolate lessons. At Scripps College, we heard, organizers had worked with a group of faculty to integrate issues of diversity into the curriculum by making social justice the theme of a community service-learning program that would extend Scripps's commitment to issues of diversity beyond the classroom. Organizers saw their Model Institute on social justice as allowing them not only to implement the idea but also to launch a faculty development program to increase the number of courses at Scripps that would have a community service component (Skubikowski, 2006). At Furman, organizers addressed the issue of faculty working in isolation and identified a core group of faculty who collaborated in implementing lively faculty–student discussions on diversity in the classroom and in campus life. Soon afterward, Furman's faculty approved a new general education curriculum that included a place for courses "flagged" as emphasizing global awareness, diversity, and social justice. As a result, beyond the grant year the organizers planned a faculty retreat on teaching social justice that would seed ideas for the imminent course designs and redesigns (Skubikowski, 2006).

As a group, the Mellon grant organizers concluded that faculty on our campuses who were already engaging diversity and difference in their teaching were doing so for the most part in isolation and needed recognition and support. Far from preaching to the choir, as we had initially feared, we found that we had no choirs and had to form them. We found that pedagogical change, curricular change, and institutional change go necessarily together: The socially just classroom needs a socially just academy in order to flourish. Faculty will take pedagogical risks in supportive environments. Thus the kinds of collaborations for which our colleagues hunger but discussed with some difficulty might best be both horizontal (among faculty across the curriculum) and vertical (among faculty, administrators, students, staff, alumni) to create such socially just educational environments.

Still, it is our observation that many faculty feel vulnerable in their efforts to teach social inequity or to try new engaged pedagogies, and they need communication, development, and support. Many still do not perceive the value of self-reflection in relation to their professional work. Some faculty resist identifying the effects of their inclusion in dominant groups on their teaching and scholarship; others feel the need to compensate for their position in subordinate groups in ways that limit their pedagogical practices. Even faculty interested in trying new pedagogies have legitimate concerns about the negative impact on their student and peer evaluations.

In order to respond to institutional and colleague resistance, it is our observation that collaborations outside the institution are helpful. On some of our campuses the term *social justice* itself (like "White privilege," or "civic engagement") invites tension. Social justice work is interruptive, yet the association of "social justice" with terms like *Mellon* or *Vassar* or *Middlebury* can give it a hearing it might not otherwise get. And based on our own experiences in the Adams and Love workshops, on our observations of colleagues from other institutions in those workshops, on our bringing in outside speakers, and based on our observations in faculty development workshops, we found that outside experts provide a reassuring context that eases faculty reservations and allows faculty to examine old assumptions in order to reflect on and play with new ideas.

The goals of the Mellon faculty development grant were the same as the missions of SOTL and of centers for teaching and learning: to enrich learning and teaching, and to help faculty colleagues expand knowledge bases and pedagogical praxis through inquiry and collaboration. Placing CTL goals within the context of social justice education across the curriculum requires that both faculty and faculty developers engage the challenge to change with self-reflection and with an awareness of the ways that power and privilege intersect with our personal histories and classroom practices. Perhaps as college faculty we have not yet begun the work of linking, as Terry Tempest Williams has linked, social justice to what we are already doing in our professional lives. Maybe we have not yet been pushed far enough out of our personal and professional comfort zones, as Paul Rusesabagina was pushed, to force us to take a stand. If, however, we do take the link between higher education institutions and social justice seriously, we must develop two additional links: individually, between our personal and our professional lives and, collectively, to our colleagues in other disciplines. Our individual pedagogies must become self-reflective, inclusive, and comparative; our students' learning must be engaged, the subject of our professional inquiry, and central to our institutions' missions; and our institutions must reflect the change.

References

Adams, M., Bell, L. A., & Griffin P. (1997). *Teaching for diversity and social justice: A sourcebook.* New York: Routledge.

Adams, M., & Love, B. J. (2005, September 24). *Model Institute for Faculty Development On Social Justice Education.* Breadloaf Campus, Middlebury College.

Bell, L. A. (1997). Theoretical foundations for social justice education. In M. Adams, L. A. Bell, & P. Griffin (Eds.), *Teaching for diversity and social justice: A sourcebook* (pp. 1–15). New York: Routledge.

Bell, L. A., Washington, S., Weinstein G., & Love, B. (1997). Knowing ourselves as instructors. In M. Adams, L. A. Bell, & P. Griffin (Eds.), *Teaching for diversity and social justice: A sourcebook* (pp. 299–310). New York: Routledge.

Clayton-Pedersen, P., Smith, D. G., Moreno, J. F., & Teraguchi, D. H. (2007). *Making a real difference with diversity.* Washington, DC: Association of American Colleges and Universities.

Encouraging students in a socially diverse classroom. (1998). Harvard University: Bok Center for Teaching and Learning and the Harvard Office for Race Relations and Minority Affairs.

Goodman, D., & Schapiro, S. (1997). Sexism curriculum design. In M. Adams, L. A. Bell, & P. Griffin (Eds.), *Teaching for diversity and social justice: A sourcebook* (pp. 110–140). New York: Routledge.

Kendall, F. (2005, June 2). *Excavating the layers of White privilege.* Presented at the National Conference on Race and Ethnicity in American Higher Education, New York.

Kendall, F. (2006). *Understanding White privilege.* New York: Routledge.

Report of the Human Relations Committee. (2006). Retrieved August 14, 2009, from http://www.middlebury.edu/NR/rdonlyres/A8244CCA-CC6F-4D60-840F -9DCBBE43BF94/0/HRCFinalDraft.pdf

Rusesabagina, P. (2007, March 3). *Address to the community.* Presented at Middlebury College, Middlebury, VT.

Skubikowski, K. (2006). Final report on the Model Institutes for Faculty on Social Justice Education. *Teaching for Social Justice in Higher Education.* Retrieved August 14, 2009, from https://seguecommunity.middlebury.edu/index.php? action = site&site = cwwright

Tatum, B. D. (1997). *Why are all the Black kids sitting together in the cafeteria?* New York: Basic Books.

Williams, T. T. (2007, March 2). *Address to the community.* Presented at Middlebury College, Middlebury, VT.

7

CIVICS WITHOUT CYNICS

A Campuswide, Ethics-Based Approach to Social Justice Pedagogy

Meryl Altman, Neal Abraham, Terri Bonebright, and Jeannette Johnson-Licon

I seem to be hearing a lot about this ethics business recently. Is it just flavor of the month, or what?

—Faculty member's mother

At this point the question of method legitimately arises. How to do it? How to develop a working situation in the classroom where trust becomes a reality, where students are writing with belief in their own validity, and reading with belief that what they read has validity for them? (Rich, 1979, p. 65)

Knowledge emerges only through invention and reinvention, through the restless, impatient, continuing, hopeful inquiry human beings pursue in the world, with the world, and with each other. (Freire, 2005, p. 72)

Looking back on all my papers, I realize I have had a personal experience and/or an opinion about almost every topic we have had in class. This is interesting to me, because prior to this class I actually thought I didn't have an opinion on anything. (Student, Introduction to Women's Studies end-of-semester self-evaluation.)

Thanks are due to many faculty members who contributed to the writing of this chapter, and to the strength of the programs it describes: Tamara Beauboeuf, Mona Bhan, Rich Cameron, Sharon Crary, Dana Dudle, Jennifer Everett, Glenn Kuecker, Richard Lynch, Keith Nightenhelser, Brett O'Bannon, Jeane Pope, and Martha Rainbolt.

ePauw University might not seem like promising terrain for a broad-based initiative in social justice. We are small; we are isolated; we are not well-known outside the Midwest; we are very expensive, and for most of our history we were very, very White. Our admissions office promotes a DePauw education as a path toward financial and career success; a very high percentage of our students participate in fraternities and sororities, with all the challenges that participation presents in terms of both exclusivity and conformity. (Yes, Dan Quayle did go to DePauw.)

And yet, as we shared experiences with other campuses through the opportunities offered by a Mellon-funded project, we heard that colleagues elsewhere often felt like lone voices crying in the wilderness, unsupported by campus culture, swimming against the tide, even mocked. Our experience has been quite different. The term "social justice pedagogy" did not create tension or cause confusion or suspicion, and faculty members from a wide range of departments and generations were eager to participate in workshops and events. Make no mistake: We still have a long way to go at DePauw. A recent taskforce report indicates that many students and faculty members of color still sometimes experience the environment as unwelcoming; we are not yet in a position to offer financial aid to all qualified students who need it; in individual classrooms and more broadly across campus, we still struggle every semester to make good on our promise that every admitted student can succeed. However, by and large, we do not experience initiatives around diversity, ethics, civic engagement, social responsibility, or teaching for social justice as impositions or interruptions to our work. These things *are* our work. (Percy Julian, Vernon Jordan, and Lee Hamilton went to DePauw, too. And so did Barbara Kingsolver.)

Our contention is that social justice pedagogy efforts work best when they are well integrated with the ongoing practices and shared themes of the institution, and when they are informed by sincere and widely shared commitments to teaching intellectual and ethical values. Here at DePauw, we have the advantage of several decades of strong, genuine commitment to diversifying the student body and the faculty, and of a very visible and well-funded Ethics Initiative, which has found a home in the programs of the Janet Prindle Institute for Ethics, which occupies a recently completed LEED (Leadership in Energy and Environmental Design) gold-certified building in the DePauw Nature Park.[1] We also have a strong workshop culture on campus, where faculty members often gather in good-sized groups to work through teaching challenges and share resources in an interdisciplinary and cooperative spirit, which is coordinated and funded through an intentional, well-resourced program for faculty development. Finally, we benefit from the work of student affairs professionals who act as educators in partnership with faculty members to support the academic mission of the university and particularly from the synergy provided by the Compton Center, a student affairs office and resource for students and faculty members interested in peace and justice activism.

Overall, we have tried to foster a range of approaches, from out-and-out activism to simple moral reflection, on topics ranging from very academic to very timely, seeing and making connections where they naturally arise. We conceive "ethics" broadly, as encompassing everything from technical issues in philosophical theory, to questions archaeologists face in excavating sacred sites, to student activism around an environmentally sustainable campus. Ethics-related projects, some for research, some for teaching, some combining both, are ongoing in nearly every discipline. We hope our students will understand that ethics is not something you think about on Sunday, not an honor code that you hear a lecture about and then have to sign, not a set of steps you have to follow to get around the institutional review board; rather, ethics is a mode of reflection, an impulse to ask certain questions, a drive to acquire the skills to answer them, and the courage to act on the answers.

However, if we want our students to be like that, we need to be like that ourselves. We must bring to bear all the specialized training and knowledge at our disposal, in a collaborative, engaged, and interdisciplinary way. Most important is opening a space for students—and for faculty members and administrators—to be serious rather than cynical. Postmodern habits of mind, inside and outside the academy, do not make that easy, and graduate education does not make much space for it. But we have to try.

Axiom One: Gather and Use the Energy and the Knowledge You Already Have

Example: Social Justice Institutes

Under the Mellon-funded faculty career enhancement grant, held in partnership with five other colleges, the "Social Justice Institute" rubric developed at Middlebury College was used to support and integrate activities at DePauw that had already been planned, such as hosting a visit by public intellectual bell hooks and the Great Lakes College Student of Color Leadership Summit Conference. One highlight of that conference was the presentation of the documentary video *Five Minority Perspectives on DePauw*, a frank and searching exploration of what it is like to be a student of color here, which student Nicole Halper produced as her senior project in the Department of Communication and Theatre. The project's impact did not end when Nicole graduated. We have used the video since as part of new faculty orientation, because it includes segments on race in the classroom, segregation in the dining hall, experiencing racism, interracial dating, and the social scene, and it is a reality check about who is sitting in our classrooms and what we are and are not accomplishing.

DePauw's Social Justice Institute also provided occasions for faculty members to share assignments and ideas. Economist Ray Burgman described an intermediate microeconomics class in which she was engaging students in a simulation exercise to create nonprofit organizations instead of profit-making corporations as she used to do (and as is more typical); sociologist Rebecca Bordt talked about an assignment she developed for her course on prisons, in which students communicate directly by e-mail with a writer who is in jail (they read his book, he reads and comments on their papers); anthropologist Mona Bhan shared a reading she assigns about how efforts to "Save the Tigers" in Sri Lanka have unintended, devastating effects on villages that rely on the forest for their livelihood. In another extremely fruitful session, faculty members and student affairs staff members talked about ways to work toward respecting and including one another. One of the most revealing sessions, in which a small group of faculty members spoke candidly about teaching difficult issues, led to a new faculty orientation session on classroom climate the following year.

The second year began with a call for people interested in a reading/discussion group to be led by three junior faculty members, a political scientist, a philosopher, and a biochemist. Over 50 people, from a wide range of departments and across generations, turned up at the first meeting. Almost more important than anything actually said at the meeting was what this turnout showed about the breadth of interest and commitment across campus. Younger faculty members in particular felt heartened that their efforts would be supported, and all of us were energized by the evidence of a context for what we were doing. Even though specific agendas differed and people disagreed (sometimes vehemently), all were part of a larger whole. That year, alongside lively and contentious interchange around readings that ranged from cosmopolitan ethics to sustainability and environmental justice, we uncovered new potential collaborations among faculty members and began developing course modules to be shared. As Terri Bonebright (then faculty development coordinator) reported at the end of that year, "The discoveries from the workshops, reading groups and discussions demonstrate that social justice issues are not solely the responsibility or interest of those in philosophy, sociology and political science; instead we found broad interest, ranging from scientists to teachers of literature. We learned that social justice issues pervade the curriculum and pedagogy at DePauw University and that there is broad interest in addressing them" (end-of-year report, June 2007).

Axiom Two: Include Everyone; Integrate Everything

Examples: Humanitarian Intervention; Sustainability

Another result of the synergy between the Mellon grant and the new Prindle Institute was a proliferation of reading groups, which then generated broader projects. For instance, the Prindle Institute sponsored political scientist Brett O'Bannon's faculty reading group on humanitarian intervention, which led in turn to the planning of a major symposium for March 2009: "Imperfect Duties? Humanitarian Intervention in Africa and the Responsibility to Protect in the 21st Century." To prepare students and faculty members for the event, Brett provided detailed information over the summer of 2008, encouraging us to incorporate the symposium in our course planning for the year. The long list of speakers for the symposium includes Amos Sawyer, former president of the Interim Government of National Unity in Liberia; Babacar Kante, vice president of the Constitutional Court, Republic of Senegal; and Karen Koning AbuZayd, commissioner-general, United Nations Relief and Works Agency. (Karen AbuZayd also went to DePauw, and was our commencement speaker in 2007.)

DePauw annually hosts a number of high-profile public events to which we invite alumni as well as the whole campus and Greencastle community. These often, and without argument or embarrassment, involve a social justice theme, as their titles show: Arts Fest 2007, "Arts and the Environment"; Arts Fest 2009, "Art and Borders"; DePauw Discourse 2008, "America's Role in the World"; DePauw Discourse 2007, "Sustainability and Global

Citizenship"; and the whole series of Boswell Symposia: 2006, "Race-ing for Social Justice"; 2007, "Grassroots Environmental Activism"; and 2008, "Ethics and Global Justice," with keynoter Cornell West. Although some might be cynical about the cost of these events, they do serve to offset the isolation of our campus, and they keep social and ethical issues in public focus, showing strong administrative and board support.

In fact, the wide range of speakers coming to DePauw each year provides opportunities for building broad coalitions and spreading resources. An event is often cosponsored by more than one interdisciplinary program or by an interdisciplinary program and a department, or by a faculty member or program in coordination with Student Life, the Office of Multicultural Affairs, or another of our many student-run groups. Events are typically publicized in ways that make them resources for teaching. Professors may require their classes to attend an event, prepare them by assigning a reading, set aside class time for debriefing, and so on. Ideally, this bridges the disconnect between what happens inside and outside the classroom, spreading a shared vocabulary and set of common experiences across DePauw and helping us develop as a teaching and learning community.

A particularly successful example of a public event that sprang from activist interests and met both social and academic community needs was DePauw's contribution to Focus the Nation's January 31, 2008, event, "the largest national teach-in in U.S. history, educating nearly a million people at more than 1,900 institutions and catalyzing the conversation on global warming solutions with 64 members of Congress, 15 governors and countless local and state politicians" (http://www.focusthenation.org/focus-nation-2008-0; retrieved December 6, 2008).[2] Led by philosopher Jen Everett and geoscientist Jeane Pope, a group of some 25 faculty members planned and presented thoughts on climate-change topics in the natural sciences, social sciences, arts, and humanities. The day's 12 public sessions included "Biodiversity Loss and Climate Change," "DePauw's Sustainable Future," "Capturing Hearts and Minds: The Power of the Arts to Battle Climate Change," "Socialism, Capitalism, and the Environment," "Going Neutral and Beyond: Carbon Footprinting and Offsets," and "Green Development vs. Social Justice: Are They at Odds?" Faculty members were encouraged not just to attend these sessions and send their students but also to find ways to adapt the day's theme to their regularly scheduled classes.

This last component had been prepared for in a workshop the previous semester, "What Does Global Warming Have to Do With the Courses I Teach?" and many of us found ways to incorporate the theme, some more obvious than others. For Introduction to Women's Studies we found and disseminated recent articles about how climate change affects women in both the third and first worlds: the theme will now become part of the syllabus every semester. For Gender in Ancient Greece, we expanded the Focus the Nation theme to include all forms of activism, and turned the schedule around to start with Aristophanes' *Lysistrata*. This was a stretch, but the discussion was intellectually productive in ways that could not have been predicted, and again the ideas we discovered will continue to be incorporated in that course. Meanwhile, students deeply concerned about global warming felt supported by the bare attempt to connect with the campus-wide theme.

Participation in Focus the Nation was broad and enthusiastic, and the impact was major. Symbolically speaking, after this no one could assert that climate change was a concern only of a few isolated crusaders, or that only scientists needed to/could be involved in sustainability efforts. Practically speaking, a number of important steps and activities have followed under the leadership of Sustainability Coordinator Jen Everett. Under the DePauw Environmental Policy Project, a pilot program funded through the Prindle Institute, student interns were responsible for researching recent environmental legislation and likely policy proposals in Indiana, working with summer study committees of the Indiana General Assembly, preparing testimony on bills pending for the 2009 legislative session, and planning a summit for Indiana college students to extend the program's civic empowerment impact statewide. They also helped create the syllabus for Environmental Policy, a course Jen Everett co-taught with community activist Kelsey Kaufmann. Everett's philosophy department course, Environmental Ethics, in her words,

> made a concerted effort to address the social, economic and environmental dimensions of sustainability challenges but also to integrate academic studies of environmental ethics with the operational challenge of putting an institution's ethical commitments into effect. . . . the experience has provided fertile ground for conceptual and personal grappling with the disciplinary subject matter of moral philosophy. (Everett, Cantrill, & Orr, 2008)

The key word is *concerted*: an intention to connect efforts across campus, and to provide an umbrella for all sorts of efforts—from an "energy wars" competition between living units to John Caraher's physics course for non-majors, in which he assigns George Monbiot's (2007) *Heat: How to Stop the Planet From Burning* and requires students to analyze Monbiot's proposals for their scientific rigor. The effort is interdisciplinary at its core, not because of a top-down mandate, but because the subject demands it. Everett writes,

> As the complexity and interconnectedness of economic, political, and climatic systems have become clear, the idea that our students can be effectively prepared to tackle their generation's most pressing problems as narrowly trained experts in one field or another rather than across a broad spectrum of knowledge and skills has come unraveled. Academics who study the world's emerging sustainability challenges continually stress the inadequacy of piecemeal, additive approaches to solving them . . . . sustainability calls for an integrative, whole systems perspective. (Everett, Cantrill, & Orr, 2008)

And—in our opinion—so does every other form of social justice.

Axiom Three: Use the Campus Culture

Examples: Workshops, Workshops, Workshops

The workshop model of faculty development—long-enduring and well-supported across the DePauw faculty—provides a helpful space for advancing and broadening social justice efforts. Orientation sessions for new faculty members have always included sessions on teaching a diverse student body and creating a classroom climate that will be welcoming and supportive to all, along with more conventional topics like designing clear syllabi, writing good assignments, and creating fair systems for assessing student work. As a more concrete example, here follows a simple exercise that has become part of the regular orientation series. The "What do you do when . . . ?" exercise is designed to help teachers develop good practices and to provide the forethought they may need in dialoguing about difficult or contentious issues with a diverse student body (or in creatively meeting student resistance to our increasingly diverse faculty!). This is an intrinsic part of orientation workshops, not an "add-on" for the usual suspects who might self-identify as interested. We begin by handing out the following worksheet, asking everyone to brainstorm/freewrite for 10 minutes.

What do you do when:

1. "I'm teaching about race, and there is only one student of color in the class. He keeps looking down at his feet when the subject comes up. How do I handle that?"
2. "The women in my class don't participate as much as the men do. Why might that be?"
3. "I'm having a hard time getting students to talk."
4. "I'm having a hard time getting students to be quiet and listen to one another."
5. "I was talking about a transgender issue and asked students for their reactions. One guy raised his hand and said, 'I'm sorry, that's just sick.'"
6. "I have a student who refuses to accept peer criticism on his paper—he doesn't think other students know what they're talking about."
7. "When I ask students to make peer criticisms, they never say anything except that they like the paper very much."
8. "I know from their papers that students in my class hold a variety of opinions about X, but when we discuss X in class, only the most conservative students speak and the others are quiet" (or "Only the most liberal students speak and the others are silent.") (Do we feel differently about these two possibilities?)

Free-writing is followed by small-group discussions in which stories about classroom experiences always emerge, and there is an opportunity to say, "What did you do?" "What should I have done?" "What would you do if it happened again?" In an effort to model the kind of teaching we are trying to encourage, we do not lecture or lay out a preferred paradigm; the idea is to access and pool the experience and knowledge that colleagues, new or experienced, already have, and to develop a shared ethos about commitment to classroom equity and a welcoming climate for all.[3]

Make no mistake: these are challenging discussions that require us to work outside our own comfort zone. For instance, the first time we discussed what you do when a GLBT issue arises and a student says, "I'm sorry, that's sick!" a social science faculty member in the group said, "But we're not trained to deal with these issues; is it really our job?" and another faculty member responded, "Well, some of us deal with those issues every day of our lives." That was an interesting moment.

Another example of how social justice pedagogy is supported by a workshop culture is the weeklong faculty workshop on Feminist Ethics that took place in June 2007. Following a model that has been common for summer workshops at DePauw for several decades, especially those training faculty members to teach courses in the competence programs (writing, speaking, and quantitative reasoning across the curriculum), we met for five days, six hours per day, and the 20 participants each received a stipend and free books and articles. This particular workshop grew out of a similar, enjoyable workshop the women's studies program ran in June 2003: an interdisciplinary and intergenerational group including some faculty members with long-term core involvement in women's studies teaching and scholarship, some who had been teaching or planning to teach departmentally based courses cross-listed with women's studies, and some for whom women's studies was a completely new area or a stretch. The goals included improving the cohesiveness of the curriculum by providing those who teach across the program a shared intellectual base, encouraging broader participation, developing new courses, and so on.

For the 2007 workshop, the topic, Feminist Ethics, was construed in similarly broad and interdisciplinary ways. Three philosophers helped the facilitator select readings and during the workshop generously shared their expertise in an open and accessible spirit. Twenty-five participants attended from across the DePauw community: faculty members from Asian studies, biology, education, economics, English, geosciences, modern languages, philosophy, political science, sociology, and anthropology; a librarian, an instructional technologist, and a community activist; and both women and men, from every academic generation. Topics included Feminist Approaches to Bioethics; Care and Dependency; Intersectionalities and Privilege; Feminism and Environmentalism; Women and Citizenship; The Nature of Oppression; and Nationalism, Colonialism, and War. Readings ranged from Virginia Woolf's *Three Guineas* (1936/1966) to Siobhan Somerville's "Scientific Racism and the Homosexual Body" (1998) to Sandra Lee Bartky's "Shame and Gender" (1990) to Jamesina King's *Gender and Reparations in*

Sierra Leone (2006)—ending with three feminist approaches to Sophocles' *Antigone.* Some participants had a great deal of professional expertise and/or teaching experience with women's studies and/or with ethics; some had almost none; but everyone had a voice and a role in generating the questions that the group would take up. And everyone made a contribution, proving that it is entirely possible to have a high-level discussion with a diverse group in a completely interdisciplinary way. Many participants emerged with ideas for new writing projects, new courses, and (of course, because this is DePauw) more workshops.

Axiom Four: Connect to Core Institutional Values and Structures

Example: Faculty Development

DePauw's website, and the brochure given to all candidates for faculty positions, describes "Faculty Development" as

> a systematic, comprehensive, well-resourced effort to help us all do our best work, to learn and grow as individuals and as an intellectual and teaching community. The Faculty Development Committee, along with the Faculty Development Coordinator, . . . maintain a range of programs that support professional achievement, teaching improvement, and the life of the mind. Our programs include short- and long-term internal funding for conferences and research travel; stipends for course development and for scholarly and creative projects; new faculty orientation, and other teaching workshops; mentoring; sabbaticals and other leaves; opportunities for a reduced teaching load to undertake research or teaching improvement; and groups that meet to read, write, and discuss topics of mutual interest. A wide variety of projects are supported every year. We see particular value in collaborative and/or interdisciplinary projects, in faculty research that involves students, in creative work as well as more traditional scholarship, in efforts that support our commitments to internationalization and diversity and (a new initiative) in work that investigates the area of Ethics. Every semester, there are numerous well-attended on-campus opportunities for faculty members to present work in progress to their colleagues and receive helpful feedback. On this site you will also find listed the awards by which the accomplishments of DePauw faculty members have been recognized, both locally and around the world.

In other words, we take this work very seriously.

Faculty development is especially important because DePauw does not have a strict publication requirement: Rather than making tenure a test that some people are intended to fail, DePauw relies on a careful search process, a rigorous interim review, and thoughtful mentoring, so that nearly all who come up for tenure achieve it. This means that, if faculty members are to be both good teachers and productive scholars, we must provide other forms of encouragement, incentives, and help: generous travel budgets, competitive opportunities for people to propose projects involving reassigned time from the normal 3–3 teaching load, and recognizing and celebrating faculty achievements on the website and through a convivial end-of-year gathering.

All this work falls within the purview of the faculty development coordinator, a three-year rotating position held by a senior faculty member who works closely with the vice president, with the elected faculty development committee (which reads and vets faculty proposals for awards and leaves), and, more recently, with the Prindle Institute, which has its own faculty programs coordinator and its own advisory committee. Yet we still ask ourselves whether we are doing enough to build community in ways that are not simply cynical—co-opted by the institution. These issues are particularly important in small liberal arts colleges, where a competitive, careerist atmosphere can become particularly poisonous and destructive. How can we encourage real scholarly and intellectual productivity and prolong generativity, change, and enrichment over long careers, while giving faculty members a sense of place and of meaningful, deep commitments not divided along departmental or disciplinary lines?

Faced with the need to explain what we do and why to an incoming president from a very different type of institution, the faculty development coordinator generated a list of four basic principles:

1. People do their best work when they can identify and engage their own intrinsic motivations for teaching, learning, and scholarship. People are different. People change. One size does not fit all. Each faculty member contributes in his or her own way, and all deserve to be treated with dignity and respect.
2. Teaching and scholarly/artistic production feed one another: they do not compete. Creation of a vital intellectual community for faculty serves both.

3. Faculty members at different career and life stages may have different needs and different goals, and may benefit from different sorts of support and require different sorts of mentoring.[4] However, faculty members at all career stages are important. We try to avoid stereotypes; we encourage colleagues to reflect on their own progress and set their own goals, to "think big" but also plan realistically.

4. In keeping with DePauw's approach to faculty evaluation and promotion, faculty development is encouraging and supportive rather than punitive or competitive. As we do in our teaching, we try to send the message that all colleagues can succeed, and to make all programs as open and inclusive as possible.

These are goals, or hopes; how far we have succeeded should be for others to say.

Although the structure of faculty development explains why and how so many events can be *planned*, it does not explain why, in spite of persistent agonizing about the lack of time to do anything properly, *so many people consistently come to them*. (It can't be just the food.) For better or for worse, Greencastle is a very small town, and DePauw is a face-to-face culture, or as one visitor put it, a "total institution." Faculty members come to one another's talks, read each other's scholarly work, volunteer to mentor junior colleagues, admit when they are struggling, enjoy finding out how other colleagues do things. We are in more reading groups than you can shake a stick at. And when a problem arises—such as the difficulty of adjusting to new populations of international students in writing classes—we organize yet another workshop. Where does this energy come from?

Axiom Five: Meet People Where They Are, and Give Them What They Need

Example: First-Year Seminars and Interdisciplinary Programs

In seeking broad faculty acceptance and buy-in to the social justice pedagogy institutes, and to the Ethics Initiative more broadly, DePauw benefited from its experience developing interdisciplinary programs, most particularly from the first-year seminar program begun in 1990. At that time, in response to a perceived need for greater student engagement with their academic work, DePauw built on the experience of the Posse program, in which students are taught not just to support one another but to be proactive and intervene: to sit in the front row, to ask questions, to ask to speak with the professor if they have a problem, to keep asking for explanations until they understand. We wanted to give all students similar first-year seminar experiences in the hope that they would all acquire these skills and investments. But rather than having a small team or committee create a first-year course and then looking for people who could be convinced or coerced to teach it, we asked faculty members to create a diverse menu of courses, whatever they felt comfortable with and had always wanted to do; we then offered students the chance to choose from that menu.

The basic insight is this: To ensure the faculty is behind a new initiative, figure out what the faculty members have been wanting to do already, and show them how the new initiative will be a way for them to do it. For the first-year seminar, faculty members were offered a chance to design their own courses, and departments were encouraged to design courses that served departmental needs such as attracting majors or making sure students acquire certain skills. Similarly, when the interdisciplinary programs began, faculty members were encouraged not just to stretch beyond their own area of graduate training and expertise, but also to use that training and expertise to develop courses that met departmental needs and were also cross-listable.

Axiom Six: Good Pedagogy Is Good Pedagogy

Finally, most faculty members would agree that teaching for social justice means examining, and changing, not just what we teach, but how we teach. The three examples of teaching projects given in our discussion of axiom one (i.e., those of Burgman, Bordt, Bhan) seem especially appropriate because they do not just deliver information or outline solutions; rather, they are problem based, and require students to engage in discussion and other activities. Those of us who have come through women's studies or Project Kaleidoscope bring to the table the idea that certain concrete classroom strategies—collaborative learning, room for all voices to be heard, goals of self-development—make up a liberatory pedagogy, to the point where it may be hard to tease form and content apart. However, as we seek to spread these ideas more broadly, it is helpful that at DePauw, and probably at most other colleges of our size and type, there has been a commitment to interactive

pedagogy across the curriculum *for other good reasons.* With only a few exceptions, DePauw's faculty members have taken on board the research that indicates that a hands-on, inquiry-based approach is most effective for getting
students to actually learn *anything.*

This inquiry-based approach has won broad acceptance in the sciences,
and is reflected in our commitment to small class size and to providing
authentic student–faculty research experiences for as many students as we
can afford, while attempting to ease new faculty members away from the
lecturing-expert model they may have learned in graduate school. It makes
as little sense to teach Intro to Women's Studies as a lecture course as it does
to teach biology without a lab, and vice versa; some big schools have to do
both of these things, but that's not what DePauw is about. In a way, even
apolitical active learning, such as hands-on, discovery-based physics labs, has
a connection to social justice, because one hope that lay behind the development of these approaches was that they would bring women and minorities
to the academy and especially to science, to help them strategize to succeed.
It turned out to work well for everyone else, too (see Steele, 1997; Project
Kaleidoscope, 1991, 2008; and Treisman, 1992).

Conclusion Without Complacency

Still, most of this "innovative" and/or liberatory pedagogy is now at least 30
years old. Far from being revolutionary, it is now the dominant paradigm in
many places and many fields: it is no longer a welcome surprise and a challenge for a first-year student to be asked to write a first-person essay or a
poem; in fact, it is likely to be part of the way he or she has already learned
to "do" school. One skeptical colleague asked whether social justice pedagogy meant "the idea that putting the chairs in a circle would change the
world." At some level, the answer is sort of "yes, it did, and it still does,"
but the question offers a helpful check on smug self-righteousness. Putting
the chairs in a circle is not enough anymore to change the power dynamics
of the conventional classroom. (And Freire wasn't really talking about our
kinds of classrooms in the first place.)

There is much more work to do. We may be irritated, for instance, by
students who interrupt us to ask, "Is it going to be on the test?" But if we
want them to stop, we must be sure we are not giving the kinds of tests that
make that an appropriate question. Rather, we must be clearer in our own

minds about the relationship between what we are teaching and what we are testing. And we should stop prevaricating between the two slightly different meanings of terms like "active learning," one directed at getting more people to do a better job of mastering a body of knowledge (with right answers), the other meaning a discussion or research question itself is fully open-ended, and the teacher herself may not have arrived at a clear answer or may have decided that there is no clear answer. That sort of pedagogy requires faculty members to be really listening, and genuinely open to the possibility of outcomes very different from what they anticipate.

In the summer of 2008, DePauw's Prindle Institute hosted a weeklong workshop called Ethics and Education. Leader Tamara Beauboeuf, who had participated in the Feminist Ethics sessions, was taking over as chair of education studies, and DePauw's education studies program was being redesigned to focus on liberal arts inquiry rather than teacher credentialing and certification. We began with a discussion of Parker Palmer's *The Courage to Teach* (1998), which reminds us that authentic teaching requires us to risk knowing, and revealing, *who we really are*—which of course is more than a little terrifying. Again, the group was drawn from many disciplines and generations. When we tended to become too abstract, Beauboeuf kept bringing us back to our own classrooms and our own commitments, and also to our persistent *worries*. We could agree, for instance, that the object of education is "to produce free subjects." But does that word "produce" point to a contradiction in terms? By teaching "ethics" are we simply sophists preparing the corporate jerks of the future to oppress their workers and consumers more skillfully? The Socratic method (the original active learning pedagogy?) was of course invented to address this, but there will always be a remainder of unease.

There are always good reasons, in teaching, for humility. Among them: If we want to change our world, we have to be prepared first to challenge and change ourselves.

Notes

1. http://prindleinstitute.depauw.edu/
2. For more information, go to http://www.focusthenation.org/
3. We have all been present at events where an expert pontificated at great length, and with no apparent awareness of irony, about the importance of avoiding

the "banking model," seemingly unaware that anyone in the room might have heard about it already and/or might have some ideas to contribute.

4. Reflection on this point was stimulated by the Mellon grant for faculty career enhancement to DePauw and Denison University, and by an opening-day exercise that asked faculty members, "What helps you do your best work?"

References

Bartky, S. (1990). *Femininity and domination: Studies in the phenomenology of oppression* (pp. 83–98). New York: Routledge.

Everett, J., Cantrill, T., & Orr, M. (2008, August 25). *DePauw University sustainability status report.* Retrieved December 6, 2008, from https://www.depauw.edu/univ/sustain/documents/DePauw_Sustainability%20_Status_Report.pdf

Freire, P. (2005). *Pedagogy of the oppressed.* New York: Continuum.

King, J. (2006). Gender and reparations in Sierra Leone: The wounds of war remain open. In R. Rubio-Martin (Ed.), *What happened to the women? Gender and reparations for human rights violations* (pp. 247–283). New York: Social Science Research Council.

Monbiot, G. (2007). *Heat: How to stop the planet from burning.* Boston: South End Press.

Palmer, P. J. (1998). *The courage to teach: Exploring the inner landscape of a teacher's life.* San Francisco: Jossey-Bass.

Project Kaleidoscope. (1991). *Volume I: What works: Building natural science communities.* Retrieved December 6, 2008, http://www.pkal.org/documents/VolumeI.cfm

Project Kaleidoscope. (2008). *Volume IV: What works, what matters, what lasts (2004–present).* Retrieved December 6, 2008, from http://www.pkal.org/collections/VolumeIV.cfm

Rich, A. (1979). Teaching language in open admissions. In *On lies, secrets, and silence: Selected prose 1966–1978.* New York: W. W. Norton.

Somerville, S. (1998). Scientific racism and the homosexual body. In L. Bland & L. L. Doan (Eds.), *Sexology in culture: Labeling bodies and desires.* Chicago: University of Chicago Press.

Steele, C. (1997). A threat in the air: How stereotypes shape the intellectual identities and performance of women and African Americans. *American Psychologist, 52,* 613–629.

Treisman, U. (1992). Studying students studying calculus: A look at the lives of minority mathematics students in college. *College Mathematics Journal, 23,* 362–372.

Woolf, V. (1966). *Three guineas.* New York: Harcourt Brace and World. (Original work published 1936)

8

ON COMMITMENT

Considerations on Political Activism
on a Shocked Planet

Vijay Prashad

I n 1944, 15-year-old Michael King traveled from Morehouse College in
Atlanta, Georgia, with a group of his college friends and acquaintances
to work in the Cullman Brothers' tobacco fields in Simsbury, Connecticut. In the early 1900s, Joseph Cullman Jr. began to grow Havana, or Cuban,
seed tobacco along the Connecticut River. This broadleaf tobacco became
the outer shell of the cigar (i.e., the maduro, with the dark, mature leaf).
Cullman formed a partnership with Morehouse to bring in college students
during the summer to work the fields: The students earned money toward
their college tuition, and Cullman benefited from the seasonal labor (a hundred Morehouse students each summer). During the summer, Michael King
wrote to his mother, telling her about how he and other Black students were
able to eat at any restaurant (even "the finest restaurant in Hartford"), to
worship in any church, and to ride anywhere in the trains. "After that summer in Connecticut," he wrote in his autobiography, "it was a bitter feeling
going back to segregation" (August 4, 1944; King, 2001, p. 11).

His Simsbury experience taught this teenager about the relative freedom
of public space. But it also taught him something else. Raised in the elite
Black circles of Atlanta, Michael King did not face the everyday racist trauma
that was the lot of the Black working class. While toiling with the workers

---

This is an amended version of a lecture given at Middlebury College, Middlebury, Vermont, on January
21, 2008.

in the tobacco fields, Michael King called his mother and told her that he wanted to be a minister; he had found his calling here, among the people who survived to struggle for a better day. Four years later he wrote, "My call to the ministry . . . came about in the summer of 1944 when I felt an inescapable urge to serve society. In short, I felt a sense of responsibility which I could not escape" (King, 1992, p. 148). Michael King became Martin Luther King Jr. and he found inspiration among those who had dirt under their fingernails. King emerges in the Connecticut River Valley out of his narrow class confines into the solidarity of generations.

King was drawn into an epochal struggle: not by theory alone, or by the drive of his social gospel, but by the brave resilience of everyday people who became extraordinary people in the struggle, people like high school student Claudette Colvin and seamstress-activist Rosa Parks. Ella Baker, who ran the Southern Christian Leadership Conference (SCLC), dismissed the idea of the leader as the "magic man" but pushed the notion that the leader must "develop individuals who were bound together by a concept that benefited large numbers of individuals and provided an opportunity for them to grow into being responsible for carrying on the program" (Morris, 1984, p. 104). Ella Baker points to two crucial elements: the ethics of an organization and the concept that motivates those within it, in other words, how it functions and what it functions for. And these two elements had to be consonant with each other. The concept was freedom, or, to give the empty word some meaning, a culture of solidarity and equality; the organization, too, had to promote this culture of solidarity within itself. That concept, the culture of solidarity, is the central lever of this chapter.

In 1988, the National Urban League reported, "More blacks have lost jobs through industrial decline than through job discrimination" (Dewart, 1988, p. 155). For a civil rights organization this was a remarkable observation. Born in the era of Jim Crow racism, the Urban League championed the aspirations for upward mobility among urban African Americans. When banks refused to lend money to Black entrepreneurs or when municipalities failed to service the Black community, the Urban League intervened. One of the demands of the Urban League was for public goods to be shared across racial lines. Although the organization was not on the frontlines of the civil rights struggle, it would have been a major beneficiary of the movement's gains. But the tragedy of the civil rights struggle is that its victory came too late, at least 30 years late. Just when the state agreed to remove the discriminatory barriers that restricted non-Whites' access to public goods, the state form changed. Privatization and an assault on the state's provision of social welfare meant that it was not capable of providing public goods to the newly enfranchised citizens. At the same time as the state withered, the industrial sector in the United States crumbled in the face of globalization. Industrial jobs, once the backbone of the segregated Black communities, vanished.

As the 1964–1965 victories closed one chapter of the Civil Rights Movement, Martin Luther King moved on. He realized that the fight ahead was just as fierce as what had come before, if not more. Returning home to the annual convention of the Southern Christian Leadership Conference in August 1967, King challenged his organization to "address itself to the question of restructuring the whole of American society. There are forty million poor people here. And one day we must ask the question, Why are there forty million poor people in America? And when you begin to ask that question, you are raising questions about the economic system, about a broader distribution of wealth. When you ask that question, you begin to question the capitalistic economy. . . . You see, my friends, when you deal with this, you begin to ask the question, Who owns the oil? You begin to ask the question, who owns the iron ore? You begin to ask the question, why is it that people have to pay water bills in a world that is two-thirds water? These are questions that must be asked" (Washington, 1990, p. 250).

King's Poor People's Movement and his blunt critique of the U.S. war on Vietnam moved this agenda. Before he could carry it further, he was assassinated. But the movement went on, below the radar screen of the media, through welfare rights organizations, tenants' rights groups, and community organizations. It would flourish in these small spaces, speaking loudly to deliver the basics of life to those whose presence seemed to give offense in a newly confident consumerist America.

The Civil Rights Movement also pushed a new generation of students of color toward college. Michael King went to Morehouse, but the next generation would go as well, and in larger numbers, to the public universities and, under pressure, to the private institutions. What these students found was that the institutions that wanted them were happy to have them on campus, to photograph them for their brochures, but were unable to or unwilling to produce the kind of broad cultural change required for a *deep* diversity. What we got instead was a surface diversity.

In 1968–1969, a diverse group of students led by the Black Students Union (BSU) at San Francisco State College laid out their agenda for the campus. The liberal cultural institutions (i.e., the academy, the museums, the media) had tread very timidly on the post–civil rights landscape. In many cases, they wanted to embrace legal equality without adopting any posture toward cultural change. It was far easier for White supremacy to compromise on the ballot box than for it to acknowledge the equality of sense and sensibility, of history and the imagination. The BSU students didn't want to play a "skin game," disassociating themselves from other students, whether White or of color. What they called for was "nothing short of a campus revolution" (Prashad, 2006, p. 162). The audacity of this demand was not simply the inheritance of the Civil Rights Movement; it was also part of the broader élan of the "Generation of 1968," fed up with the promises of liberalism and needing to be enchanted with a new project.

For anti-racist students on the campuses who drew from this new energy, the point was not to celebrate their various cultures but to transform the social power relations that oppressed people and the cultural worlds of those thought of as minorities. "The black students at San Francisco State," writes scholar Robert Allen, "knew that black studies could not be complacent; that it must be consciously disruptive, always seeking to expose and cut away those aspects of American society that oppress black people; that it could not be modeled after other departments and accept the constraints imposed on them, because one function of these departments is to socialize students into a racist and oppressive society" (Allen, 1969, pp. 261–262).[1] The space to exert cultural presence had to be *constituted*; the masquerade of cultural diversity within a genteel racist institution would not suffice. Anti-racism, for them, was the ethos, not cultural diversity: The point was to dismantle inherited structures rather than to simply graft on their story as a footnote of the *real* march of civilization. Crucially, the point was to *socialize students* into a different kind of society, to abjure the hierarchical racist society.

The cruel tragedy of these demands was that they were radical in the context of Jim Crow racism, but they would become impenetrable in the world of post–Civil Rights racism. In the latter, the "skin game" would be central, and the revolution of campus institutions would be seen as unrealistic, even juvenile.

The guardians of the academy met the radical challenge to racism and to the culture of upwardly mobile hierarchy not with recalcitrance but with finesse. When the demands outpaced the willingness of the establishment, they adopted a social compact that was less than the hopes of the activists. It is this compact that we have come to call multiculturalism. Brought to the surface in the 1980s during the revisions of school textbooks and college canons, national holidays and street names, Martin Luther King Day and year-end holidays, multiculturalism opened up space for those who had previously been put to the side, and it has matured into an impediment for the construction of an anti-racist polity.

Multiculturalism as adopted by the major cultural institutions of the nation is a bureaucratic approach to the problem of diversity. The arrogance of "White supremacy from below" (i.e., overt racism and the Klan) received a well-deserved snub from the purveyors of national culture and from society in general. Few felt, or feel, comfortable in the skin of unreconstructed racism (even the most wretched among them now speak of "White rights," as if Whites are an oppressed minority, rather than of White supremacy). What remained untouched, however, was "White supremacy from above," the association of Judgment and the Sublime with the history of European civilization. Such genteel White supremacy would allot others some value, but it would arrogate to itself the great philosophical, technological, and political advances. Not for nothing would the term "Western civilization" mark the space of this greatness and also be the adversary of many of those of us who want to create a fairer curriculum. Forgotten in the disputes over the "culture wars" was the centrality of diversity. The defense of diversity on administrative terms contributed to the reduction of anti-racism to bureaucratic multiculturalism.

Multiculturalism emerges, in its own clumsy way, to preserve this White supremacy from above. The cultural logic of this ideology is that the world is constituted by a diversity of cultures, each of which has relatively impermeable boundaries, and each of which has its own logic. Thus, "Chinese" culture can be identified as Confucian, whereas Indian culture can be trotted up to being Hindu (or some such incarnation). Importantly, the gatekeepers of what counted as the culture of the lesser were often the guardians of "Western civilization." Colonial anthropology adopted the prejudices of the orthodoxy in each of the spaces of the world and developed their contested views as the cultural consensus. This orthodoxy was often prone to a masculine and hierarchical worldview that favored theological explanations for the world over any others. In India, the Brahmin worldview stood in for an "Indian" one, and the historical and sociological challenges from others could not be accommodated into this view of Indian culture. Modernity would then be the preserve of Western civilization, and this or that tradition would smother others. The idea of "respect" and "diversity" became an alibi to constrain any critique of these cultural worlds. Such is the paucity of the category of "culture" mobilized within the mainstream strands of multiculturalism.

Multiculturalism allows the entry of various forms of cultural life into the curriculum and into campus life, but only in this guise: as separate and different, as well as obviously inferior to the heritage of Europe and of Western civilization. Martin Luther King anticipated this in his 1967 speech, when he asked his country to see integration not as a "problem but as an opportunity to participate in the beauty of diversity" (Washington, 1990, p. 251). This beauty is in the resources of these traditions, in their wisdom as well as the struggles to reform and reconstruct social and theological life. "It is good," Gandhi wrote in the mid-1920s, "to swim in the waters of tradition. But to sink in them is suicide" (Gandhi, 2001, p. 64). The histories of interchange and subordination and the contradictions within the delineated cultural worlds are generally ignored in the mainstream rendition of multiculturalism. We are told to *respect* each other, as if condescension is a social relation we should prize. I would prefer to struggle with cultural elements in someone else's society rather than to bow down before it in the name of cultural relativism.

Analogously, on college campuses (a major site for the transfusion of culture in our society), upwardly mobile students found a college administration in line with the creation of "cultural organizations," which are often mapped onto racial formations: the Black Students Union, La Raza or La Voz Latina, Asian Americans Students' Association, and others. Colleges tend to accept these organizations, often provide space for them, even if grudgingly, and tender them the hands-off respect they have come to expect. The campus's overall hierarchical culture is not disrupted, but in sheltered zones these "cultures" have been allowed, even encouraged, to express their diversity. It is this expression that provokes the bad-faith query, Why are all the Black kids sitting together in the cafeteria? (Tatum, 1999). Few ask, Why do the White kids sit together? or, more deeply, What kinds of social compacts are forged on the college campus to welcome a superficial diversity alongside, but beneath, the preservation of a White supremacist culture? What we have is what King called "the stagnant equality of sameness"; integration with resentment is not a community. It is stagnant because there is little hope of transcending the resentment; it is sameness because it contains no understanding that historical inequalities cannot be wished away.

Multiculturalism did not enter the cultural imagination of the post–Civil Rights era in a vacuum. It came alongside two other ideologies: color-blindness and the model minority. These three operated in tandem, and indeed, none of them can be seen without being aware of how they are in conversation with each other. We are told that with the demise of state sanctioned racism each individual must be treated on his or her merits (color-blindness); we are also told that each individual is a member of a cultural group, and that this culture should be accorded respect and dignity (multiculturalism); and yet at the same time we are told that certain cultures produce individuals who stand out and who become the "models" among the minorities (model minority). In other words, and after all the bromide about equality before the law and of culture, it is established by the model minority thesis that certain cultures are inferior to others, and that the litmus of this is not "Western civilization," which stands apart, but other minority cultures. If Indians and Jewish Americans can make it, the drill sounds, why can't African Americans and Latinos? The specific histories of how certain sections of these communities "make it," and what the terms of "making it" are, remain unmentioned. State selection stands in for natural selection.

For institutions, multiculturalism and the model minority population provided an important function: It allowed them to enjoy the measured diversity of their staff, student body, or platoon. For individuals, color-blindness functioned as an awesome means to deny any structural conditions for inequality, as well as to allow those individuals who make it to enjoy their success "without any assistance." This ideological complex permitted segments of the population of color to strive for upward mobility in the unequal system. A culture of hierarchy has enveloped this matrix and further occluded the immense structural inequality of our country. Multicultural individual advancement has become the norm, and any discussion of the racialization of poverty is being discounted as itself racist. Upward mobility in a culture of hierarchy perpetuates inequality without any real confrontation of it. Upwardly mobile people of color do not want to be mistaken for janitors, just as they don't want to abolish the condition of janitor itself. And, it turns out, one is always to be mistaken for the janitor, whatever one's vocabulary or uniform. In addition, the rifts between the janitors and the upwardly mobile within the world of color widen. This is a perversion of the wide demand for dignity that motivated the Civil Rights Movement.

That we have deciphered the problem is only one part of the discussion. How do we restart the dynamic run aground by multiculturalism? To make things legible, let me divide this part into two pieces: theory and practice.

Theory

In the 1980s, as multiculturalism made its appearance within the groves of academe, hip-hop tore through the streets and housing projects. Hip-hop—the culture, not simply the music—had an epistemology different from multiculturalism. It did not believe that cultures were spatially sealed, or rather, it could not believe this. In the congested multiethnic working-class areas, with immigrants cheek by jowl with other residents, cultural purity was a conceit, not a reality. Artists borrowed liberally from resources around them. In music this was to "sample," but the same could be said about fashion and indeed about hip-hop aesthetics in general. I learned from this vision and for about 10 years now have argued against multiculturalism from the standpoint of hip-hop, or what I call *polyculturalism*. There are three principles of polyculturalism:

- Cultures are not spatially sealed. Cultural worlds are created in relationship with other cultural worlds. Cultures are not hermetically sealed. They interact; they are alive. There are no boundaries, only centers.
- Cultures are not temporally sealed. Cultural worlds expand, contract, grow, and desiccate. They are not formed once, in an ancient past, and then carried forward out of time, as an essence, as what is authentic about a people. Culture is what we live in, what we fight over. It is alive, and therefore it changes. Cultures are living resources, not dead heritages.

- Political economy of culture, and the culture of political economy: We have to tend to the way starvation constrains dreams, and the way dreams of the powerful enforce the starvation of others.

The most encouraging thing about hip-hop aesthetics is the idea that, even if everything has been done before, it can be transformed. There is no cynicism here. There is only the future.

Once Martin Luther King emerged as the leader of the Civil Rights Movement, he often told his audiences, "Christ furnished the spirit and motivation, while Gandhi furnished the method" (Washington, 1990, p. 117). If King borrowed from Gandhi, the Indian master learned from the New England recluse, Thoreau, who himself learned from his extensive reading of the *Bhagavada Gita*, which was itself a reaction to Buddhism, and backward into the mists of unrecorded history. Interactions and borrowings—it is only inauthentic if it does not work once borrowed, but if it sticks then it is real.

Practice

So how does this exalted vision enter the world of our practice? I want to lay out four principles to help translate it into practice and then offer some capsules.

1. Celebrate differences but also put each cultural world into the other. Never allow anyone to become complacent about his or her culture.
2. Always seek the grounds of solidarity or interconnection, and then seek the barriers that need to be overcome. We have tensions we should talk about and push before our adversaries exploit them.
3. Solidarity should be based on a scrupulous attention to the interests of different pan-ethnic formations in the rat race of bureaucratic multiculturalism.
4. Always put the spotlight on White supremacy.

Some Modest Proposals

We cannot be anti-racist and not be in an organization committed to the culture of solidarity. So first, join or create an anti-racist organization. In addition, I've found in my work in the United States, now over 20 years in the struggle, that any organization that starts all-White will always substantially remain all-White. So once you have an organization, here are some things to do:

1. Campus clean-up. Each weekend and after major sports events, some students typically trash the campus, with no sense of the clean-up required. This is a characteristic example of the upward mobility culture of our campuses. To borrow from W. E. B. Du Bois, vulgar exhibitions of liquor, extravagances, and sports cars are an indicator of one's graduation into the culture of impunity. Your anti-racist group should mobilize students to join in solidarity with the physical plant workers to conduct the clean-up the following morning.

2. Geography of fear. Periodically, our campuses produce e-mails or maps to inform us about crimes committed on the campus. Most of these lists are about incidents that involve people off campus doing something illegal to students, faculty, or staff. Join with the Women's Center, feminist, and LGBT Queer organizations to transform the campus's self-understanding of the geography of misogyny, racism, and homophobia. Who feels safe where, and what is this safety premised on? Do a survey with your students; make alternative maps.

3. Good jobs. Struggle with the administration to ensure that the Career Services office promotes social justice organizations and non-profit organizations as legitimate careers for students. If the career fair is basically a Corporate Fair, contest this. Also, most students tend to go toward money-making jobs because of the vise of student loans. Start campus discussions about the link between student loans, the disempowerment of the imagination, the upward-mobility culture around you, and your students' futures.

4. Just food. Encourage students to link with local sustainable farmers to create a plan for the campus dining hall in line with the 100-mile meal campaign. A culture of solidarity must run across the town-gown divide but also across the mind-body one!

5. To counter the culture of hierarchy and the culture of criminality with impunity, your organization has to connect the insistence on U.S. primacy around the world with the growth of inequality globally (including within the United States). What are the planet's priorities, and what kind of world are we to inherit if unsustainable priorities continue? In 1967, King said that the United States would

never take issue with poverty and inequality as long as warfare, that "demonic destructive suction tube," dominated the agenda. The war, he said, "is an enemy of the poor." And it is the enemy, therefore, of the culture of solidarity. "A nation," King said, "that continues to spend more money on military defense than on programs of social uplift is approaching spiritual death" (Washington, 1990, p. 241).

Note

1. For a broader study of the Black studies movement, see "Some Implications of the Black Studies Movement for Higher Education in the 1970s," by Wilson Record, March 1973, *Journal of Higher Education*, *44*(3), pp. 191–216; as well as "Media for Change: Black Students in the White University," by Frederick D. Harper, Summer 1971, *Journal of Negro Education*, *40*(3), pp. 255–265.

References

Allen, R. (1969). *Black awakening in capitalist America: An analytical history.* Garden City, NY: Doubleday.

Dewart, Janet (1988). *The state of Black America.* Washington, DC: National Urban League.

Gandhi, M. K. (2001). *Navajivan,* June 28, 1925. In *Collected Works of Mahatma Gandhi*, Vol. 27. Ahmedabad: Government of India.

King, M. L., Jr. (1986). *Testament of hope: The essential writings and speeches of Martin Luther King, Jr.* San Francisco: Harper.

King, M. L., Jr. (1992). "Admission to Crozer Theological Seminary for the academic year beginning September 1948." In C. Carson, R. Luker, & P. Russell (Eds.), *The papers of Martin Luther King, Jr.: Volume 1. Called to serve, January 1929–June 1951.* Berkeley: University of California Press.

King, M. L., Jr. (2001). *The autobiography of Martin Luther King, Jr.* Clayborne Carson (Ed.). New York: Warner Books.

Morris, A. (1984). *The origins of the Civil Rights Movement.* New York: The Free Press.

Prashad, V. (2000). *The karma of brown folk.* Minneapolis: Minnesota University Press.

Prashad, V. (2006). Ethnic studies inside out. *Journal of Asian American Studies,* *9*(2), 157–176.

Tatum, B. D. (1999). *Why are all the Black kids sitting together in the cafeteria, and other conversations about race.* New York: Basic Books.

Washington, C. C. (1990). *A testament of home. The essential writings and speeches of Martin Luther King, Jr.* San Francisco: HarperCollins.

PART THREE

SOCIAL JUSTICE PEDAGOGY ACROSS THE CURRICULUM

9

MATHEMATICS OF, FOR, AND AS SOCIAL JUSTICE

Priscilla Bremser, Chawne Kimber, Rob Root, and Sheila Weaver

What Is Math and Social Justice?

Our goals are to reconsider the way new skills are applied and practiced in college mathematics courses and to promote an understanding of the role that mathematics plays in the lives of all students in other types of classes. We begin with an attempt to define these goals formally and follow with brief classroom examples that may further clarify.

We approach the definition of *math and social justice* (MSJ) inclusively: It should be understood to include *math of social justice, math for social justice*, and *math as social justice*. That is, a teacher may have one or more of the following goals for her or his students:

- Students should achieve a certain level of functional quantitative literacy that is necessary to understand social and political issues using mathematics. Depending on the course, the math *of* social justice is a set of raw computational and/or conceptual skills that could include, for example, basic algebra, probability, statistics, or calculus, but may require the methods of more advanced topics such as differential equations or evolutionary game theory. This level of competency may be assumed as a prerequisite or may be part of the curriculum of the course.
- With the skills in place, students should learn how to use mathematical tools to analyze social issues. Ideally, this leads to the recognition

that possession of this power of math *for* social justice may allow one
to effect change.

- Students should be aware of the social injustice that results from inad-
equate functional quantitative literacy, which impedes one's ability to
understand and navigate the social and political world in which she
or he lives. In other words, they should see math *as* social justice.

Trickling up, in a sense, our movement on the college level follows more
than 20 years of K-12 efforts; we describe two of them. The Algebra Project
(Moses & Cobb, 2001) works to introduce algebra in middle school so that
more students will have the chance to complete a college preparatory curriculum in high school. Developed by Robert P. Moses, the pedagogy can be
described as cultural and experiential; for example, students progress from
an actual physical experience of a subway trip to an exercise in creating artistic (drawn and written) representations of the trip that, finally, help them
generate their own symbolic abstraction of the descriptive qualities (such as
speed and distance) they encountered. Also working with middle school students, and influenced by the "problem-posing approach" to co-constructing
knowledge in adult literacy programs advocated by Paulo Freire (1970), Eric
Gutstein (2006) seeks to teach mathematics in a sociopolitical context,
emphasizing through question-rich writing projects that one may "read the
world" with mathematics.

Examples of Courses

Generally, there are three types of college courses in which one finds MSJ
approaches. First, the "liberal arts math" courses for students with non-
quantitative majors typically include a mix of math topics such as modeling,
probability, statistics, logic, and more recently, voting. Second, regular math
courses such as statistics, calculus, and differential equations provide opportunities to emphasize applications. Third, first-year seminars that are discussion and writing based provide for a different teaching environment that is
conducive to talking about math *as* social justice. In any type, the professor
may choose to use a service-learning project to reinforce traditional classroom learning.

To make mathematics relevant to the students in his liberal arts math
course at Belmont University, professor Andy Miller introduces students to

mathematical and economic models for and measurements of income inequality. Game theory, expected value, and the mean value theorem are taught and then applied to gain an understanding of "winner-take-all" markets. Strategically chosen data sets for use in statistics courses can open the door to discussions of social and political issues. Larry Lesser at University of Texas–El Paso, a leader in the effort for teaching statistics with social justice (Lesser, 2007), has his students use expected values to understand the way lotteries work (Lesser, 2004). He suggests that students then proceed to research proportions of state lottery budgets that go to education and address the income and educational level of lottery ticket purchasers; this is a nice example of teaching the issue of math *as* social justice.

Traditionally, calculus texts use as "context" a simplified physical world, asking students to calculate the impact time of a ball dropped off the roof of a tall building (neglecting the presence of air) or to make predictions about the population growth of some unnamed bacteria colony using sanitized data. At Ithaca College, Thomas Pfaff filters in examples that raise awareness about sustainability (Pfaff, 2008). Using the same skills required to understand the population of a colony of bacteria, students use actual data on ozone depletion during 1979–1987 (prior to the UN Montreal Protocol) to predict the status of the ozone layer in the year 2050. The students then follow up by modeling the depletion using all current data and, by comparison, learn the positive effect that regulation can have on the environment (National Oceanic and Atmospheric Administration, 2006).

Service-learning can be integrated with social justice issues in mathematics courses in a range of ways. The recent book *Mathematics in Service to the Community* (Hadlock, 2005) is a guide to designing modeling, statistics, and education projects that are community based, some of which lend themselves to our ends. Some of the modeling projects at St. Olaf College, for instance, described by professor Steve McKelvey are for public health (e.g., predicting the spread of AIDS), the environment (e.g., managing air quality) and social services (e.g., exposing racial inequalities in child welfare services). The bulk of the statistics projects involve students with community organizations, where they apply statistical methods to data sets to provide needed information. For example, in the book, Deborah Hydorn at the University of Mary Washington mentions a client demographic study done for the Association for Retarded Citizens in Rappahannock.

In a recent first-year seminar on mathematics education, Priscilla Bremser of Middlebury College included a unit on standardized testing in K-12 mathematics, which formed the basis of a service-learning project. After conducting background research and then interviewing students, teachers, and parents at a local elementary school, as well as the assessment director for the Vermont Department of Education, students designed and wrote a guide to the state's standardized mathematics test, intended for use by parents in the community.

The MSJ Network

We are building and growing a community of both faculty who actively engage in incorporating MSJ into courses and those who support the effort. As professionals, we work within a larger society that may view mathematics as strictly objective and, consequently, somehow removed from human concerns. In our own departments, there are established curricula and mathematical learning objectives that usually don't include the word "justice." Although we are convinced as individuals that addressing justice questions can serve mathematical learning, exchanging ideas with each other will allow us to do so more effectively. Our experience so far bears this out.

Robert Root, a mathematics professor at Lafayette College, organized an MSJ course development workshop in 2006 that was fully funded by the college. From nationwide mailing lists and word of mouth, 20 participants came from a wide variety of institutions across the nation. The focus was on establishing identity, exploring the tools (including writing assignments and service-learning), understanding the pitfalls of teaching innovation, and exploring the "next steps."[1] The main next step was an effort to design course modules and experiment with them in courses. Several participants did incorporate MSJ into their teaching in the 2006–2007 academic year.

With this foundation set, Priscilla Bremser, a professor at Middlebury College, and Chawne Kimber, a professor at Lafayette College, co-organized a second MSJ workshop with the main goal of producing modules. Twenty-two math and statistics educators convened for four "voice of experience" presentations[2] and a panel on service-learning. They spent the bulk of the three-day workshop working in small groups to research and develop course modules on the topics of mathematics education, lending and access to money, food security, the environment, healthcare, and criminal justice. The modules (in various stages of completion) are posted on a password-protected website accessible to all participants. Revisions on the modules continue, benefiting from experimentation with implementation in classrooms. The workshop ended with a wide-ranging conversation about outreach.[3]

For both workshops, we had more applicants than slots for participants, which indicates that there is a demand for professional development of this kind. Our group has looked to national professional organizations for outreach opportunities, and some of us have participated in panel discussions and offered workshops at meetings of the Mathematical Association of America and the American Association of Colleges and Universities. Plans for more such activities continue.

We can see a few obstacles to going forward. The most mysterious is the suggestion that we should consider "math *or* social justice," which is based on the public perception that mathematics courses ought to remain the last unbiased frontier. Interviewed in the *New York Sun* for a dissenting reaction to the April 2007 workshop Creating Balance in an Unjust World: Math Education and Social Justice (organized by Jonathan Osler and attended by more than 400 educators), New York University education professor Diane Ravitch said, "one of the things children learn in mathematics is how to review evidence and come at questions with a nonpartisan, dispassionate perspective" (Shapiro, 2007). We would challenge the assumptions that there can be any class that is presented in an unbiased fashion and that mathematics is only used to address nonpartisan issues one can't or shouldn't get excited about.[4,5] There will always be detractors for any teaching innovation; we must accept this and continue to try new methods responsibly. Our students must adjust to the notion that knowledge is interconnected and that it is okay to discuss the real world in a mathematics course to develop new perspectives.[6] Further, for students otherwise not attracted to the study of mathematics, explicit connections with issues that move them may provide valuable motivation to acquire important analytical skills.

Understanding that there can be a balance of "math" and "social justice" in a course without sacrificing curricular standards is a challenge for all faculty, both those who actively address questions of social justice and their colleagues who do not. Again, this is a challenge that crops up with any teaching innovation;[7] in taking on a new approach one must remain mindful of issues of tenure and promotion. In regular math courses with set departmental syllabi, the faculty member must always put the mathematics first

and be sure to emphasize the social justice component as a valid enhancement that may reinforce learning of the math content.

The inclusiveness of our network—embracing all forms of MSJ and faculty from all sorts of educational institutions—creates a challenge. We must
be sure to address the issues that may be specific to a particular kind of school
(e.g., K-12, community college, 4-year liberal arts college, or large university).

Case Studies

Case Study I.

Sheila Weaver teaches a liberal arts mathematics course at the University of
Vermont, and she covers much of the typical content, including probability
and statistics, financial math, voting theory, and fair division. However, this
course is called Mathematics and Social Justice. Weaver's reasons for this
pairing include the attraction that questions of social justice have for students and the fact that "a quantitatively literate person should understand
the mathematical reasoning often involved in social justice issues" (personal
communication, January 16, 2008). Moreover, in the process of learning
quantitative reasoning, students discover that "many mathematical ideas
themselves involve 'fairness,' for example, random sampling, random assignment to treatments, equally likely outcomes and probabilities" (personal
communication, January 16, 2008).

Unlike a typical finite mathematics course, Weaver's begins with an
exploration of the idea of quantitative literacy: What IS it? What should a
citizen know to function in society? The answer includes many mathematical
ideas that logically intersect with social justice issues. Before the class
embarks on quantitative reasoning topics, a unit on the philosophy of justice
introduces the complexity of the concept of "fairness" and "equality" in
context.

The themes of poverty and hunger form a thread through the entire
semester. Here we examine the weaving of that thread with some of the
mathematical content and describe how a service-learning project for a community agency reinforces and builds on that content. To begin the quantitative topics and as an introduction to data, students are asked to construct
their own frequency distributions and histograms using data on percentages
of households suffering undernourishment in different countries. Along the

way, students examine how the Food and Agriculture Organization of the United Nations defines and measures undernourishment. Next, students are invited to explore a dynamic scatter plot relating nations' average life expectancies to their per capita incomes, including animations showing changes over time and the effects of shifting between logarithmic and linear scales (Gapminder Foundation, 2008).

Adding a local perspective to the global, the class meets representatives from its community partner early in the semester. For two iterations of the course, that partner has been the Vermont Campaign to End Childhood Hunger (VTCECH).[8] Students in the first group generated a "data snapshot" of each Vermont county on issues related to hunger, including the number of people who qualify for food stamps, the proportion that actually use them, resources available, and how many are served. The second group will build on that knowledge and investigate some issues for low-income residents. For example, since transportation is a crucial barrier to eligible individuals' actually receiving food stamps, students find the correlation between the percent of eligible residents using food stamps in each town with the distance that the residents must travel to an office of the state Department of Children and Families.

A close examination of how policy makers measure poverty begins in the fifth week. By this time, students have worked with both definitions of justice and techniques of measurement, so they are ready to engage the interplay between them. In the United States, the poverty rate is calculated by means of a formula developed in 1963 and simply adjusted each year for inflation since then. Is this satisfactory, or should a whole new measure be considered? Should poverty be measured absolutely, so that a standard of basic necessities sets a threshold? Or should it be measured relatively, in comparison to an average? Should measures focus on income or consumption in a particular society, given the particulars of its economy? (Klass, 2008).

Using tax data from the IRS website, the class estimates the Gini index, a measure of income inequality, in the United States. Students read "The Inequality Conundrum" (Lowenstein, 2007), and focus on pros and cons of the unequal distribution of wealth in the United States. A lively discussion follows the author's claim that "the United States has a pretty high tolerance for inequality. Americans care more about 'fairness' than 'equalness.' We boo athletes suspected of taking steroids, but we admire billionaires" (p. 11).

In considering poverty around the world, Weaver's students pay attention to questions such as the reliability of data collected by government agencies with varying capacities and agendas from citizens who may or may not trust their leaders. Given the connections that are often made between poverty and other issues, such as literacy, gross domestic product, and life expectancy, this ground is rich with material for discussion about the difference between correlation and causation and the possible interpretations of correlation statistics by policy analysts with different viewpoints.

Weaver highlights links between the course material and the communities around the students. She brings colleagues from other disciplines into her classroom. Early on, it might be a philosopher who discusses theories of justice; later, an economist whose expertise includes the relationship between gender and poverty. She also includes discussions of relevant local issues. For example, recently the Burlington, Vermont public school administrators confronted the relationship between poverty and test scores. Weaver's class discussed the quantitative analyses of that relationship, as well as proposed responses such as redistricting.

After presenting and discussing various voting systems and their properties, Weaver explores *Voting and Registration in the Election of November 2004* (U.S. Census Bureau, 2006), a report of the U.S. Census Bureau based on survey data. The report examines rates of voting and registration broken down by various characteristics, including sex, "race and Hispanic origin," educational attainment, annual family income, and employment status. In addition to reinforcing what students have learned about statistical studies, this investigation leads naturally to consideration of fair division and apportionment at the end of the course.

Although hunger and poverty are by no means the only social justice issues considered in Weaver's course, they do tie together what might otherwise appear to students to be unrelated mathematical topics. More generally, the students in the class seem to respond well to its premise. Here are some of their comments:

I like feeling as though I'm not just dealing with a math problem, but if outside the classroom someone spoke of these things I would be able to contribute and understand the discussion. . . .

I'm not the biggest math person, so the idea of a Math and Social Justice class appealed to me. I thought it was really cool when we ended up doing readings along the lines of race and gender inequalities, such as the racial profiling article. . . . I feel like I spent most of my life denying the applicability of math, but that is not always true.

Since everything we do relates to real life, it is not a burden to work through the problems, and interesting to see what different answers mean for the problem. The answers are relevant, compared to other math classes that take word problems and just change the wording to appeal to different crowds.

Case Study II.

Every entering freshman at Lafayette College must complete a writing-intensive, discussion-based first-year seminar (FYS) course. According to the college catalog, the goal of the course is "to introduce students to intellectual inquiry through engaging them as thinkers, speakers, and writers" (Lafayette College, 2008). Faculty members from every department contribute to the program by directing seminars on a wide variety of topics. Rob Root offered his seminar, FYS 141: Social Justice through Quantitative Literacy, during the fall semesters of 2006 and 2007. In short, as stated in the syllabus, the goal of Root's FYS is to "examine quantitative literacy and its role in understanding and achieving social justice." To this end, the course offers alternative definitions of social justice and of quantitative literacy; investigates the teaching and learning of quantitative literacy; considers access to credit, bankruptcy, and the distribution of wealth and income in the contemporary United States as quantitatively rich issues of social justice; and frames the act of acquiring quantitative literacy as an issue of social justice. Students in the FYS completed several reading assignments, including Frank (2007), Warren and Tyagi (2003), and Moses and Cobb (2001) (with a writing log), three "process writing" assignments, and a service-learning project.

Although Weaver's math course has a primary goal of improving her students' quantitative skills, Root's FYS does not earn students credit for a mathematics course; however, his students indeed reported increased quantitative literacy as a result of completing the class. The writing requirements of the course are another distinguishing factor. Students in the FYS must complete 20 pages of "process" writing. Root divides this writing over three assignments. The first two writing assignments of the semester address students' personal sense of quantitative literacy. The first is a narrative of a student's understanding of quantitative literacy and its relation to fairness demonstrated by a personal experience of quantitative learning that will have long-term effects. With this in mind, the second paper examines a student's own "QL radar." That is, students are asked "to consider the strengths and weaknesses of [their] own quantitative literacy as a tool for identifying unfairness and for resolving unfair treatment." The third paper is a more traditional research paper in which the students investigate the quantitative aspect of some issue of social justice.

The first few reading assignments focus on setting the definitions of "social justice" and "quantitative literacy." *The Encyclopedia of Community* (Christensen & Levinson, 2001) provides a tidy reading on various interpretations of social justice, but Root settles on the broad and politically neutral Aristotelian consideration of "fair distribution of a society's benefits and burdens among its members" (Erickson, 2001, p. 1309). With this in mind, students are free to explore how societies actually behave in practice. For instance, they read Olivia Judson's article "The Selfless Gene" (2007), which suggests evolutionary bases for behavior and alludes to the economic games that are described in detail in Robert Frank's book, *What Price the Moral High Ground?* (2005). In particular, on the first day of the class, students play the Ultimatum game, which demonstrates that many would prefer to go without resources in order to punish others who do not share fairly. Students are introduced to the many definitions of quantitative literacy that are in use by reading "Mathematics and Democracy: The Case for Quantitative Literacy" (National Council on Education and the Disciplines, 2007) and then proceed to the concept of the ability to and habit of continually "reading the world through mathematics."

Root uses the text *What the Numbers Say* (Niederman & Boyum, 2003) to familiarize students with some methods for understanding the world quantitatively. The book is a popular account of pervasive quantitative methods used to describe social phenomena and support particular positions. The book is a cornerstone for the course in that it is a tutorial on the pragmatic benefits of a numerate approach to life. For instance, the authors spend a chapter explaining the nature and value of nonlinear curves for understanding population growth and compound interest. Most topical at this time is their discussion of taxation in general and the inherently regressive nature of flat tax schemes in particular.

Reading current news articles helps students try out these new skills. Root uses a pair of opinion pieces on taxes that provide for interesting discussion: The first involves a speech on the injustice of our tax code: "Last year,

Buffett said, he was taxed at 17.7 percent on his taxable income of more than $46 million. His receptionist was taxed at about 30 percent" (Tse, 2007, p. D3). To unpack this sentence is an exercise that induces students to learn about compensation and taxation in the United States; they read the companion response by Larry Elder (2007), who disputes Buffet's claim. Wading through Elder's article requires that students doubt data, build models, and ask further questions. Root notes that the underlying social justice issue can get tangled up in politically motivated doubts about data, but that students appreciate the situation more fully when provided more background information on compensation and taxation in the United States.

The final chapter of *What the Numbers Say* (Niederman & Boyum, 2003) addresses reform movements in math education and attempts to raise awareness of the connections between quantitative learning and the reform of K-12 math education. The authors take a firm stand against calculators but otherwise offer a surprisingly evenhanded arbitration on the merits of traditional memorization and student construction of mathematical ideas. They make clear that quantitative literacy requires the engagement of mathematical ideas beyond the mathematics classroom. The debate about the need to teach problem solving versus traditional memorization of rote procedures continues, and balance is elusive. This segues into the segment of the seminar devoted to a reading of Liping Ma's *Knowing and Teaching Elementary Mathematics* (1999). Ma's book is a rich comparison of teacher training in China and the United States that illustrates the profound differences in the depth of the teachers' conceptual understanding and, in turn, the way students learn elementary math. With awareness of this gap and some new comprehension in hand, Root's students tutored at-risk middle school students at Easton Area Academy for a service-learning project. The experience allowed one student to observe, "It has shocked me. I did not expect to see so much quantitative illiteracy in the population of the U.S." Another remarked, "Working with the EAA students I realized that there aren't that many people who have a great understanding [of math]."

Although it was not part of the syllabus, a discussion of the cost of war in Iraq was particularly effective. Instigated by a visit to campus of the American Friends Service Committee (AFSC) art exhibition *Eyes Wide Open,* the conversation led Root to find more articles for students to read: one, a source of data (Iraq progress reports, 2008), and the others on estimates of monetary and short- and long-term human costs (Bilmes & Stiglitz, 2006). The *Eyes*

Wide Open exhibition is an effort to represent the magnitude of the human cost of the war and "features a pair of boots honoring each U.S. military casualty, a field of shoes and a Wall of Remembrance to memorialize the Iraqis killed in the conflict" (AFSC, 2008). The conversation in class that followed transcended the red-blue divide, with students earnestly exploring the distribution of the burden of the human cost of the war and considering quantitative comparisons of the sacrifices versus benefits. The immediacy of the war and its costs were much more familiar to the students than the increasing frequency of bankruptcy in the United States or the increasing disparity in incomes over the past 40 or so years, topics that the course was planned around.

Student reactions to the course as a whole can be summed up in the following quotations from the evaluations:

> *[The course] has made me realize that the U.S. could be a lot stronger and wealthier if average citizens had quantitative literacy.*
> *. . . I never thought math could be used [to evaluate fairness].*
> *[The course] has helped me understand that social justice is very important and must be acted upon. You can't just sit around hoping things will change.*
> *I see far more injustice at a deeper level after taking this course.*

The 15 students enrolled in the course in fall 2007 assessed their levels of quantitative literacy through a brief survey on the first day; they returned to reconsider the survey in an evaluation at the end of the course. The results and responses are interesting, so we spend some time on them here. The survey showed that the students enter with a high degree of quantitative learning skill, but have great room for growth. Even though instilling these skills is not a goal of the FYS, at the end of the semester, 13 students said that the course improved their quantitative learning, and the remaining two responded that the course had not helped with their ability to answer the quantitative learning survey. We discuss a few representative questions here:

- *Offer an example of a situation you might encounter in everyday life when you might want to perform a division by one half.*
  This was surprisingly difficult for them and generated ongoing conversation for weeks. Only four students were able to come up with an

acceptable scenario; nine gave instances of multiplication by one half; and the other two offered nothing. On the evaluation at the end of the course, 8 students recognized that they could better respond to this question since reading Liping Ma's book.

- *In the 2000 presidential election, the Democratic candidate, Al Gore, won the popular vote with 51,004,000 votes to President George W. Bush's 50,460,000. Nonetheless, President Bush won the electoral vote 271 to 267 once the Supreme Court decided the result for the state of Florida. Explain how a candidate can win the electoral vote despite losing the popular vote.*

In the abstract, there are two ways for such a win to occur, and 13 students were able to describe at least one of the two. However, just 4 of them accurately described the particular way that Bush won the 2000 election. It is surprising that such a high-profile case is known by so few of the students.

- *In his* New York Times *column of July 24, 2007, David Brooks notes that politicians are claiming, "CEOs are seeing their incomes skyrocket while the middle class gets squeezed." He asserts that "This story is not entirely wrong, but it is incredibly simple-minded." He offers a series of complicating facts that this story ignores. The first is "Real average wages rose by 2 percent in 2006, the second fastest rise in 30 years." How does rising average wages complicate the situation described by the politicians?*

Only four of the students were able to demonstrate that the average may be increasing solely because of the increasing incomes of the CEOs. One of the other responses was "The middle class makes most of the average wages." This misconception can lead to an interesting discussion of income distribution, which Root includes near the end of his course using articles by Krugman (2007) and Crook (2006).

- *Put the following nine causes of death in the United States in the year 2004 in order from most likely to least likely: cancer, terrorist attack, murder, heart disease, Mad Cow disease, diabetes, stroke, shark attack, suicide.*

Students found this question unfair, but the goal is to see if they can at least form three groupings of the causes, one including the top three causes of death in the United States, another with three frequent killers, and the last group of the three that caused no deaths in the United States in 2004. Estimation is a tactic discussed in *What the*

Numbers Say (Niederman & Boyum, 2003). Assessing the responses on the basis of accurate groupings, students did fairly well identifying the top three, but only eight students knew that heart disease is at the top. Results in the middle grouping were muddled, with three students identifying Mad Cow disease as a medium cause even though there have never been any U.S. deaths because of this disease and another couple promoting shark attack into the middle group. Most encouraging is that no student failed to include terrorist attack in the bottom grouping. At the end of the course, students commented in the evaluation, "The readings we did helped me to have better intuitive sense for approximate amounts," and "I have enhanced my ability to critically think up a rational approximation."

Thinking Like Mathematicians

We are often met with puzzlement when we use *mathematics* and *social justice* in the same sentence. Yet, on some level, it is a natural pairing: *Justice* suggests a search for fairness, which may well require measurement and, hence, quantitative analysis.

Still, there is more to mathematics than comparing quantities. A mathematician's habits of mind also include using well-defined terminology, sorting what is known from what is not, identifying assumptions, and employing principles of logic. In asking our students to apply these practices to social justice questions, we aim to assist their development as quantitative and analytic thinkers, to enrich discussions of equity, and to convey the importance of quantitative literacy in a democratic society. The student responses cited in our case studies suggest that our approach has promise for all three of these goals.

Our young network is already serving one of its purposes, that of providing community to instructors with similar objectives on campuses across the country. It will necessarily take longer to evaluate the success of our outreach efforts in terms of both new or modified courses and student learning. There is interest in more course development workshops, and we hope to build the capacity to offer them. The course module website is naturally easy to maintain; its impact is more difficult to gauge. Nevertheless, we are optimistic that our growing core of dedicated participants will find ways to share their ideas that we haven't yet imagined.

Notes

1. Mathematics speakers included Victor Donnay (Bryn Mawr), Dennis Ebersole (Northampton Community College), Lawrence Lesser (University of Texas–El Paso), Jonathan Osler (El Puente Academy), and Catherine Roberts (Holy Cross).

2. Voices of experience were Charles Hadlock (Bentley College), Andy Miller (Belmont University), Thomas Pfaff (Ithaca College), and Sheila Weaver (University of Vermont).

3. This second workshop, hosted at Middlebury College, was funded by a subgrant from the PA/NY Campus Compact Consortium's Learn and Serve America grant, Building on Our Strengths (Academic Discipline Network), with matching funds from partner institutions: East Stroudsburg University, Lafayette College (lead institution), Middlebury College, Moravian College, and West Chester University.

4. This is nicely illustrated in the introduction to *Rethinking Mathematics* (Gutstein & Peterson, 2005).

5. Manhattan Institute Fellow Sol Stern (2007) attempts counterpoint, starting with "There's a fifth column in New York City's public schools—radical teachers who openly undermine Schools Chancellor Joel Klein's curriculum mandates and use their classrooms to indoctrinate students in left-wing, anti-American ideology" (p. 31).

6. Gutstein (2006) spends an entire chapter on (the almost wholly positive) parental reactions to his efforts that were misunderstood by his principal; throughout, he emphasizes his students' range of responses expressed in journals and writing assignments.

7. The "Calculus Reform" movement of the 1990s fueled intense debates within mathematics departments, and we continue to grapple with, for example, the role of technology in our courses.

8. See VTECH's website: www.vtnohunger.org.

References

American Friends Service Commmittee (AFSC). (2008). *Eyes Wide Open*. Retrieved October 20, 2008, from http://www.afsc.org/eyes/ht/d/sp/i/38782/pid/38782

Bilmes, L., & Stiglitz, J. (2006, December). Encore: Iraq Hemorrhage. *The Milken Institute Review*, 76–83.

Brooks, D. (2007, July 24). A reality-based economy. *The New York Times*. Retrieved September 3, 2009, from http://select.nytimes.com/2007/07/24/opinion/24brooks.html?_r=1

Christensen, K., & Levinson, D. (Eds.). (2001). *The encyclopedia of community* (Vol. 3). Thousand Oaks, CA: Sage.

Crook, C. (2006, September). The height of inequality. *The Atlantic Monthly, 298*(2), 36–37.

Elder, L. (2007, July 5). Billionaire Warren Buffet—A case of the guilts? *Real Clear Politics* Retrieved September 3, 2009, from http://www.realclearpolitics.com/arti cles/2007/07/billionaire_warren_buffett_a_c.html)

Erickson, P. E. (2001). Social justice. In K. Christensen & D. Levinson (Eds.), *The encyclopedia of community* (Vol. 3, pp. 1309–1314). Thousand Oaks: Sage.

Frank, R. (2005). *What price the moral high ground? Ethical dilemmas in competitive environments.* Princeton, NJ: Princeton University Press.

Frank, R. (2007). *Falling behind: How rising inequality harms the middle class.* Berkeley: University of California Press.

Freire, P. (1970). *Pedagogy of the oppressed.* New York: Continuum.

Gapminder Foundation. (2008). *Gapminder.* Retrieved October 20, 2008, from http://www.gapminder.org/

Gutstein, E. (2006). *Reading and writing the world with mathematics.* New York: Routledge.

Gutstein, E., & Peterson, B. (2005). *Rethinking mathematics: Teaching social justice by the numbers.* Milwaukee: Rethinking Schools.

Hadlock, C. R. (Ed.). (2005). *Mathematics in service to the community: Concepts and models for service-learning in the mathematical sciences.* Washington, DC: The Mathematical Association of America.

Iraq progress reports. (2008). *The New York Times.* Retrieved July 7, 2009, from http://topics.nytimes.com/top/news/international/countriesandterritories/iraq/ iraqprogressreports/index.html?scp = 1-spot&sq = iraq%20progress%20reports& st = cse

Judson, O. (2007, October). The selfless gene. *The Atlantic Monthly, 298*(2), 36–37.

Klass, G. (2008). *Presenting data: Tabular and graphic display of social indicators.* Retrieved October 20, 2008, from http://lilt.ilstu.edu/gmklass/pos138/datadis play/sections/poverty/poverty.htm

Krugman, P. (2007, September 18). *The conscience of a liberal: Introducing this blog.* Retrieved October 20, 2008, from http://krugman.blogs.nytimes.com/2007/09/ 18/

Lafayette College. (2008). *Lafayette College catalog.* Retrieved October 20, 2008, from http://www.lafayette.edu/academics/catalog/search.php

Lesser, L. (2004, Winter). Take a chance by exploring the statistics in lotteries. *The Statistics Teacher Network, 65,* 6–7.

Lesser, L. (2007). Critical values and transforming data: Teaching statistics with social justice. *Journal of Statistics Education, 15*(1). Retrieved September 3, 2009, from http://www.amstat.org/publications/jse/v15n1/lesser.html

Lowenstein, R. (2007, June 10). The inequality conundrum. *The New York Times Magazine,* p. 11.

Ma, L. (1999). *Knowing and teaching elementary mathematics: Teachers' understanding of fundamental mathematics in China and the United States.* Mahwah, NJ: Erlbaum.

Moses, R. P., & Cobb, C. E., Jr. (2001). *Radical equations: Math literacy and civil rights.* Boston: Beacon.

National Council on Education and the Disciplines. (2007). *Mathematics and democracy: The case for quantitative literacy* (L. A. Steen, Ed.). Retrieved July 7, 2009, from http://www.maa.org/ql/mathanddemocracy.html

National Oceanic and Atmospheric Administration. (2006). *Twenty questions and answers about the ozone layer: 2006 update* (World Meteorological Organization Global Ozone Research and Monitoring Project—Report No. 50). Retrieved October 20, 2008, from http://www.esrl.noaa.gov/csd/assessments/2006/chapters/twentyquestions.pdf

Niederman, D., & Boyum, D. (2003). *What the numbers say.* New York: Broadway Books.

Pfaff, T. (2008). *Tom Pfaff's sustainability page.* Retrieved October 20, 2008, from http://www.ithaca.edu/tpfaff/sustainability.htm

Shapiro, G. (2007, January 24). Do social issues belong in math class? *New York Sun.* Retrieved September 3, 2009, from http://www.nysun.com/new-york/do-social-issues-belong-in-math-class/47301/

Stern, S. (2007, March 20). Math and Marxism: NYC's whack-job teachers. *New York Post*, p. 31.

Tse, T. M. (2007, June 27). Buffet slams tax system disparities. *The Washington Post*, p. D3.

U.S. Census Bureau (2006, March). *Voting and registration in the election of November 2004.* Washington, DC: U.S. Department of Commerce. Retrieved October 20, 2008, from http://www.census.gov/population/www/socdemo/voting.html

Warren, E., & Tyagi, A. E. (2003). *The two-income trap: Why middle-class mothers and fathers are going broke.* New York: Basic Books.

10

VALUED CONTINGENCIES

Social Justice in Foreign Language Education

Roman Graf

T he shift in the last several decades from structuralist approaches in
language teaching focused on grammatical accuracy to communicative models focused on communication within a cultural setting
introduces the potential for social justice education into the foreign language
curriculum. Once the center of students' attention and classroom activities,
teachers have moved out of the limelight of the "omniscient" lecturer to a
more marginal position as moderators of communicative situations in a
student-centered classroom. If we add an element of transparency and self-
reflection to this kind of foreign language teaching, we can align the pedagogies of social justice education and foreign language acquisition. Students
and teachers become members of a group that consciously creates and re-
creates multiple layers of cultures.

Theoretical Framework

Based on a study by Weinstein and O'Bear, Bell, Washington, Weinstein,
and Love (1997) explore the role of the teacher in the social justice classroom
and arrive at the following observation:

> In most traditional classrooms, our particular social and cultural identities
> as teachers usually remain in the background, but in the social justice class-
> room where social identity is central to the content, the significance of who

we are often takes center stage. . . . Whether we are members of the privileged or targeted group with respect to particular issues inevitably influences how we react to material under discussion as well as how our students are likely to perceive us. (p. 300)

Such recognition and introspection affects the educational process directly, especially the student–teacher relationship. Paolo Freire (1998) remarks:

> By speaking about their fears or insecurities, educators move gradually toward overcoming them, and at the same time they gradually win the confidence of learners. This way, instead of trying to hide fear with authoritarian disguises easily recognized by learners, teachers humbly admit it. By speaking of their feelings, they accept themselves as persons, they testify to their desire to learn with the learners. (p. 48)

At the same time as the personal assumes a pivotal role in this pedagogical approach, the teacher's function moves from the center of the students' attention to the periphery. The ideal pedagogue now mediates and channels students' interactions with each other and the course materials. Thus, students and teachers become equal partners in a common pursuit.

In the social justice classroom students develop from recipients of messages and information to active participants in the educational process, whose attitudes, values, convictions, and belief systems interact. In order to facilitate this shift to personal engagement, we need to ensure students receive and recognize an increased structural flexibility in the educational process. Only then can they utilize their specific learning styles and bring their personal situations to bear on classroom activities. In turn, they will personally engage in the educational process and not only absorb knowledge but create it, through a personally differentiated interaction with the learning material. This also means that "knowledge" is not predetermined before class starts. It develops during class and automatically filters into so-called "real" life. In fact, because individual learning styles and life experiences permeate this classroom learning experience, there no longer exists a separation between classroom learning and life learning or between class and life. The liberal arts education has become a lifelong engagement. Freire (1998) stipulates that

> teachers understand that the students' syntax; their manners, tastes, and ways of addressing teachers and colleagues; and the rules governing their

fighting and playing among themselves are all part of their *cultural identity*, which never lacks an element of class. All that has to be accepted. Only as learners recognize themselves democratically and see that their right to say "I be" is respected will they become able to learn the dominant grammatical reasons why they should say "I am." (p. 49)

This new general understanding of the roles of teachers and learners in a socially just classroom necessarily also applies to foreign language education. Under these new premises, simple familiarity with a foreign language or culture per se does not qualify as an engagement in a social justice endeavor. A student or teacher's mere knowledge of a different language and culture is not sufficient. It would simply constitute an accumulation of knowledge and skills. In order to arrive at a pedagogical setting that reveals and explicates social attitudes and norms and simultaneously engages the personal values of students and teachers in a constructive collaboration, both students and teachers alike have to acknowledge the multiple contingencies of cultural formation. The allusion to Barbara Herrnstein Smith's *Contingencies of Value* (1988) in the title of this chapter gains relevance here. It is key to any (e)valuation. Explicating Shakespeare's sonnets, Herrnstein Smith (1988) suggests:

> Evaluation is always compromised because value is always in motion: a never-fixed mark, whose worth's unknown although his height be taken: "unknown" not because, like true love, it is beyond mortal cognition, but because it is constantly variable and eternally indeterminate. (p. 9)

Beyond literary analyses, this insight holds consequences for investigations into cultures as well. Herrnstein Smith continues:

> If we recognize that literary value is "relative" in the sense of *contingent* (that is, a changing function of multiple variables) rather than *subjective* (that is, personally whimsical, locked into the consciousness of individual subjects and/or without interest or value for other people), then we may begin to investigate the dynamics of that relativity. (p. 11)

In the socially just classroom and, by extension, in the socially just academy, contingencies of value have become valuable contingencies. It is these contingencies that enable us to engage in the process of social justice education.

Teachers and educators specifically need to be aware of the educational processes, the language-teaching pedagogy underlying their daily classroom practices. These processes and structures must become transparent to our students. In the following I argue that the shift in foreign language pedagogy from grammar-translation models and structuralist approaches to communicatively oriented models that focus on cultural meaning, content, and form already implicitly aligns with a concern for social justice. Yet, in order for these implicit structures to effect social change, they have to become explicit and transparent.

Claire Kramsch, in *Context and Culture in Language Teaching* (1993) specifies the changed roles for teachers and learners in the foreign language classroom:

> in the foreign language classroom teacher and learners are both participants and observers of a cross-cultural dialogue that takes place in the foreign language across grammatical exercises, communicative activities, and the discussion of texts. The language classroom should therefore be viewed as the privileged site of cross-cultural fieldwork, in which the participants are both informants and ethnographers. (p. 29)

Kramsch's (1993) ensuing discussion of dialogic principles applied to the foreign language classroom may be a bit too static,[1] but her inclusion of Mikhail Bakhtin's notion of the "dialogic" into an exploration of sociolinguistics is crucial for a better understanding of the cultural forces prevalent in cross-cultural discourses. In its wake, the discussion in second language acquisition has moved from a focus on "linguistic competence" to an emphasis on "intercultural communicative competence" (see Byram, 1997). The theoretical ramifications of Bakhtin's principle of a "dialogical heteroglossia" are essential to the following elaborations on social justice and culture in foreign language education. Bakhtin (1975/1981) theorizes:

> The living utterance, having taken meaning and shape at a particular historical moment in a socially specific environment, cannot fail to brush up against thousands of living dialogic threads, woven by socio-ideological consciousness around the given object of an utterance; it cannot fail to become an active participant in social dialogue. After all, the utterance arises out of this dialogue as a continuation of it and as a response to it—it does not approach the object from the sidelines. (p. 276)

Accordingly, any conversation among speakers within a single culture or of differing cultural backgrounds is always already multivoiced. It contains a multiplicity of cultural referents, a heteroglossia that needs to be engaged by the speakers involved in the dialogue. In general, within the second-language-acquisition context, a speaker's first culture colliding with a second culture forms what Kramsch (1993) calls a "third domain."

In terms of Bakhtin's dialogic (1975/1981) and Herrnstein Smith's (1988) contingent values, every encounter already inhabits many other encounters, thus bringing not only two cultures in contact with each other but also many culturally contingent positions. Therefore, in addition to remaining focused on the colliding cultures, we need to shift our attention to the contingent positions that enable multiple reflections within and across cultures. If we consider only the context of two overarching cultures, a "native" and a foreign culture, forming a third, we obliterate individual contingencies that form specific cultural vantage points. There are many voices within a single culture, that is, group affiliations that influence specific "cultural" reactions. For example, does an encounter between two gay men, one from the United States and one from Germany, foreground their affinity with the same subgroup, gay men, or their belonging to different national groups, the United States and Germany? The short answer is that *all* group affiliations are involved in the creation and re-creation of cross-cultural encounters. In this specific example, cross-cultural understanding can be facilitated through the common background of being gay.[2]

Group affiliation that escapes the confines of languages and national cultures, if meaningful to the individuals concerned, can advance cross-cultural learning. Thus, in the foreign language classroom these group ties must not be overlooked or remain unmentioned. They are an influential force in communicative situations and, therefore, in cultural understanding. Although students are encouraged to bring their individual cultural contingencies into the classroom, they are also enabled to gain better access to the foreign culture because they can use a group membership they share with the "other" to connect more readily to it. At the same time, this connection fosters a questioning of the similarities and differences of the shared group ties, which in turn allows for an easier critical analysis of the foreign culture as well as one's own. Within this framework and its awareness of cultural contingencies, social justice enters the foreign language classroom and makes explicit already implicit critical analyses of group dynamics, inter- and inner-group power relations, and stereotyping. Michael Byram (1997) summarizes:

The advantages of an FLT [foreign language teaching] approach emphasizing analysis of the interaction is that it allows learners to see their role not
as imitators of native speakers but as social actors engaging with other
social actors in a particular kind of communication and interaction which
is different from that between native speakers. (p. 21)

The Beginning Foreign Language Classroom

In a second semester, beginning German classroom where students are primarily introduced to lexical items pertaining to professions, the teacher,
instead of having students memorize and repeat vocabulary, now situates the
newly acquired words in a specific context pertaining to their common use
in the target culture. This restructuring in and of itself reflects the transition
from a structuralist approach in foreign language education to a communicative one. Students learn about the daily routines of several professions in the
target culture, talk about likes and dislikes of young people as they pertain
to their choices of professions, and try to recreate communicative situations
in which they have to apply newly acquired vocabulary and grammatical
structures. Some cultural differences may arise; however, if merely attempting to (re)create specific communicative situations, it remains far too easy for
students simply to project their own preferences and ways of living onto the
target culture and its people. The students are not forced to enter into a
dialogic relationship with that culture or their own. They may do so by
chance, but the very structure of the curriculum does not foster such inquiry.
In addition, most textbooks reflect this "traditional" approach to language
teaching, relegating culture to notes in the margins or little boxes filled with
general information about the target culture. Cultural items remain issues
for the curious. In fact, these notes in the margins romanticize the target
culture and allow students to remain detached from it. Consequently, no
understanding of one's own cultural contingencies is gained, and the interaction with the target culture continues to be on a superficial level that encourages rather then discourages cultural stereotyping.

In contrast, when we make use of principles of social justice pedagogy,
students and teachers gain a differentiated understanding of cultural contingencies and recognize the essential instability of cultural norms. Thus, social
justice pedagogy destabilizes worldviews previously assumed stable. Although
it is true that, in a foreign-language-acquisition context, such destabilization

conflicts with the goal of communicating a general sense of the target culture, I contend that it is possible and necessary to present a consistent picture of a target culture while at the same time challenging its stability.

Continuing with the previous example, the German teacher distributes handouts in his second semester language classroom with statistical information about the job choices of young Germans. He introduces the respective sequence of the class with an explanation of this pedagogical choice, thus shifting the students' attention from a mere communicative framework of reenactment to an open acknowledgment of pedagogical choices, on the one hand, and a realization of the contingencies of specific job selections in a German cultural environment on the other. The statistical material divides the professional choices of young Germans (who did not want to attend a university) along geo-political lines, focusing on a comparison between former East and West German states. While introducing lexical items pertaining to the world of professions, this teacher creates a class setting in which a discussion about the reasons for certain choices among young people is firmly embedded in the structure of the lesson. Consequently, students immediately ask why young Germans in the former Eastern states want to become cooks and why the Westerners tend to choose jobs as mechanics and sales clerks. Instead of giving an authoritative response and therefore a specific reason for these choices, the teacher in this case joins the students in an informed inquiry into this question. A lively discussion about socioeconomic conditions in the former East and West ensues. The class talks about the divided Germany as well as its reunification. At one point during the lesson, students begin to reflect and report on their own individual situations and those in their home communities. While some English is spoken, most of the conversations remain in German, the target language.

In this example, the teacher introduces new material in a form that necessitates social justice questions from the students. The students determine the direction of the class. They use new lexical items within an informed discussion of cultural specificities and differences between the target culture and their own environment and individual situations. The teacher allows for a free-flowing dialogue, suspending his position of authority on the specific cultural topic. However, he remains authoritative and knowledgeable about the material with which he wants to work, supplying information, for example, about former East and West Germany. The difference between authoritarian and authoritative positions in an educational framework gains importance here. If we view this classroom scenario within a Bakhtinean framework of "heteroglossia," we can elaborate with Gary Saul Morson (2004):

> In any given culture or subculture, there tends to be what Bakhtin would call an "authoritative" perspective. However, the role of that perspective is not necessarily authoritarian. . . . Authoritative words in their fully expressed form purport to offer an alibi. They say, like Dostoevsky's Grand Inquisitor: we speak the truth and you need not question, only obey, for your conscience to be at rest. Yet, every authoritative word is spoken or heard in a milieu of difference. It may try to insulate itself from dialogue with reverential tones, a special script, and all the other signs of the authority fused to it, but at the margins dialogue waits with a challenge: you may be right, but you have to convince me. Once the authoritative word responds to that challenge, it ceases to be *fully* authoritative. To be sure, it may still command considerable deference by virtue of its past, its moral aura, and its omnipresence. But it has ceased to be free from dialogue and its authority has changed from unquestioned to dialogically tested. Every educator crosses this line when he or she gives reasons for a truth. (pp. 318–319)

Social justice education and Bakhtinean theory merge at the point of intentional transparency. I stated earlier that it is important for a social justice educator to continuously engage in self-reflection and to encourage students to do the same. Process gains importance *vis-à-vis* a specific outcome, and the question *why*, and all its ramifications, takes center stage. The German instructor in the example explains why he has chosen this very set of data in order to demonstrate to the students that course material is always contingent on specific choices by the teacher. Consequently, all course material remains contingent on the instructor's point of view concerning foreign language education. The instructor values these contingencies and makes transparent what Barry Kanpol (1990) calls a "hidden curriculum":

> The "hidden curriculum" refers to implicit, moral, and ideological assumptions routinely passed on to students. In its strongest and least emancipatory sense, the hidden curriculum refers to the hegemonic body of knowledge that places students in subordinate social positions. (p. 248)

Thus, social justice pedagogy is aware of the cultural contingencies alluded to by Barbara Herrnstein Smith, acknowledges them, and reveals them openly in order to incorporate them into the learning and teaching process.

Transparent Pedagogy

I contend that we foster learning when our pedagogy becomes transparent to our students. "Nobody proves the Pythagorean theorem by saying Pythagoras said so" (Morson, 2004, p. 319). In other words, it is not enough to force students to memorize facts. They need to understand how one arrives at new knowledge. Then they will be able to better utilize their newly acquired insights. Students in a foreign language classroom become more involved in their own educational processes once they know why the educator uses specific pedagogical tools. For example, when in a workbook exercise I want my students to ask questions of other students in class, I always tell them to first ask the question and then say the name of the student they want to answer the question. This ensures that everyone listens to each question. If they first were to state the name of the student, the other class members would not have to focus on the question anymore, because they would know that someone else will answer. This way I not only familiarize them with an educator's trick but also draw their attention to the learning process. They can reflect on their peers' reactions and on their own behaviors in the educational process, and become included in the common goal of teaching and learning. At the same time, the process of foreign language education has gained transparency.[3]

Again referencing Bakhtin, Morson (2004) reminds us, "We not only learn, we also learn to learn, and we learn to learn best when we engage in a dialogue with others and ourselves" (p. 331). Students direct their own learning and become responsible for the outcomes. They are better able to reflect on their position and function in the learning process, which can then inform their investigations and interactions with the new cultural paradigms. They are more conscious of the contingencies of their points of view *vis-à-vis* new cultural encounters, a prerequisite for social justice awareness. At the same time, students engage in "active learning,"

> which is achieved by acquiring "organized knowledge structures" and "strategies for remembering, understanding, and solving problems." . . .

Additionally, active learning entails a process of interpretation, whereby new knowledge is related to prior knowledge and stored in a manner that emphasizes the elaborated meaning of these relationships. (Active learning, 2007)

Introducing students to the process of learning through an explicit reflection on pedagogical tools used inside and outside of the classroom contributes to "active learning." Students' explicit knowledge of foreign language pedagogy facilitates the transition to an active engagement with the content of the courses.

In addition to the changed roles of students and teachers, the selection of course materials and forms of cultural interaction in the classroom play an important role in the success of socially just foreign language education. With the appropriate choice of textbooks and course materials and the explicit use of social justice pedagogy, students and teachers try to interact with the target cultures. They realize the contingencies of their individual interactions with the many facets of the target culture and are able to deconstruct both the target culture and their own.

The Advanced Foreign Language Classroom

An example from the German School at Middlebury College highlights these structures. In a third-year, undergraduate-level German culture course, instead of selecting a textbook created and produced in the United States, the instructors in the German School opted for a sociology text developed in Germany by Germans for the advanced levels in German high schools: (Gymnasien): *Die Gesellschaft der Bundesrepublik Deutschland* (Blumoehr, 2001). Susanne Niemeier (2004) states:

> Autonomous learning can thrive best when the learners are offered authentic learning situations (which involve insights into foreign thinking patterns and into the foreign culture) in a classroom environment where the above-mentioned principles of language awareness and intercultural competence are present as well. (p. 97)

Thus, choosing this text for a culture course allows both students and teachers to interact with a cultural product of the target language. Consequently, German cultural paradigms, norms, prejudices, and so on, remain in the text. It has not been censored or filtered through a specific U.S. ideology. In an atmosphere of increasing diversification of students and faculty, no preference is given to any cultural interpretation or orientation before the encounter with the text. Students and teachers can interact with this text, bringing their own cultural paradigms, their contingencies, into the mix.

Each participant in this interaction meets "Germany." Thus, the tasks in the classroom change. First, the contingent nature of the choice of instructional material is immediately foregrounded. It becomes a topic of discussion. Second, no individual cultural outlook is privileged. Everyone encounters this text from his or her specific cultural vantage point. Third, these individual cultural positions become highlighted, and students are encouraged to view the material through their specific cultural lenses, which in turn fosters cultural self-reflection. Their own cultures become constructed, destabilized, and heteroglossic. These are the conditions that now enable students and teachers to approach the text as a construction of a German culture. As a result, this culture becomes automatically destabilized because the class has already explicitly engaged in a cultural deconstruction of their own. Thus, *Die Gesellschaft der Bundesrepublik Deutschland* (The Society of the Federal Republic of Germany) becomes multifaceted and multivoiced. Rather than harboring a "truth" about Germany and the Germans, this text now forms the basis for active reflection on its constructedness and its nature as a cultural product and producer. After all, this text is the result of an accumulated German cultural knowledge as well as the creator of such, because it is used to teach young Germans on their way to the university what it means to be a member of their society. In the German classroom at Middlebury College, it assumes the function of an initiator of discussions about forms of societies, their value systems, and their cultural contingencies in general; ". . . it helps learners to not try to look for equations between their native language and the foreign language, but that they are open for other conceptualizations within the foreign language and its culture" (Niemeier, 2004, p. 113).

In addition, in this course students work online twice per week. They select an Internet project that pertains to any aspect of German culture they find interesting. After searching the web for pertinent information, they create a website on the chosen topic and share it with their classmates in presentations at the end of the term. Their narratives reveal a higher level of analytical skill than their traditional essays did, and the presentations reflect their newly acquired intercultural savvy.

Thus, in this course, students develop into conscious participants in the construction of cultures. Reflecting on cultural contingencies, they destabilize the target culture as well as their own, and offer views of the target culture that are consciously filtered through their own perspectives. All this is explicit. One student, for example, developing a website on German soccer shifted his focus from sports to German identity and the importance of soccer to a more confident German national self-awareness. At the same time that he explicated German social, political, and economic history he also repeatedly referred to U.S. connections to that German cultural construction, beginning with an explanation of the brand name Adidas and its impact on the world of sports and finishing with a picture of his own soccer shoes. He started from a point of personal interest, shifted to an involvement with the target culture, and returned to the personal that now was informed by his preceding analysis of German culture. Thus, students and teachers leave this course not only having gained knowledge about Germany but able to recognize contingencies of cultures, an important goal of social justice education.

The Middlebury College German department also uses a social justice education approach in one of its upper-level courses. One colleague introduced an adapted version of "deliberative dialogues"[4] to her course on identity politics. Pairs of students selected topics of interest, such as political parties, underrepresented groups, immigrants, and others. Instead of presenting their findings on the subjects, they were asked to produce at least three approaches to the topic that could be used in a deliberative dialogue in class. In one concrete example focusing on the situation of immigrants in Germany, students created a set of supporting and refuting arguments to each of the following approaches: immigrants should segregate, immigrants should assimilate, immigrants should integrate. This setup fosters a deliberation of positives and negatives to each approach, ideally resulting in a common ground among all of the approaches. Class discussion becomes not a debate but a deliberation of specific issues that is founded in knowledge about the specific situation of immigrants in Germany. While students and teachers exchange and engage information about the culture, this class format models social justice behavior: deliberation instead of debate.

Finally, service-learning courses can round off the social justice and foreign language curriculum by bridging the lives of students and the communities that surround them. In a service-learning environment, students and teachers react to specific needs of the surrounding language communities, for example, teaching language to heritage speakers. Students study the conditions of the community, interact with its members, and return to the classroom with newly acquired insights, feeding back into the course design and assignments. A reciprocal relationship between the college students and the foreign language community off campus develops, avoiding a hierarchically perceived interaction that privileges the students as knowledge bearers and condescends to the community as help seekers. In this scenario, both parties profit and learn from each other.

Social Justice Learning

The examples discussed here clearly demonstrate that it is possible to consistently apply the principles of a socially just education to the foreign language classroom. We simply have to take this task seriously and we can affect change, a change that has finally been called for in the report of the Modern Language Association's (2007) Ad Hoc Committee on Foreign Languages:[5] "In the course of acquiring functional language abilities, students are taught critical language awareness, interpretation and translation, historical and political consciousness, *social sensibility*, and aesthetic perception" (p. 238; emphasis added).

The relationship between social justice and foreign language education suggests that a language pedagogy based on the notion of a "critical pedagogy" engaged by Paolo Freire and informed by a "dialogic" developed by Mikhail Bakhtin allows for the incorporation of social justice issues into the foreign language curriculum. This kind of social justice pedagogy activates learners as well as instructors and creates a potential for social change. It transforms a historically authoritarian discourse into a dialogic one and acknowledges the multiplicity of voices participating in the educational process while at the same time it shifts the focus and goal of language education from a pseudo-stable production of a linguistic "near native proficiency" to an eternally developing cultural hybridity. While retaining lexical, morphological, and syntactical accuracy as one of the goals in foreign language education, this kind of pedagogy recognizes the power of comparative cultural thinking that creates a multiplicity of points of view and reveals the contingencies of any cultural perspective. Thus, it ultimately allows for the possibility of an active interaction with traditional "others" that does not generate stereotypical thinking and generalizations but facilitates a differentiation of cultural perspectives.

Notes

1. See Susanne Niemeier's critique of Kramsch's use of "intercultural competence" in "Linguistic and Cultural Relativity—Reconsidered for the Foreign Language Classroom" in *Cognitive Linguistics, Second Language Acquisition, and Foreign Language Teaching* (p. 115) edited by M. Achard & S. Niemeier, 2004, Berlin: de Gruyter.

2. Of course, this is true for any group affiliation but becomes especially pertinent when based on race, ethnicity, gender, sex, ability, religion, and other legally protected categories of discrimination.

3. This longing for transparency may be reflected in students' renewed interest in the study of linguistics as an explanation of language systems. They gain access to how languages work and how they developed, which is not the case in a traditional foreign-language-acquisition scenario.

4. Compare Kamakshi Murti's contribution in this book (chapter 13).

5. This "outcome" corresponds to the European Union's affirmation of multiculturalism and European values expressed in a report by the Commission of the European Communities in 2005:

> It is this diversity [of cultures, customs and beliefs] that makes the European Union what it is: not a "melting pot" in which differences are rendered down, but a common home in which diversity is celebrated, and where our many mother tongues are a source of wealth and a bridge to greater solidarity and mutual understanding. (Com. 596 final)
>
> Contrary to the United States, the European Union rejects the notion of a "melting pot" in favor of a community that encourages intercultural understanding based on the very idea that cultures are different. In turn, these differences enable intellectual and social growth and development, which are denied in a "melting pot" where differences simply melt away.

References

Active learning: A perspective from cognitive psychology [Electronic version]. (2007, March). *Faculty Focus*. Retrieved March 21, 2008, from http:www.magna pubs.com/issues/magnapubs_ff/4_3/news/600016-1.html?type = pf/

Bakhtin, M. (1981). *The dialogic imagination* (C. Emerson & M. Holquist, Trans.). Austin: University of Texas Press. (Original work published 1975)

Bell, L. A., Washington, S., Weinstein G., & Love, B. (1997). Knowing ourselves as instructors. In M. Adams, L. A. Bell, & P. Griffin (Eds.), *Teaching for diversity and social justice: A sourcebook* (pp. 299–310). New York: Routledge.

Blumoehr, F. (2001). *Die gesellschaft der bundesrepublik deutschland.* Bamberg: C.C. Buchner.

Byram, M. (1997). *Teaching and assessing intercultural communicative competence.* Clevedon: Multilingual Matters.

Commission of the European Communities. (2005, November 22). *Communication from the commission to the council, the European parliament, the European economic and social committee and the committee of the regions: A new framework strategy for multilingualism.* Retrieved March 23, 2008, from http://www.hm.ee/index.php?popup = download&id = 4312/

Freire, P. (1998). *Teachers as cultural workers* (D. Macedo, D. Koike, & A. Alexandre Oliveira, Trans.). Boulder, CO: Westview. (Original work published 1993)

Herrnstein Smith, B. (1988). *Contingencies of value: Alternative perspectives for critical theory.* Cambridge: Harvard University Press.

Kanpol, B. (1990). Political applied linguistics and postmodernism: Towards an engagement of similarity within difference. *Issues in Applied Linguistics, 1*(2), 238–250.

Kramsch, C. (1993). *Context and culture in language teaching.* Oxford: Oxford University Press.

Modern Language Association. (2007). Foreign languages and higher education. *Profession 2007,* pp. 234–245.

Morson, G. S. (2004). The process of ideological becoming. In A. F. Ball & S.Warshauer Freedman (Eds.), *Bakhtinian perspectives on language, literacy, and learning* (pp. 215–333). Cambridge: University of Cambridge Press.

Niemeier, S. (2004). Linguistic and cultural relativity—Reconsidered for the foreign language classroom. In M. Achard & S. Niemeier (Eds.), *Cognitive linguistics, second language acquisition, and foreign language teaching* (pp. 95–119). Berlin: Walter de Gruyter.

II

SHAKESPEARE MEETS SOCIAL JUSTICE

Incorporating Literature in the Social Sciences

Carolyn F. Palmer

And earthly power doth then show likest God's
When mercy seasons justice. Therefore, Jew,
Though justice be thy plea, consider this:
That, in the course of justice, none of us
Should see salvation . . .

—*The Merchant of Venice*, IV.i.195–199

So states Portia, a wealthy Christian woman masquerading as a male legal expert. She asks Jewish Shylock to be merciful, then shows little mercy to him as tables turn. Shylock describes prejudice and abuse at the hands of Christians; men describe greater love for one another than for their wives; money makes the power dynamics go 'round. In this single scene, Shakespeare offers us social justice provocations in poetic meter.

This chapter explores how teaching with literature in the social sciences can stir the blood, fire the imagination, and set up a safe space for exploring diverse perspectives on social justice issues. Literature and art take us into another's world and foster empathy more directly than much scholarly material, thus providing flesh and feeling for theory and evidence. Teachers routinely ask students to report on scholars' viewpoints; doing this with a literary text begins the exercise from a more accessible frame. For example, when a student reads Alex Kotlowitz's *There Are No Children Here* (1992) in an introductory sociology course, the novel draws students quickly and viscerally into the sociological issues—more so than scholarly fare, which will have its place farther on.

As a psychology and cognitive science professor, I address social justice teaching that draws on literature and art by considering, respectively, social justice education principles; a faculty development workshop held at Vassar College that provides a model for experiential classroom activity; how literature engages the whole person; and a sampling of social justice questions applicable to literary texts (specifically applied to *The Merchant of Venice*, Act IV, scene i).

Social Justice Education

Social justice envisions that all people and groups should live safely, with equitable distribution of resources and participation in society. Toward this goal, social justice education assesses the exploitation of one group by another, through individual and institutional structures and processes, as well as the processes by which social justice can be achieved (Bell, 1997). Individual and group identities, intra- and intergroup relations, systems of privilege, history and sociocultural contexts, resistance, and collaboration are all major facets of understanding power and empowerment.

Handling social justice materials and discussion is not easy. Adams (1997) asks teachers to consider several principles of teaching for social justice purposes. She urges us to teach in ways that acknowledge both emotion and cognition, to notice personal experience as well as system dynamics, to be mindful of classroom processes, to encourage reflection on experience, and to overtly appreciate developing awareness and change as consequences of learning. Although it is not the purpose of this essay to delve into the principles of social justice educational practice per se (as, for example, the contributors to Adams, Bell, & Griffin, 1997, do so well), it is useful to remember that students bring multiple identities, beliefs, and different stages of development to classes. Teachers will need to balance their goals of analyzing target materials with fostering students' development. This chapter focuses particularly on features of target material, but it acknowledges that teachers need to monitor students and classroom dynamics continually, and invite students to connect the material to themselves and contemporary social processes.

The approach described here emerges from a liberal arts orientation in which students examine values, integrate learning across fields, and take their learning into the world. College mission statements speak to the humane purposes of a diverse curriculum, faculty, and student body. For example, liberal arts institutions seek "to educate the individual imagination to see into the lives of others . . . to meet the challenges of a complex world responsibly . . . working toward a more just, diverse, egalitarian, and inclusive college community where all members feel valued and are fully empowered. . . ." (*Vassar College Mission Statement*, 2004); "engage students in the liberal arts, which fosters self-determination and demonstrates the transformative power of education" (*Denison University Mission Statement*, 2004); and recognize that "developing a global perspective and an appreciation and tolerance for a more diverse society are vital for living in an increasingly interdependent world" (*A DePauw Education*, 2006).

Social justice teaching fulfills these missions by examining particular sets of (power) values and using learning to make a difference in the world. When faculty bring to class something unexpected and different—poetry or movement or film or music—students discover that they can apply the social justice frame to any human endeavor.

Faculty as Explorers in a Teaching Development Workshop

A characteristic feature of social justice education is an awareness of one's experience, in life and in learning. The "Shakespeare Meets Social Justice" workshop offered by the Office of Teaching Development at Vassar College in 2005 provided campus faculty an experience that integrated text, movement, voice, acting, history, and discussion in a two-hour session. Faculty attended from across the liberal arts curriculum. Some taught courses focused explicitly on social justice issues, and others sought ways to introduce social justice questions into their courses and classrooms. (I interviewed a number of these faculty thereafter, and their practices are presented throughout this chapter.)

The organizers recruited professional actors to facilitate exploration of dramatic text. The actors described how they prepare for playing a scene, such as the trial from *The Merchant of Venice* (MV), in which Shakespeare depicts various power dynamics. (Faculty prepared by reading, in advance, part of Act IV, scene i). What methods could help faculty and students bring forward social justice issues? Two themes emerged across the variety of methods the actors used: staying concrete, such as staying connected to the body, and grounding everything in awareness of social positions and power relations among diverse groups.

Stay concrete and aware, in body and place: Who are we? Where are we? In simple gestures such as creating an inclusive circle, announcing names, and shaking hands with every workshop member, each person revealed a bit of self and lost some privacy; the actors considered this crucial if the group members were going to encourage one another to reveal themselves. Making a safe place for failure and glory, participants "unbuttoned" themselves. The actors commented that everything they do in drama is *practical*. "You start reading, you do it *quickly*. You then stand up, and *get the scene on its feet!*" They asked faculty to read different parts and serve as the audience. Everyone played a role, and everyone moved according to role. They demonstrated how, in a few short minutes, teachers could warm up a class, in body, voice, emotion, and mind.

Ground every activity in awareness of social positions and power dynamics: Who's an insider, who's an outsider? Are the power dynamics stable, or do they shift? What cultural myths and stereotypes are active? Are my contemporary and/or personal interests *not* the interests of those in the literature? Faculty in the workshop explored answers to these questions through awareness of voices in the play. The actors encouraged participants to speak certain lines multiple times, using different voices and attitude, drawing out different features of text. How does it feel to take a strong versus weak stance while delivering lines? How do others react to the different stances? The actors noted that using a script can set up a "safe space" for trying out different values and emotions, and that it's critical for understanding script and experience to rehearse such different approaches.

After faculty enacted different approaches to the scene, they readily wanted to consider social justice issues such as, What constitutes justice (e.g., the justice of the court enforcing the bond vs. social justice)? What does mercy have to do with justice? What is the ethical nature, interpretation, and enforceability of a contract? How do female and male roles and ethnic stereotypes play out? How quickly do we come to judge another? What power structures marked my upbringing? How do power structures function in this play? Are these power dynamics stable or shifting? If they shift, what's the effect?

The actors concluded this lively workshop by asking faculty to remember what a difference it made to speak, shout, and move from the very outset, thereby establishing connections with one's body, one another, one's environment, and with the text. Faculty took the experience back to class.

Asking Social Justice Questions Using Literature: Arousing Attention and Emotion

This single play, and even the single trial scene, has potential use in any number of courses in which social justice questions arise, such as those about gender, religion, economic class, legal structures, histories of empowered and marginalized groups, or about the notion of justice itself. For purposes of this discussion, MV will serve as the central text, but the social justice approach exemplified is applicable to any relevant art.

A teacher may raise social justice questions periodically in the context of a course focused on other topics (e.g., the introductory course to a major discipline) or address social justice as a theme throughout a course. Whether used once or repeatedly in a course, a teacher's use of literature or arts for social justice discussion startles students out of a passive stance. Literature takes people inside experiences, intentionally tapping emotions and exciting curiosity. Literature thus helps the teacher open up everyone's receptivity to a topic.

To begin, a teacher starts with a social justice goal for a class. She or he finds a piece of literature or art to arouse students' attention and feeling. What the teacher chooses as an activity will emerge from his or her goals for the class. For example, on an identity theme, the teacher may want to explore the idea of "marginalized voices in contemporary communities." To use the MV scene as a launching device, the teacher asks students to consider the primary characters, Portia and Shylock, as marginalized voices in their culture. Students might point out, for example, how both characters sought to control what they could, given the enormous constraints around them (Oldrieve, 1993). Portia found several ways to show men how smart she was, and in the end elicited their acknowledgment of her power as a woman.

In order to arouse the students, the teacher selects parts of the play that highlight the characters' struggles and constraints, and everyone takes a role in a group enactment. (Everyone gets concrete; everyone plays a role and thus explores a perspective; everyone uses a voice right from the beginning of class time.) Immediately following the enactment, students gather in small groups to brainstorm, first about how Portia and Shylock may be marginalized voices in their community and then about who have marginalized voices in our contemporary communities (such as the college campus or environs or the students' hometowns). Are there parallels across the centuries? What are differences? The small groups (whose small design continues the opportunity for more voices to participate and minimizes risk taking in front of an audience) then return to the whole class, each offering (for a start) one meaningful point they discussed. This may be adequate for the teacher's goals. If further work is desired, students can do their own outside-of-class analysis of another text or piece of artwork, perhaps from a list the professor provides. Literature or any art form can be used as extensively or as lightly as serves one's goals. Merely starting every class with a poem or a paragraph or a film clip will arouse attention and emotion.

Why is arousing emotion important? Social justice teaching aims to provide clarity about the experience of diverse social groups, and to balance cognitive and emotional aspects of learning. Emotion marks the value of experiences; it marks an encounter as something to pursue or avoid, fight or accept. Emotion marks *every* encounter: every reading of a text, every class meeting, every assignment, every topic. How does a professor approach emotion during social justice teaching? Although some teachers are skilled at managing explicit emotion work during class, many others do so more indirectly yet effectively.

Clarity of emotional experience can be enhanced through exercises aimed at articulating the range of emotions we experience. Simply asking small groups of students (1) to choose one emotion, such as "happiness," "anger," "sadness," "fear," "disgust," or "curiosity," (2) to generate as many terms as they can, from weak to intense, to evoke that quality (e.g., delight as well as ecstasy, wariness as well as terror), then (3) to report their list to the whole class, leads quickly to a rich lexicon of terms pertaining to emotion that will be useful in subsequent discussions throughout the course. The teacher has simultaneously raised awareness of the range of emotional experiences and provided a vocabulary for that awareness.

Clarity of emotional experience also comes from being grabbed by art. For example, one colleague chooses certain texts because she expects them to elicit students' empathy. She does not have to invite empathy with a heavy hand, because students naturally react emotionally to the characters portrayed. What is a woman's life like, if living on welfare? What is the experience of a Native American navigating between the reservation and town?

How does an incarcerated man connect with his children? This is not a Pollyanna tale; students are sometimes, initially, critical or judgmental of characters' situations. Many feel multiple, even difficult, emotions, including some empathy, but minimally recognize that there are different perspectives afoot. Students may hold on to a more sustained empathy especially if other events (i.e., readings, activities, assignments) reinforce their evolving view, and sometimes they come to a wholly new worldview. At its base, the encounter with literature offers a new way to look at something (e.g., a welfare recipient's view, an economic view, a political view, etc.).

Using literature in a social science setting broadens classroom tools for connecting with students who have a variety of learning styles. This is consistent with the social-justice-education perspective. It is one thing to read text; it is another thing to stand up, speak in character, gesture and strut, and attend to your fellow characters. Such full-body participation calls on not only students' intelligence with words, but also their intelligences of movement, rhythm, intonation, and social encounter. Educational practices that engage the whole person are more likely to encourage student exploration (see, e.g., Adams, Jones, & Tatum, 1997; Bell & Griffin, 1997; Gardner, 1993; Goleman, 2006).

Asking Social Justice Questions Using a Specific Literary Text

The following are examples of social justice questions in a social science course that can be addressed by means of the Shakespearean text *The Merchant of Venice*. A professor in psychology might be covering *stereotypes* specifically, or group dynamics in general, and could start with the MV trial scene. The teacher would ask students to read the scene aloud, taking both character and audience roles (stirring their blood! using voices!). Students readily perceive the *identity* focus on Jew and Christian, laden with power and prejudice; Shylock is referred to throughout as "the Jew." Other religion-based cultural references include "A Daniel," "Barabbas," "infidel," "if thou dost shed one drop of Christian blood . . . ," and "alien"; and Shylock is coerced to convert to Christianity in the end.

The professor could also orient students to basic structures of the writing, asking, What do these structures convey about social justice? For example, Shakespeare here writes in lines of iambic pentameter, and the end of a line is visually compelling. What words show up at the end of lines? Asking this question about references to Shylock during the trial prompts students to count how many times different characters use the word "Jew" as the last word of a line, thus emphasizing his identity. (Five different characters use it thus, two of them on several occasions.) What effect does this emphasis have on Shylock, the trial proceedings, and a reading of both?

This initial read-through and discussion serves both the "stay concrete" and "ground everything in perspectives" purposes of experiential, social justice teaching within a social science framework. The dramatic reading, with everyone playing some role, uses concrete voice and body in social interaction with the whole group, all organized by the scene's script. "Jew" and "Christian" identities explicitly contrast one another. Having brought in an example of identity issues at a trial where identity is supposedly not at issue but where it clearly matters, the professor has enticed students to delve further into stereotyping processes and effects in general.

Additional activities could expand consideration to other identities within the text or invite students to choose a further text that addresses ethnicity, class, gender, or sexuality. Students could apply group dynamic and stereotyping processes to a select piece of literature, for example, through writing an essay. The professor could also ask whether there are any forces dismantling exploitation. Such discussions will benefit from student familiarity with an introductory article on social justice tenets.

In addition to addressing identity issues, social justice focuses on the *broader contexts* for specific events. Attention to contexts could provide a basis for a larger project in a psychology course (e.g., an essay, class presentation, poster, or term paper). Students could consider "context" to include the text of the entire play; the playwright himself; the audience of Shakespeare's day; the sociopolitical and historical context of Elizabethan London; or our own, contemporary context (both personal and sociopolitical) that we bring to the encounter with the text. For example, reading the scene within the context of the *entire play* brings out more depth in Portia's views and actions regarding her female place in society, and one can see both Portia and Shylock as outsiders in the culture's power centers. Reading the whole play provides many more examples of stereotyping, prejudice, and violent or coercive behavior beyond just those related to gender or religion. Characters who might otherwise be seen as sympathetic in one way are clearly unsympathetic for other reasons. Shylock, for example, sees no problem with owning slaves when he likens his ownership of Antonio's flesh to the merchant's slave owning. All of the characters are flawed, ambivalent, even nasty, and embody the complexities of personality, motivation, and power machinations.

Asking about the *playwright* leads to questions about Shakespeare's personal experience, motivations, and livelihood. Shakespeare's parents were probably Catholic, and he may have maintained some connections with Catholicism, or at least other Catholics, throughout his life (see Greenblatt, 2004, for a recent perspective on Shakespeare's family, community, and views regarding Catholicism and religion as expressed in his plays).

Regarding his livelihood, who might have provided Shakespeare with the money to produce the play, and how did a patron's interests affect the text? Could a playwright expect patronage for a play that questioned existing power structures? If there appear to be tensions in the text about power, how is the playwright handling them so as to allow the patron and the audience to feel entertained, yet even enlightened and ennobled, in the process? Shakespeare presents wealthy Venetian Christian men who abuse Jewish Shylock, and Shylock rebukes them for their hypocrisy as Christians. Shakespeare also took pains to embed the Christian men's unethical behavior in larger contexts of their (supposed) generosity and love under most circumstances. A patron could thus feel superior, as an enlightened Christian, by acknowledging that Antonio's and others' abuses *were* sinful while still taking comfort in the larger point that these were hopefully generous, loving, responsibly superior citizens.

Similarly, by contextualizing Jewish history in England leading up to Shakespeare's day, students and teachers can interpret more elements in the Venetian courtroom, such as the larger resonance of Shylock asking for a pound of flesh and the judge's pronouncement that Shylock cannot "shed one drop of Christian blood" (thus resonating with "blood libel" myths). Also, depending on the country and crown, over a few short years Catholics were forced to be Protestant, Protestants were forced to be Catholic, and throughout this time Jews were forced to be Christian. Students will grasp why requiring Shylock to convert to Christianity is not merely racial/religious violence. Coercing Shylock's religious conversion drew a parallel, for the audience, with contemporary coercions among Catholics and Protestants, thus making an unexpected, perhaps tense, connection for Elizabethan Christians to a Jew's experience. And, because Christians could not be usurers, at least prior to the Puritans and other Reformers, the enforced conversion also deprived Shylock of his lifelong livelihood.[1] Students can appreciate how Shakespeare crafted a far more complex Jewish person in Shylock than was the tradition in the theater, and how Shakespeare posed (at least briefly) ethical challenges to his audience about the Christian abuse of Shylock. (See also Weinstein & Mellen, 1997, for an anti-Semitism curriculum design and further ways to develop social justice themes with such literature.)

These identity and context questions could orient students to social justice issues in economics, history, political science, psychology, sociology, women's studies, Jewish studies, and religion courses. As one Vassar faculty member notes from her experience, literature is so rich that it will take students in a hundred directions. If a teacher so chooses, she or he can invite the students to take the investigation further. When they have questions for which the teacher doesn't know the answers, she or he can ask them to investigate on their own and come to the next class with information to offer to the group. Any teacher can, on the spot, pause from focus on the precise details of a known issue and ask the class to construct a much larger set of questions to raise about power and context. It's likely that some combination of professor's perspective and knowledge and students' knowledge will allow for a tentative framework of questions and answers to grow.

Supporting Faculty Pursuing Social Justice Education

As social science faculty choose to use more literature or art to engage social justice education, they may want to design their courses more deliberately. Full courses that incorporate some literature and arts will take considerable work and probably multiple iterations to come to maturity. A Vassar colleague who uses fiction, poetry, journalism, film, photography, and music in teaching social justice courses in sociology notes that, for a course on war and art, it took a full sabbatical's work, another year's honing, and fully teaching one version to feel that it was in hand.

For teachers who wish to build a course explicitly using social justice processes, Bell and Griffin (1997) describe the sequencing of features in materials that develop student awareness and skill. Low-risk activities build acquaintances and surface analysis before attempting high-risk activities that probe feelings and explore conflicts. Concrete, single-level analyses of power dynamics precede more abstract, multilevel dynamics. Focus on personal content balances understandings of institutional patterns. Understanding difference leads to understanding that some differences are privileged. Faculty choosing to bring literature, arts, or any number of rich materials into social justice teaching in the social sciences will be much more effective when they are clear about where that material fits within such sequencing in their courses. Literature such as *The Merchant of Venice* could be introduced early in the semester for low-risk, concrete, surface activities and brought back at a later point for students to explore with their developing skills of recognizing identities, group processes, and dominance relations at multiple levels. Once students have seen a model from class, they are in a better position to apply the interdisciplinary approach outside class in projects that continue the theme without the instructor orchestrating the experience.[2]

Although many topics can be approached with a social justice view, transfer of learning takes work. Asking about the historical context of one feature from the MV trial scene, the role of "the Jew" in Elizabethan times, led this author in a short time to learn a great deal about Jews' roles, power, vulnerabilities, and caricatures, from their arrival in England (in the historical record) in 1066 through their official expulsion in 1290 and their unofficial welcome back to England years after Shakespeare's day (see Rogers, n.d.; Shapiro, 1996; Stirling, 1997). In English theater from the Middle Ages through the Elizabethan years, Jews were presented as stock, isolated, often villainous, and almost always one-dimensional figures. Elizabethan theatergoers would have been familiar with, and even have experienced directly, religious tensions of the day.

This transfer of learning is nearly as true for faculty as it is for students, and it points to the value of learning from one another and in group settings. Readers are encouraged to organize faculty workshops, wherein professors get a chance to listen and learn from each others' contributions. It is extremely useful for faculty to experience the discovery process as participants, akin to what students experience every day. Faculty who routinely use plays, poetry, and other literature in active engagement with students could facilitate the gathering. Visiting one another's classes also inspires new approaches and gives faculty the chance to be the student again.

A particular point about this collegial development mode is that there are many faculty who feel their disciplines are not obvious candidates for social justice education; they might feel that literature is an even farther stretch from the core curriculum. Social justice educators, however, see that perspectives on power and context are relevant to any discipline. Whether acknowledged or not, the professor and students (and textbooks) all bring personal and cultural histories to classroom dynamics that affect coverage of the core curriculum. Faculty are eager to deepen their disciplinary coverage and connection with students. A science professor, for example, who already uses literature and art could offer a welcome opportunity for faculty development by hosting a discussion about literature in the science classroom.

Finally, liberal arts teaching in the 21st century is an increasingly interdisciplinary endeavor. Interdisciplinarity can be simultaneously empowering and disempowering, as it requires multiple perspectives, less certainty, and greater nuance as people seek meaning in events. As teachers move outside their comfort zones, they stretch and question their own authority and face limits of expertise. Interdisciplinary social justice teaching takes great effort but yields empowering results for both teachers and students.

Conclusion

The Merchant of Venice resonates on many levels. Even across hundreds of years, Portia's decision to dress and act like a man in order to manage her destiny speaks to people about women's concerns in the world. She also speaks from a position of power, as a wealthy woman and as a judge, asking for a merciful stance from Shylock but offering little mercy to him.[3] Portia, Shylock, and so many others in literature flesh out complexities of individual and institutional responsibility and action.

In this chapter I focus on the use of literature as teachers pursue social justice in social science classrooms at liberal arts institutions. Introducing literature that evokes emotions; providing activities that engage the whole person and invite collaboration; scaffolding students' reflections on both personal and systems levels of meaning, or historical and contemporary meanings—these are all processes that not only serve to arouse student attention and concern around a topic but that also embody social justice practices (Adams, 1997). Faculty who engage in such processes report that their students are energized, inspired, provoked, expanded, discomfited, and empowered by their engagement with literature. Students may listen to, and remember, a message well in a social science classroom if it first arises through art.

> How far that little candle throws his beams!
> So shines a good deed in a naughty world.
> —Portia, in *The Merchant of Venice*, V.i.90–91

Notes

1. However, Oldrieve (1993) notes that, in actual practice, Christian merchants did charge interest, and Shakespeare's audience knew this, thus the conversion may not have seemed so crippling.
2. See also Griffin (1997) for further useful points about facilitating classroom process.
3. However, see Oldrieve (1993) for a "shared oppression" view of Portia's orientation to Shylock.

References

Adams, M. (1997). Pedagogical frameworks for social justice education. In M. Adams, L. A. Bell, & P. Griffin (Eds.), *Teaching for diversity and social justice: A sourcebook* (pp. 30–43). New York: Routledge.

Adams, M., Bell, L. A., & Griffin, P. (Eds.). (1997). *Teaching for diversity and social justice: A sourcebook.* New York: Routledge.

Adams, M., Jones, J., & Tatum, B. D. (1997). Knowing our students. In M. Adams, L. A. Bell, & P. Griffin (Eds.), *Teaching for diversity and social justice: A sourcebook* (pp. 321–325). New York: Routledge.

Bell, L. A. (1997). Theoretical foundations for social justice education. In M. Adams, L. A. Bell, & P. Griffin (Eds.), *Teaching for diversity and social justice: A sourcebook* (pp. 3–15). New York: Routledge.

Bell, L. A., & Griffin, P. (1997). Designing social justice education courses. In M. Adams, L. A. Bell, & P. Griffin (Eds.), *Teaching for diversity and social justice: A sourcebook* (pp. 44–58). New York: Routledge.

Denison University mission statement. (2004). Retrieved March 18, 2007, from http://www.denison.edu/catalogs/missionstatement.html

A DePauw education. (2006, January). Retrieved March 18, 2007, from http://www.depauw.edu/catalog/section1.asp

Gardner, H. (1993). *Multiple intelligences: The theory in practice.* New York: Basic Books.

Goleman, D. (2006). *Social intelligence.* New York: Bantam Books.

Greenblatt, S. (2004). *Will in the world: How Shakespeare became Shakespeare.* New York: W. W. Norton.

Griffin, P. (1997). Facilitating social justice education courses. In M. Adams, L. A. Bell, & P. Griffin (Eds.), *Teaching for diversity and social justice: A sourcebook* (pp. 279–298). New York: Routledge.

Kotlowitz, A. (1992). *There are no children here.* New York, Anchor.

Oldrieve, S. (1993). Marginalized voices in *The Merchant of Venice. Cardozo Studies in Law and Literature, 5*(1), 87–105.

Rogers, J. (n.d.). Shylock and history. Retrieved March 12, 2007, from http://www
.pbs.org/wgbh/masterpiece/merchant/ei_shylock.html

Shapiro, J. (1996). *Shakespeare and the Jews*. New York: Columbia University Press.

Stirling, G. (1997, February). Shakespeare and anti-Semitism: The question of Shylock. Retrieved March 12, 2007, from http://www.geocities.com/Athens/Acropo
lis/7221

Vassar College mission statement. (2004). Retrieved March 18, 2007, from http://presi
dent.vassar.edu/mission.html

Weinstein, G., & Mellen, D. (1997). Antisemitism curriculum design. In M. Adams,
L. A. Bell, & P. Griffin (Eds.), *Teaching for diversity and social justice: A sourcebook*
(pp. 170–197). New York: Routledge.

12

WRITING FOR SOCIAL CHANGE

Building a Citizen–Scholar Discourse
That Combines Narrative, Theory, and Research

Catharine Wright

We need to teach in such a way as to arouse
passion now and then; we need a new camara-
derie, a new en masse. These are dark and
shadowed times, and we need to live them,
standing before one another, open to the world.

—Maxine Greene (1996)

Because language can never be situated outside of history, power, and struggle, languages
of resistance and possibility (that is, resistance
to various forms of oppression and the possibility of transformation of the status quo) must
always be productive (critical and inclusive, producing new meaning) rather than simply
reproductive.

—Pepi Leistyna, Arlie Woodrum,
and Stephen Sherblom (1996)

S cholars in composition and rhetoric have long advocated for a change
in the way writing is taught in higher education, working to "reclaim
a form of expression that really matters" (Miller, 2005, p. 30). In *Writing at the End of the World*, Miller (2005) calls for academics to "think anew

about writing as a place where the personal and the academic, the private and the public, the individual and the institutional, are always inextricably interwoven" (p. 31). These goals have much in common with a history of liberatory education theory that calls for "objectivity and subjectivity in constant dialectical relationship" (Freire, 1996, p. 32). And they are neatly aligned with principals of contemporary social justice education, which include "balancing emotional and cognitive components of the learning process; acknowledging the personal while illuminating the systemic; utilizing personal reflection and experience as tools for student-centered learning, and valuing the development of awareness and personal growth" (Adams, 1997, p. 30). All of these calls for a new academic discourse, a discourse that draws on both the personal and theoretical, the public and private, are ideally suited to the purpose of a liberal arts education. Our role as educators, former dean of Harvard College Harry Lewis (2006) asserts, is to engage students and ourselves in the moral issues of the day.

As academics, we view the personal with suspicion. We *study* narratives, observe the ways that they cross and change genre boundaries, draw on them for critical analyses of cultures and intercultural relations, and research their relationship to memory and the mind (Chamberlain & Thompson, 1998). But we do not personally and honestly converse, as scholars, or as world citizens, through first-person narrative. Our discipline-specific discourse in the third person fails to provide an arena in which to bring together our personal and scholarly selves. The binary is one that we would be quick to point out in our subjects for research, but which we willingly maintain in our practice of communication. Born in the separation between body and mind (hooks, 1994, p. 136), the divide widens with our focus on specialization. Students, colleagues, communities, and our own worried mind at night recognize that the gap between scholarly discourse and public life is probably not so necessary, that the stakes are exceedingly high. Yet we push on, producing specialized papers, caught in an institutional web that is increasingly driven by commercial concerns, honing our scholarly craft. We articulate paths of knowing that Macedo (1996) describes as "fragmented" and "reduced" (p. 42).

For most of us, these divisions are necessary to ensure our success in the academy. We are rewarded when we "do not teach against the grain" (hooks,

1994, p. 203), when we subscribe to the idea that scholarly practices are objective rather than culturally, historically situated. But subscription comes with a price. Our methods of discourse were conceived and refined in elite, White institutions. The methods are elegant, penetrating, and can be learned. When those new to the institution learn these methods, the infusion of new cultural strains should naturally change not only the content but the very modes of discourse. Yet this has hardly occurred. "Creative writing" programs offer creative expression in three standard genres, "writing programs" teach the norms of academic prose, and departments guide young scholars to follow specialized forms of expression. Why is this so? If we fail to ask this question, we are like figures in Beverly Tatum's metaphor for passive racism (1997, p. 11): We stand still on a conveyor belt of a culturally prescribed discourse rather than walk against it, just as passive immersion in a culture based historically on racist practices makes us passive racists. Our way out, like Tatum's anti-racists, is to walk *against* the movement of the belt, to resist a hegemonic discourse by cultivating in our students and ourselves hybrid, complex forms of expression that mirror what we understand about the fluidity of culture. In Miller's (2005) words, we must urge our students to "play the personal against the theoretical, the fictional against the real, and facts against interpretations, not to establish the primacy of any one of the terms in these binary oppositions, but rather to forestall for as long as possible slipping into the simple and satisfying binarism that allows anyone the comfort of relaxing into a settled position" (p. 48).

We have a wealth of models on which to draw. Not only have the social sciences made efforts to include narrative through ethnography, and not only have writing programs embraced multiple literacies, for example, but major thinkers and writers of the 20th century have alternately theorized, narrated, and argued in the first person. Said, Bhaba, and Foucault are just a few whose writing is fluid, urgent, personal, theoretical (H. Vila, personal communication, November 10, 2008). Du Bois, Baldwin, hooks, and Silko, among others, straddle literary genres and/or fields of study while being self-reflexive. Examining the works of these writers with our students helps us perceive the possibilities for a more exciting discourse in academia, one in which we can all participate in small or large ways according to our goals and our willingness to take risks. Such a discourse demands attention to a range of ever-shifting rhetorical concerns, and is reinforced by the work of colleagues already engaged in the transformation of academia through cross-disciplinary conversations, student-centered classrooms, service-learning courses, and new curricular ventures in sustainability and mindfulness.

A Dialectical Discourse: Models and Theory

In his 1946 essay "Why I Write," George Orwell (1995) says that good writing involves facing unpleasant truths. He models this ability to face the truth about his own social group, White imperialists, in his 1936 essay "Shooting an Elephant," in which he asserts that "when the white man turns tyrant" he "wears a mask, and his face grows to fit it" (1995, p. 38). This insight into the nature of the social group of which he is a part comes from "a tiny incident in itself" that "gave a better glimpse . . . of the real nature of imperialism" (p. 36). The situation, involving the Burmese, the English imperialists, and an elephant's death, is politically revealing. But his understanding of those politics is conveyed through first-person narration, his insights the result of "a glimpse" into something that happened "one day."

Prior to Orwell, in his 1903 "Of the Sons of Master and Man," W. E. B. Du Bois (1903/1982) set out to analyze the "actual relation of whites and blacks in the South" (p. 189). Unlike Orwell's, his insights are not the result of a glimpse but derive from a "conscientious study" of contact between races. His "line of study" is structured by categories of observation rather than a single story. Yet like Orwell, Du Bois (1903/1982) draws on the intimacy of narrative, assuring readers that questions about race contact will be answered by means of "a plain, unvarnished tale" (p. 189), making observations that do not "require any fine-spun theories of racial differences" (p. 191). He attends to the "little things which are most elusive to the grasp and yet most essential to . . . the whole" (p. 203) and invites his readers to observe as closely as he: "now if one notices carefully one will see . . ." (p. 204).

The kind of discourse about racial domination and subordination into which these two great 20th century writers and social critics invite their readers is simultaneously personal and scholarly. It is personal in that both writers use the first person. Orwell (1995) locates himself within his narrative: "here was I, the white man with his gun" (p. 38). Both writers exhibit emotion, through metaphor and directly. "It is, in fine," Du Bois (1903/1982) reflects, "the atmosphere of the land, the thought and feeling, the thousand and one little actions which go to make up life" (p. 203). They attend to the spiritual landscape of their subjects, evoking images of life and death, shadow and water, naming "spiritual turmoil" as a human concern. The discourse is scholarly in that both writers include critical perspectives on imperialism and race relations. Kenan (1995) points to "Du Bois' pioneering . . . approach to race relations in psychological and philosophical terms" (p. xxxi). Orwell "is the narrator created to demonstrate the dehumanizing effect of Empire on all within its reach" (Gornick, 2001, p. 17). He observes the psychological state of both "the white man with his gun" and the "unarmed native crowd" in ways that anticipate later studies in White privilege. Both writers attend closely to the physical, psychological, and spiritual conditions of both oppressive and oppressed groups—pinpointing what Bell (1997) calls "defining features of oppression" (p. 4). In a cross-listed class called Writing for Social Change, I use these essays and others not only as models of a hybrid discourse but to develop Bell's "theory of oppression" in class.

In Writing for Social Change we analyze texts for their rhetorical strategies and their content. What are the arguments, and to whom are they addressed? Do the authors' social positions and types of knowledge inform their arguments or not? With a background in both creative and critical writing, I enjoy examining the hybrid nature of the discourse. I realize that not all teachers have this advantage, yet I believe that as critical thinkers we are prepared to negotiate the divide. We know that the how and why of narrative belongs to citizens throughout the world and is regularly shared outside the academy and beyond the genre of creative nonfiction. Intercultural and intergenre, personal narrative belongs to an older, community discourse, a discourse of storytelling, "the truest of all modes of discourse to our experience of being alive" (Sobol, 1999, p. 15). A critical discourse that *includes* storytelling situates us in ways that, as academics, we are used to situating subjects. It locates us within the human world, as "social location (positionality) affects the stories we construct" (Bell, 2008). And within the natural world, as well, by bringing together what Barry Lopez (1996) calls "two landscapes . . . the exterior landscape . . . organized according to principles or laws or tendencies beyond human control" and "the interior landscape . . . the speculations, intuitions, and formal ideas we refer to as 'mind'" (pp. 686–687). Situating us within social and ecological systems, then, a storytelling discourse observes relationships between larger systems and individuals, the impersonal and the personal. *Participating* in a critical storytelling discourse requires the ability to step back and observe ourselves as outsiders. This aligns with a major element of social justice education, to "acknowledge the personal while illuminating the systemic" (Adams, 1997, p. 30).

Student Discourse in Informal and Formal Writing

Perhaps the most challenging principle of social justice education is to balance emotional and cognitive aspects of learning. We know that our course content can provoke emotion, and we hope for some passion in student response. In literature classes we acknowledge emotion via discussion of characters in a text. Only recently have I begun to explicitly address emotion as a category of response. When asked to identify the range of feelings that class readings provoke, students list anger, shame, sadness, pride, hope, despair. Sometimes they connect their emotional response with their social position(s). At some point we might observe that, for different reasons, shame is a response experienced by members of both dominant and subordinate social categories. In acknowledging the emotional aspect of the texts, we begin to explicitly both analyze a hybrid discourse and simultaneously engage in it.

This hybrid discourse can be further legitimized in informal response papers in which students respond privately to both academic and personal questions. The following excerpt is an informal student response to McIntosh's (1988) "White Privilege and Male Privilege: A Personal Account of Coming to See Correspondences Through Work in Women's Studies."

> *I probably related a little too easily to McIntosh's discussion of her childhood and her schooling. I was raised in a primarily white suburb of New York City, where we were certainly taught about slavery, racism, the Civil Rights era, and oppression, but we were never taught to see ourselves as morally damaged. We were reminded of this history once or twice a year, usually during the month of February—as Black History Month coincides with Martin Luther King Day. We'd quickly review the history of the Civil Rights Movement, talk briefly about current issues of racism, attend an assembly—though never one too shocking—and then move on to math class. And so we continued living in our little bubble . . . there were enormous amounts of White privilege . . . in this sense, I can relate to what McIntosh says about both White privilege and gender relations.*

In the excerpt, the student "relates" to a first-person narrative in her own first-person voice. Her intimate reflection is connected to critical content—"we were never taught to see ourselves as morally damaged"—which responds to McIntosh's point that White people are negatively affected by our own privilege. The student reflects on her previous schooling in relation to color and power, which gives her a chance to evaluate and revise her knowledge base. In this way she makes the learning her own and invites its relevance into her life.

The informal response is sufficient for students to make connections between course material and their own lives, and many faculty will successfully confine a hybrid discourse to that space. My goal, however, is to develop students as serious writers in multiple capacities, knowing that development in one area of writing informs another. Historically, I have met this goal by assigning, at the beginning of the semester, one formal paper that is a personal narrative with analysis. Students love the assignment, but for years it was a struggle to get them to sufficiently analyze their experience from a critical perspective. In the late 1990s, inspired by colleague Hector Vila, co-author of "Digital Stories in the Liberal Arts Environment" (Ganley & Vila, 2006), and aided by the way that new technology breaks down our perceptions of writing—for example, weblogs are nonlinear, and digital videos layer text, image, and soundtrack—I asked students to cluster or layer a personal narrative, scholarly research, and critical responses to texts in a single, online, nonlinear "space." This fostered connections, but new challenges emerged. Students failed to adequately develop and synthesize ideas. Where were the sustained arguments? After a few semesters I brought the concepts inspired by the technology back into the formal paper and assigned "research essays" in which students combined narrative and research. This produced the results I was after. In the following excerpts from a 14-page research essay written in 2007, one student successfully explores her interstitial experience with language. She begins with a narrative:

> *I spent five years at Nishimachi International School, which is the longest I have stayed at any one school or in any one neighborhood. There, I picked up a language that everyone seemed to be using—what my friends called mix-go (mixed language). Not only did our conversations consist of English and Japanese sentences, but even our individual sentences were made of both English and Japanese words. It all seemed very natural, and I soon started imitating*

my friends, stringing English verbs with Japanese prepositions. It became my dominant language within weeks.

She reveals herself emotionally to the reader and also brings in research on the topic:

I . . . remember having a conversation with a teacher . . . in which we were talking about mix-go. *I told her that I was ashamed of it, and I tried hard to stop because I thought it made me sound inarticulate. She told me, however, that we often mix languages because there are many words that we simply cannot translate, and we pick the word, irrespective of the language it is in, that is most appropriate to what we want to say. Being bilingual simply meant having a bigger repertoire, more tools, a larger dictionary. In an article that discusses the pros and cons of "global nomads," a term used for children who grow up abroad, Debra Carlson (1997) notes: "Languages offer different people a variety of ways of expressing themselves creatively. Who wants only one kind of art? Why would we want only one kind of language?" I never considered my* mix-go *to be something that was smart, something that made linguistic sense.*

As the paper develops, her nonemotional, scholarly persona dominates the discourse:

In a series of studies conducted on adult Third Culture Kids, or TCK's who are at least 25 years old, Useem and her colleagues found that 90% of their adult TCK respondents felt "out of synch [sic]" with their American peers—a feeling that is especially painful for an adolescent (Useem & Cottrell, 1993). Similarly, in a case study of four Japanese students . . .

In her conclusion, subjective and objective discourse are in full dialectical relationship:

There are clearly many advantages of being a Third Culture Kid too, and despite all the confusion and the loneliness I have felt because of it, I am glad I grew up that way. According to Global Nomads International President and founder Norma McCaig, TCK's are "cultural chameleons" who carefully observe their environment and then modify their behavior accordingly (McCaig, 1994). Carlson lists many "cross-cultural skills" that TCK's have, such as flexibility, tolerance, strong observation skills, a multi-dimensional worldview, and a feeling of connectedness with the world (Carlson, 1997).
(excerpts by Aki Ito)

In her essay, the student draws on diverse modes of discourse, discusses the realities of insider/outsider status, and reflects on her academic history using her current academic skills. The form of the writing mirrors the interstices that she knows so well in her life. Rather than dividing or fragmenting her relationship to the knowledge she has acquired both in her research and in her composition process, the essay stitches together types of knowledge: self-knowledge, scholarly knowledge, knowledge of Japan, knowledge of the United States, and knowledge of language as ever evolving and productive.

Not only do assignments that encourage hybrid student texts help students to connect information, critical perspectives, and personal meaning, but they help us avoid privileging any one type of writer. Standard academic papers assume standard English; most affected are first-generation college students and students with learning differences, but we are all morally affected by maintaining dominant forms. hooks (1994) asserts, "It is difficult not to hear in standard English always the sound of slaughter" (p. 169). She acknowledges the need for students to master standard English but also outlines the need for language to serve as a "site of resistance" and a "space for alternate cultural production" (pp. 170–171). When we separate spaces of resistance and production from the academy, we leave resistance and production vulnerable to the values of the marketplace. Why not integrate critical knowledge and cultural production? Why not validate languages of resistance that integrate scholarship and imagination? There is room for all of these languages in the academy, an appropriate site for voices representing diverse histories, perspectives, questions, and goals. Although including new forms and voices may initially destabilize some teachers and students not trained in the practice, the strategy ultimately benefits all. It challenges students from both privileged and less privileged backgrounds by bridging the dichotomy between their study of social systems and their discourse *across* social differences.

Shifting to a new discourse requires steps that validate the process and that invite discussion of criteria for evaluation. Narrative in formal essays needs to be well written, concise, and worthy of an audience. To get past the surface material, students benefit from writing informal "discovery drafts." I assign three separate discovery drafts because the first one or two tend to tell stories on which the writer has already reflected (Bertolini, 2007). By the third narrative, students confront material about which they have more questions than answers. The narratives grow deeper and the voices more distinct.

To engage their critical faculties in narration, I follow the advice of Julia Alvarez and assign the opening chapters of Gornick's *The situation and the story: The art of personal narrative* (2001). Gornick (2001) helps us understand that, if we write from a particular persona, or aspect of ourselves, that is engaged in a particular way with the situation we describe, our story achieves greater intimacy, complexity, and intensity. With my input, students choose one discovery draft on which to critically reflect. They are now ready to tackle a hybrid discourse that they will develop and revise with the critical feedback of our writing community, the class.

Throughout the years, Writing for Social Change has attracted an even mix of White students and students of color. Typically, one or two students are sexually "out," and a few question their sexuality in the privacy of their narratives. I acknowledge my Whiteness and privilege on the first day of class, along with my interstitial position as "writing instructor" who occupies the margins of the arts, humanities, and social sciences. These features strike me as relevant to their trust in me and to their learning experience. I also feel that, because I'm teaching a class that explores the intersection of the personal and theoretical and because so few faculty come out as queer, I ought to come out to my class. Yet, despite—or perhaps because of—a background in literature and the arts, I am no more comfortable in sharing personal information with students than are faculty in other disciplines. I came out in class for the first time by sharing a digital story I made called "Gender Habits," and after showing the three-minute video along with examples of student work, I abruptly turned on the lights and asked whether students had questions about their homework. Two queer students teased, "We liked the video," acknowledging my discomfort. I share this to say that there is no easy way to forge a new dialogue with our students. I now, in the words of my partner, "come out like a grown up" to my class, casually and without the video, at no particular point in the semester. However, going through the process helps me understand student vulnerability in sharing their narratives with me and their classmates, and the vulnerability that other faculty must feel in making space for the personal in the classroom. Because of the constraints of class time and the need to discuss course content, I still share little about myself, and student sharing is likewise brief. The hybrid discourse is acknowledged in discussion but attains its real length and depth in writing, discussed in individual conferences and in writing workshops.

The research essay makes a good second paper in Writing for Social Change, but I saw that students needed more practice early on in navigating unacknowledged differences when talking or writing about social issues across social groups. Tatum (1997) points out that it is easier to acknowledge our membership in subordinate categories than dominant ones. White students reflect honestly about their Whiteness in response papers, but in class discussions pertaining to color they tend to either fall into guilty silence or assume a position of color-blindness, referring, for example, to White populations as "they." Unacknowledged relationships to power structures can create distrust and inhibition on all sides. Not wanting to put students on the spot in discussion, or to "place their identities on trial" (Leistyna, Woodrum, & Sherblom, 1996, p. 198), I needed a place for them to practice applying their understanding of domination and subordination as it pertains to dialogue across social groups. Diplomacy is not required; we read examples of confrontational voices. But students who lack confidence, experience, and skills with intercultural dialogue have a tendency to either overaddress or underaddress what they are likely to represent to others, creating unease for everyone in the dialogue.

The author of *Reading the mountains of home* (Elder, 1998) brought my attention to narrative criticism as a form in which writers can engage in a close reading of a text through the lens of personal experience. Inspired by reader response theory, the form is flexible and works well not only in a literature class but across the disciplines as a place to apply theory to real life. Outside of a literature class students might engage in a close reading of a landscape, a memory, or a service-learning experience. They might use a theoretical lens as one way to understand or interpret their experience. I call these "critical narratives," rather than narrative criticism, to distinguish them from the more literary form. In the early part of the social change class, before students start service work, they might draw on discovery drafts and on response papers for a critical narrative. Because response papers address readings on difference and power, students gravitate toward critical narratives in which they wrestle with themselves, their communities, and their readers as "subjects in history" (hooks, 1994, p. 139). They strive to understand the effects of domination and subordination in particular instances and also to explore the fluidity of identity, the "in-between" places (Bhabha, 1994).

One middle-class White student grappled with a recent emotional experience during a year of study abroad by placing it in a critical context that drew on texts read in class:

> *I've thought a lot about social class and how it plays into my dilemma. Surely the men who robbed me did not do so out of pure malice. Unemployment is rampant throughout Ecuador, so people have to find creative sources of income just to get by. That situation has simply never existed for me. When my father's employer went out of business, he found a new job in a new state and we bought a house and hired trucks to move all of our belongings. I'm sure my parents were concerned about finances, but we never did without basic necessities and I never felt unsafe or hopeless. In contrast to my situation, writer Dorothy Allison (1994) describes her experience growing up as the "bad poor . . . not noble, not grateful, not even hopeful" (p. 18). In her U.S. family, as in many poor Ecuadorian families, generations of experience show that the outlook doesn't change, that conditions of poverty will persist no matter how hard one might try to resist them. Allison addresses people like me, people who were raised with the idea of meritocracy, in her comment on entitlement: "You think you have a right to things, a place in the world, and it is so intrinsically a part of you that you cannot imagine people like me, people who seem to live in our world, who don't have it" (p. 14). When one begins to recognize the disparity between those who feel entitlement and those who lack it, "The horror of class stratification, racism, and prejudice" comes to light (p. 35).*

In her initial draft, this student writer was so concerned with being critical about her experience that she revealed no vulnerability as a victim of a crime at gunpoint. Diverse readers in her workshop group urged her to reveal some of the details pertaining to her difficulty—to balance the critical distance. In revision, she both added layers of the story that she had withheld and researched psychology journals to contextualize those layers. A biochemistry major, she stretched herself across the disciplines in her essay, which grew to 14 pages of scholarly and personal inquiry into class structures, fear and trauma, intercultural relationships, and privilege.

When students from dominant social positions identify their own areas of privilege, in class, gender, sexuality, or ability, they create points of connection with those outside of their group. Students from clearly identified, subordinate social positions are often drawn to examine their own dominant characteristics or to explore intersections. The point is not to reify social categories or create a hierarchy of social oppressions (Adams & Marchesani,

1997, p. 269) but to acknowledge differences rather than assume blindness, to explore the relationships among our scholarly knowledge, what we represent to others, and how we know ourselves. In doing so, we acknowledge a "real life" social and political context for our work, one that is ever-changing, in which knowledge is not fixed but being produced by the very subjects that attain it. This self- reflexive aspect of knowledge is critical to our understanding of social issues as well as our survival as a species. Our human future depends on our ability to understand our relation to one another, the earth, and ourselves—past, present, and future.

Acknowledging a real-life context for our work demands that we inquire into the relationship between a hybrid discourse and praxis. Despite the advantages of a hybrid discourse that brings our whole selves to the classroom, there are limitations. Critical thinking that starts with personal reflection is time-consuming. It must be monitored to avoid having participants lapse into identity politics or depression. Also, in the end, there are issues that cannot be tackled by narrative and theory combined. If we are to confront the issues of the day, and synthesize the various aspects of our being in the process, we must engage in praxis. Macedo (1996) explains, "the sharing of experiences must always be understood within a social praxis that entails both reflection and political action. . . . a dialogue as a process of learning and knowing must always involve a political project" (p. 203).

In the second half of Writing for Social Change, students form collaborations around service-learning projects. Here we bridge divisions, not between aspects of ourselves, but between educational institutions and community organizations; there is also a shift from individual to collaborative work. In connection with nonprofits and armed with theory, research, self-knowledge, and experience, students take practical steps to create change. Whether working on issues pertaining to poverty or environmental conservation, they deepen their sense of commitment to their studies and gain a sense of connection and empowerment. Service-learning projects can range from social action within the college community to partnerships with community nonprofits to global initiatives. Students might reflect on such service in narrative criticisms or research essays, or produce writing that the nonprofits actually need. Because they do not have access to media labs, nonprofits connected to my classes have begun to ask students to create digital videos or construct websites. Students have made websites for refugee artists by working with the Vermont Folklife Center Apprenticeship Project (Kissinger,

Coleman, & Antonson, 2006); created videos on violence against women for a student-run Women for Global Peace organization (Rokey, Garewal, Schaffer, & Seth, 2006); and filmed documentaries that celebrate civic engagement in the local community for community television (Huusko, Janis, & Li, 2006). They have also explored definitions and understandings of sexual "consent" within the college campus, educated local residents on a unique local forest type that needs protection, and educated the public about child soldiers through digital video (Singh & Basij-Rasikh, 2007). They bring to these projects their skills in hybrid discourse, combining statistics and stories, emotion and analysis, word and image. Their tales are gruesome, real, and hopeful, engaging both our minds and our hearts.

Conclusion

Like ourselves, students need confidence, purpose, and permission to articulate their deepest concerns in writing and to synthesize their scholarly, creative, and social selves. Self-imposed silence in those who feel they do not have a specialized voice is very real, and is a waste of human energy. Individuals from all sorts of backgrounds censor some of the deepest parts of themselves: the part that longs to be a scholar, an activist, a community worker, a political diplomat. We can take small steps to nurture a new dialogue by assigning just a few informal response papers that inquire about emotion, a formal paper that invites students to synthesize experience with theory or research or to write for a nonprofit. Assignments like these, including multimedia assignments for a critical audience, will give our students the confidence and tools they need in this 21st century.

The call for a more versatile discourse, one that brings disparate communities into conversation rather than dividing academics from nonacademics, one type of citizen from another, is a discourse of hope (Miller, 2005). It relies on a community in order to flourish. In return, a hybrid discourse will feed community in ways that we can hardly imagine. Dialogue that integrates experience and theory, personal position and public politics, connects our learning to ourselves and to the world and creates a community of learners in which various types of knowing are valued. No one voice is privileged—the scholarly voice, the personal voice, the creative voice, the voice from one social category or another—but all work together. This creates a socially just learning environment in which the strengths of our citizens will forge exciting local and global communication in academic, political, and social spheres. The goals of such a discourse finds roots in the past with Orwell's exhortation to "tell the truth." The foundation for such a discourse is also found in the past, in Du Bois's synthesis of "study" with a "plain, unvarnished tale."

References

Adams, M. (1997). Pedagogical frameworks for social justice education. In M. Adams, L. A. Bell, & P. Griffin (Eds.), *Teaching for diversity and social justice: A sourcebook* (pp. 30–43). New York: Routledge.

Adams, M., & Marchesani, L. S. (1997). Multiple issues course overview. In M. Adams, L. A. Bell, & P. Griffin (Eds.), *Teaching for diversity and social justice: A sourcebook.* (pp. 261–271). New York: Routledge.

Allison, D. (1994). *Talking about sex, class and literature.* New York: Firebrand Books.

Bell, L. A. (1997). Theoretical foundations for social justice education. In M. Adams, L. A. Bell, & P. Griffin (Eds.), *Teaching for diversity and social justice* (pp. 3–15). New York: Routledge.

Bell, L. A. (2009). Learning through story types about race and racism: Preparing teachers for social justice. In K. Skubikowski, C. Wright, & R. Graf (Eds.), *Social justice education: Inviting faculty to transform their institutions.* Sterling, VA: Stylus.

Bertolini, M. E. (2007, Fall). *Responding to dd's.* Retrieved December 16, 2007, from https://segue1.middlebury.edu/index.php?&site=wrpro100a-f07&section=17282 &page=80185&action=site

Bhabha, H. K. (1994). *The location of culture.* New York: Routledge.

Carlson, D. (1997). *Being a global nomad: The pros and cons.* Retrieved July 4, 2009, from http://www.worldweave.com/procon.htm

Chamberlain, M., & Thompson, P. (1998). *Narrative and genre.* New York: Routledge.

Du Bois, W. E. B. (1982). Of the sons of master and man. In *The souls of Black folk* (pp. 189–204). New York: Penguin Books. (Original work published in 1903).

Elder, J. (1998). *Reading the mountains of home.* Cambridge, MA: Harvard University Press.

Freire, P. (1996). *Pedagogy of the oppressed.* New York: Continuum.

Freire, P., & Macedo, D. P. (1996). A dialogue: Culture, language and race. In P. Leistyna, A. Woodrum, & S. Sherblom (Eds.), *Breaking free: The transformative power of critical pedagogy* (pp. 199–228). Cambridge, MA: Harvard Educational Review.

Ganley, B., & Vila, H. (2006). Digital stories in the liberal arts environment: Educational media communities at the margins. In B. Hipfl & T. Hug (Eds.), *Media Communities* (pp. 322–338). New York: Waxmann.

Gornick, V. (2001). *The situation and the story: The art of personal narrative.* New York: Farrar, Straus and Giroux.

Greene, M. (1996). In search of a critical pedagogy. In P. Leistyna, A. Woodrum, & S. Sherblom (Eds.), *Breaking free: The transformative power of critical pedagogy* (p. 29). Cambridge, MA: Harvard Educational Review.

hooks, b. (1994). *Teaching to transgress: Education as the practice of freedom.* New York: Routledge.

Huusko, S., Janis, K., & Li, C. (2006). *Civic engagement: Not mere social capitol, a documentary* [Television broadcast]. Middlebury, VT: Middlebury Community Access Television.

Kenan, R. (1995). Introduction. In W. E. B. Du Bois, *The souls of black folk.* New York: Penguin Books.

Kissinger, J., Coleman, B. A., & Antonson, J. With Studioperdue webdesign. (2006). For *The Vermont Folklife Center Traditional Arts Apprenticeships. http:// www.vermontfolklifecenter.org/education/apprenticeship/dance/*

Leistyna, P., Woodrum, A., & S. Sherblom (Eds.). (1996). *Breaking free: The transformative power of critical pedagogy.* Cambridge, MA: Harvard Educational Review.

Lewis, H. (2006). *Excellence without a soul: How a great university forgot education.* New York: Perseus.

Lopez, B. (1996). Landscape and narrative. In L. Kirszner & S. Mandell (Eds.), *The Blair reader* (pp. 684–690). New Jersey: Prentice Hall.

Macedo, D. P. (1996). Literacy for stupidification: The pedagogy of big lies. In P. Leistyna, A. Woodrum, & S. Sherblom (Eds.), *Breaking free: The transformative power of critical pedagogy* (pp. 183–206). Cambridge, MA: Harvard Educational Review.

McCaig, N. (1994, September). Global nomads. *Foreign Service Journal,* pp. 32–41. Retrieved July 4, 2009, from http://www.kaiku.com/nomads.html

McIntosh, P. (1988). *White privilege and male privilege: A personal account of coming to see correspondences through work in women's studies.* (Working Paper No. 189). Wellesley, MA: Wellesley College.

Miller, R. (2005). *Writing at the end of the world.* Pittsburgh: University of Pittsburgh Press.

Orwell, G. (1995). Shooting an elephant. In W. Smart (Ed.), *Eight modern essayists* (6th ed., pp. 35–41). New York: St. Martin's Press.

Orwell, G. (1995). Why I write. In W. Smart (Ed.), *Eight modern essayists* (6th ed., pp. 62–68). New York: St. Martin's Press.

Rokey, E., Garewal, K., Schaffer, A., & Seth, P. (2006). Not just numbers. *Abroad View Magazine*. Retrieved March 16, 2009, from http://www.abroadview.org/stories/media/video/watch/notjustnumbers.htm

Singh, R., & Basij-Rasikh, S. (2007). *My gun was as tall as me: Voices of child soldiers* [Motion picture]. Retrieved March 17, 2009, from http://www.youtube.com/watch?v=Q3OVMafpZQE

Sobol, J. D. (1999). *The storyteller's journey: An American revival*. Chicago: University of Illinois Press.

Tatum, B. (1997). *Why are all the Black kids sitting together in the cafeteria?* New York: Perseus.

Useem, R. H., & Cottrell, A. B. (1993). TCKs four times more likely to earn bachelor's degrees. *Newslinks, 7*(5). Retrieved July 4, 2009, from http://www.tckworld.com/useem/art2.html

13

DELIBERATIVE DIALOGUE AS A PEDAGOGICAL TOOL FOR SOCIAL JUSTICE

Kamakshi P. Murti

Turkish woman in carsaf: It is my will [to wear a scarf]. Now I'm working for Allah. It is now my idea, my belief. I welcome all religions. Everyone is free to choose . . . Allah is great that way.

Tom Ashbrook: Did you wear your habit in Iraq?
Sister Olga Yaqob: All the time.
Tom Ashbrook: Openly, without *burqa* over it?
Sister Olga Yaqob: Openly.
Tom Ashbrook: Identified you as a Christian? You weren't afraid of that drawing . . .
Sister Olga Yaqob: Not at all, because I wanted the Muslim people, particularly of Iraq, that they would know that I was approaching them, and I wanted, as I said before, I wanted to make it to the Middle East for their feast, Eid al-adha, to show them that I am there as a Christian woman, I love them as a Christian woman. (Ashbrook, 2008)[1]

Why "Deliberative Dialogue"?

In my search for an effective way to integrate issues of social justice into my own classroom, I came across a pedagogical strategy that has possibilities for classes across the humanities. I decided to adopt what the New England Center for Civic Life (NECCL) terms *deliberative dialogue*—a process of careful deliberation that ultimately leads to civic action and that would certainly have found Paulo Freire's approval.[2] The Brazilian educationalist's *Pedagogy of the Oppressed* (2001) for social justice has transformed my understanding of popular literacy education. Freire's concept of *praxis*—informed action—is especially challenging and necessary in the humanities classroom where the symbiosis of language and thought, the fact that language is imbedded in complex systems, is often ignored, distorted, or suppressed by traditional notions of learning. It is my contention that the humanities teacher has an even greater responsibility to make transparent the effects of these systems on teaching and learning, especially when they are oppressive.

Based on Freire's philosophy, I began to ask myself the following question: "What sort of critical thinking skills should be integrated with learning so that the student is able to understand cultural 'othernesses' as an enriching experience, and grow as an individual and citizen of the world community?" Michael Byram's question was also one that I needed to frequently ask: "How, where, when and to what effect are the shared meanings of particular groups produced, circulated and consumed?" (Byram, 2000, p. 163). Byram's words seem to imply that it is as much the students' as the educator's responsibility, with the latter functioning as mediator/facilitator, each to define for him- or herself what cultures are or can be or ought to be. Such an approach would allow students to critically question the monocultural/ethnocentric world in which they are caught and learn to see the world, as Byram advocates, from many different perspectives.

Deliberative dialogue seemed able to provide a space for these multiple perspectives, a space where all students could "come to voice" (bell hooks, 1989). The African American writer and social activist bell hooks has these incisive words on teaching:

> Unlike the stereotypical feminist model that suggests women best come to voice in an atmosphere of safety (one in which we are all going to be kind and nurturing), I encourage students to work at coming to voice in an atmosphere where they may be afraid or see themselves at risk."

The passion and challenge in hooks's words were irresistible. However, my students' realities were not those of Black children growing up in the segregated South, within a White-supremacist culture (a very unsafe space), which was hooks's own experience. I understood why she resisted the notion of "safety" as a prerequisite for agency. Most of the students in my class-room, however, were born into privilege, have grown up in a safe space. How was I to create "an atmosphere where they may be afraid or see themselves at risk"? When I talked about White privilege at workshops organized by the annual National Conference on Race and Ethnicity in American Higher Education, some White participants reacted with a mixture of surprise and disguised hostility. A couple of them—White male and female colleagues from institutions of higher education—"reminded" me that the mere fact of their presence at a predominantly non-White conference proved that they had either cast off this privilege or had never possessed it. Such a sharp reaction gave me pause about my naïve belief that I was preaching to the converted! My White colleagues had internalized their privilege to such an extent that they were not even aware of it. Because privilege comes in different forms (until I came to the United States, I did not acknowledge my own privileged life as a middle-class Brahmin educated in an exclusive English-medium school and college), a first crucial step in the classroom would be to make my students aware of how difference can be used as a tool for othering and marginalizing. Deliberative dialogue provided an excellent medium for this purpose.

One of my reasons for adopting deliberative dialogue as a pedagogical tool in preference over debates lay in the fact that deliberative dialogue goes beyond these adversarial forms of communication that see their *raison d'être* in the dichotomy of winner/loser. Discussions as we know and experience them also emphasize opposition, albeit on a more informal level.[3] Deliberative dialogue involves thinking and reasoning together and working through conflicting possible choices with others in an effort to reach even a few common understandings and decisions about how to address and take action on an issue.

It was not enough, however, to create a challenging space that would enable the students to recognize their privileges. The dialogic nature of delib-eration—structured conversations in small groups—would satisfy a further significant component of my pedagogical goal, namely to lower what is known as the "affective filter" in second-language-acquisition theory—a learning blockage because of a negative emotional ("affective") attitude that students experience typically in second language acquisition but could equally affect women and other disenfranchised groups in the classroom (Krashen, 2003). Most of my students came from privilege, but five of the eight women (eight women and six men had enrolled for the course) encountered sexism compounded by racism on a daily basis. My own experiences as a female student, initially in the environment of the Indian educational system and later as a nontraditional non-White graduate student in a U.S. university—both systems tainted by racial and sexual imperialism—had prompted me to seek out ways to encourage underrepresented women to make their voices heard in the classroom. bell hooks (1989) has this to say of the remarkable women who were her teachers:

> They offered to us a legacy of liberatory pedagogy that demanded active resistance and rebellion against sexism and racism. . . . Most specifically, I understood from the teachers in those segregated schools that the work of any teacher committed to the full self-realization of students was necessarily and fundamentally radical, that ideas were not neutral, that to teach in a way that liberates, that expands consciousness, that awakens, is to challenge domination at its very core. It is this pedagogy that Paulo Freire calls "education as the practice of freedom."

Freire's "education as the practice of freedom" resonated powerfully with me. Deliberative dialogue, I was persuaded, would empower not only women but also all those other learners in less privileged educational environments who suffered under domination in some shape or form. Deliberative dialogue as a pedagogy would consequently be truly inclusive.

Schulz, Lalande, Dykstra-Pruim, Zimmer-Loew, and James (2005) point out that

> all communication has a cultural dimension. All communicative acts have a minimum of three components: (1) information (i.e., some kind of message); (2) some form of interaction (i.e., the process of conveying and/or receiving messages within a particular communicative relationship and context—either face to face or at a distance, synchronous or over time); (3) and some form of code or text (i.e., language, including verbal, non-verbal, paralinguistic and visual elements that convey messages). (pp. 172–181)

The issue of power as a common denominator remains unmentioned in this list, the kind of power that I, for example, had as a teacher over my students. I wanted to ensure that I used this power to enrich students' learning experience and expand their horizons. Moreover, the format of a deliberative dialogue would, fortunately, oblige me to relinquish my role as an omnipotent teacher coercing students to regurgitate what I imparted to them and to adopt the much more unsettling, albeit consequential, role of a mediator/facilitator who acknowledged the importance of seeing multiple paths to knowledge. Deliberative dialogue would facilitate such communication. The participants (i.e., students) and I (as mediator/facilitator) would jointly produce a knowledge base for our course. Schulz et al. (2005) rightly cautioned, "it is unrealistic to expect practicing teachers or their students to create their own knowledge base through time-consuming searches on the Internet where quality control (including a check on veracity of information) is often lacking" (pp. 172–181). However, I was convinced that students *do* learn to question these sources of information in terms of their reliability as part of the process of honing their critical skills. When regularly challenged, they *do* discover the many variables that influence/govern how a particular country/nation presents itself or is presented. The NECCL defines deliberative dialogue as part of its project for strengthening democracy through public deliberation and dialogue:

> These practices enable people to talk about difficult issues not only on the basis of knowledge, facts, and professional expertise, but also from the perspective of their deeper concerns, values and personal experience. (NECCL, 2008)

In order to test the efficacy of deliberative dialogue for teaching social justice, I had to be careful in my choice of an appropriate issue. The following characteristics for a frameable issue that would be suitable for public debate, as laid out by the National Issues Forums (NIF), were very helpful in narrowing my choices (Belcher, Kingston, Knighton, McKenzie, Thomas, Wilder, & Arnone, 2002, p. 17). According to the NIF, the issue should be of broad concern within a community, on which

- choices must be made, but there are no clear or "right" answers;
- a range of people and groups must act in order for the community to effectively move forward;
- new approaches may help the community to move forward;
- citizens have not had the opportunity to consider different courses of action and their long-term consequences; and
- decision making of officeholders and other leaders are to be informed by public judgment, as well as by experts' views.

The Muslim Headscarf and Deliberative Dialogue

The topic of the Muslim headscarf for women had the promise of offering students and me the opportunity to engage in and take ownership of a very controversial issue. The horrendous events of 9/11 had led to an increasing demonization of Islamic culture as a regressive, violent, and misogynistic society, opposed to modernity as defined in and by the West. Consequently, visible symbols gathered under the homogeneous term "veil" were being debated more and more contentiously. My interest in this topic was further intensified by the case of a German Muslim woman of Afghani origin, Fereshta Ludin, who was forbidden to wear her scarf when she entered a public school in 1998 to take up her teaching duties. On September 24, 2003, Germany's highest court ruled that Ludin could not be banned from wearing a head scarf in a public school. In ruling five to three in favor of Ludin, the court basically maintained that there was no law prohibiting her from wearing a scarf, leaving it, however, to the discretion of the states to decide whether to pass such a law.[4]

A comment made by a Turkish teacher, Emine Öztürk, made me pay even closer attention to the issue: "So many things are projected onto the headscarf without anyone ever asking the women who wear them" (Tzortzis, 2003). Western women's rights groups and conservative politicians argue that many Muslim women have no choice but to wear a headscarf because their families demand it. Alice Schwarzer, one of the most forceful voices in recent years within what is perceived to be a unitary German feminism, has dangerously popularized and trivialized this debate. For the July/August 1993 issue of *EMMA*, one of Schwarzer's correspondents, Ursula Ott, wrote an article entitled "Fundamentalismus mitten unter uns" ("Fundamentalism Amongst Us") and begins her article with the following words: "*Türkische Mädchen werden im Namen der 'Familienehre' ermordet. Deutsche Richter haben dafür Verständnis. Deutsche Frauen tragen aus 'Solidarität' den Schleier. Und saudische Gelder finanzieren die Koranschulen.*"[5] (Turkish girls are being murdered in the name of "family honor." German judges appreciate this. German women wear the veil out of "solidarity." And Saudi money finances Quranic schools.)

Adelson (2005) points out:

> Schwarzer responded with outrage to the murders of Turkish women and
> girls in Solingen in an essay targeting patriarchy as the root cause of such

violence. Turkish men are made to bear the burden of German history in an odd twist of rhetoric in 1993. Although it was German men who killed Turkish women in Solingen, Schwarzer uses the occasion to equate Islamic fundamentalism and German fascism. "Both are men's domain." (35) It is hardly a coincidence that this issue of *Emma* features an article decrying German tolerance for Muslim headscarves with the words, "A Turkish Woman: I am a Human Being Like You," or that it includes a vivid photograph of dark-haired men slaughtering sheep whose blood runs red from one page onto another. (p. 129)

Statements such as "A Turkish Woman: I Am a Human Being Like You," lay claim to humanitarian and balanced reporting. However, such a title merely hides a lack of understanding of the issue. Adelson (2005) rightly concludes that Turkish women who discard their headscarf as synonymous with Islamic hegemony are seen as symbols of female emancipation *thanks to German superiority.*

I found Azade Seyhan's (2001) consideration of the Mexican critic and performance artist Guillermo Gómez-Peña to be very useful in this context. Gómez-Peña stresses the need to create cultural spaces for others. He defines intercultural dialog as "a two-way, ongoing communication between peoples and communities that enjoy *equal negotiating powers*" (as cited in Seyhan, 2001, p. 5; emphasis added). This definition of dialogic processes resists the kind of "solipsism that threatens a simplistic idea of 'dialogue,' i.e., intercultural understanding, 'as universal equalizer' " (Seyhan, 2001, p. 5) and against which Seyhan warns.

Given the tensions underlying the debate about the "veil," I wanted to ensure that students across all kinds of divides (i.e., racial, gendered, cultural, and socioeconomic, to name a few) felt *equally* confronted to voice their opinions, making transparent underlying anxieties and fears. My goal was to help my students with deliberative dialogue to discover new perspectives or to honestly explain the ones they had, consider different options, and even formulate civic action to change public policy. Accordingly, I offered a course in the fall semester of 2007 entitled To Veil or Not to Veil: Germany and Islam. The following is a narrative of how I concretely applied deliberative dialogue to this course, how students profited from this specific pedagogical tool, and what the results were for a socially just classroom experience.

Deliberative Dialogue in the Classroom

On the first day of class, I distributed copies of a book published by NIF entitled *Racial and Ethnic Tensions* as an example of how deliberative dialogue is used in talking about social justice (Mitchell, 2000). I assured the students that I would not employ this tool if there was even one dissenting voice. Students read the material in class, talked about it in groups and with me, then *unanimously* voted for the opportunity to try out this new method of learning and exchanging knowledge. We concurred that the goal for the course would be to articulate diverse approaches to talking about Islam and its role in Western and non-Western societies, especially in the aftermath of 9/11. I also made sure that students understood their role in the classroom as equal contributors to the learning process, and mapped out the following pattern for each class meeting:

- Short informational lecture (about ten minutes long), initially by me, then increasingly by students.
- Response to questions raised about assigned texts (as a rule, participants would prepare for class by reading the assigned text and writing at least one question about it. At the beginning of the following class, I would collect these questions and we would jointly respond to them).
- Group work (students formed their own groups) to deliberate further (as the facilitator my role was to listen and take notes).
- Wrap-up with each group sharing its findings with the rest of the class.

Additionally, I ensured that group work adhered from the start to the format that the NECCL recommends for conducting deliberative dialogue:

- Participants conduct dialogues in their respective groups.
- Participants come together and share their group's findings with the others. (What measures does this group recommend? What are the political, social consequences of these measures?)
- Participants make concrete recommendations about possible action, discuss trade-offs and drawbacks.

My experience in the German language classroom had taught me that group work was vital in coaxing all voices to become audible. Gradually, groups solidified and took on distinct identities depending on their shared values and concerns. However, contrary to my fears, they simultaneously and steadily gained a readiness to thoughtfully listen to others' opinions and to engage in a productive dialogue with them. I attribute this willingness to two things:

1. A visual demonstration of this atmosphere of teamwork—I never occupied a frontal position in the classroom, nor did I claim the "head" of the oval table at which we all sat.
2. My acknowledgment that I did not have all the answers and that they shared the responsibility of complementing the knowledge that I offered. (Those who had understood this as a "confession" of inadequacy, of intellectual deficit, began to appreciate it as a gesture of respect for the knowledge that they brought to bear on the course.)

Short versions of deliberative dialogue have become an integral part of Middlebury College's orientation for first-year students since the academic year 2004–2005, when the Office of Institutional Diversity first sponsored such dialogues. This is sufficient to sow the first seed of curiosity in students about new ways of approaching divisive subjects. However, in my classroom I wanted to take students through the entire process of framing an issue for public deliberation: from the collection of factual information about an issue, through interviews and conversations with people from the college and the community about individual concerns, to the final step of creating various approaches to the issue, ensuring that "each approach is pulling in a quite different direction than the others" so that one captures "the different, even conflicting ways of dealing with a problem" (Belcher et al., 2002, p. 43). I planned to use the whole semester for the process.

Given the atypical format of the course and my insistence on delegating authority to them, students were curious and anxious about how I would grade their work. The ultimate authority of the teacher lies in her or his control over grades and, by extension, over the future of students— something that students and I could not ignore despite my protestations of egalitarianism. bell hooks talks about a student who said she was influenced by the courses she had taken with hooks:

I am reminded of the power we have as teachers as well as the awesome responsibility. Commitment to engaged pedagogy carries with it the willingness to be responsible, not to pretend that professors do not have the power to change the direction of our students' lives. (bell hooks, 2000)

I told them that I would evaluate precisely those aspects of collaborative learning that I was trying to promote, that is, their ability to

1. talk about difficult issues from the perspective of their deeper concerns, values, and personal experience (this ultimately took the shape of a short presentation);
2. listen thoughtfully and respectfully to other opinions and ask questions;
3. write short response papers about the texts discussed in class (these were not research papers grounded in outside theories but rather their personal reactions to the texts);
4. interview people from the community (townspeople, students, staff, and faculty at Middlebury College) and submit written analyses; and
5. formulate with members of their group an approach for the final deliberative dialogue.

It seemed almost impossible to achieve some degree of integrity and reliability in the modes of evaluation mentioned in points 1 and 2. However, my role as mediator gave me enough time to carefully listen to each and every student within groups and to take extensive notes. As far as written assignments were concerned, although I attended to grammar and spelling, style and organization, I primarily graded them on the students' ability to write coherently, cohesively, and—most important—with passion and conviction. All comments and questions that I wrote on these papers were dialogic, that is, they encouraged students not only to improve their ability to express their innermost convictions but to critique my remarks in turn, and thus transform the papers into miniature deliberative dialogues. The majority of participants rewrote their papers multiple times in this spirit.

We had roughly 12 weeks for the course. As I already mentioned, there were 14 students–8 female and 6 male—enrolled in the course. They were a very diverse group in terms of race and nationality. They were also different in academic terms, from freshmen to seniors. We met twice a week, each time for one and a half hours. During the first three weeks I provided the 14 participants in the class with information about the headscarf, the three Abrahamic religions, issues of immigration, and women's clothing as an instrument for containing the female body. I had identified five texts as "prescribed" reading for the course (an enriching way of using the power that we as teachers have, to paraphrase bell hooks!) to provide students with some background information.[6] In fact, I regularly sought spontaneous oral and short written evaluations of this material throughout the semester. Students in their turn enriched this data base not only with their own knowledge about the headscarf and Islam but also with articles and texts that they had read on their own or in other courses. By the end of the course, our syllabus had radically changed to include their opinions and texts.

During the following weeks, the actual work of processing all this information and bringing the issue of the headscarf into focus began. Weeks four and five were devoted to analyzing the transcripts of interviews I had conducted in Turkey (in 2006) and Germany (in 2007) with covered and uncovered Muslim women, and to viewing and critiquing *Young and Muslim in Germany*,[7] a film with recorded interviews with young Turkish Germans about the Muslim headscarf and Islam in a Judeo-Christian environment. During the next couple of weeks, participants went out into the community and interviewed members of the extended Middlebury community, as well as students, staff, and faculty of the college. I urged them to ensure as much diversity as possible in their sample.

Transcripts of these conversations were particularly illuminating because they clearly showed to what extent my students had changed in the previous weeks. Students and I had jointly come up with a list of possible questions for the interviews (see Appendix 13.A). In order to get opinions about clothing as a symbol of oppression or liberation, we thought it best to begin the interview with a general question: "What do you think about the topic of dress codes?" or "How do you think you define yourself in terms of what you wear?" Depending on the response, other questions closer to the issue of the headscarf could be posed. The following are a few remarks participants made about the interviews they conducted:

[Interview with U.S. female student:] *As X. said in her interview, "Islam evolved in the Middle East, that's where it came from, it's only natural that they would have different values than us. I mean with world globalization people think it's just the westernization of the world but I don't necessarily think that should be the case." I think our job as a nation, as a state, as a town, as a school, is to stop reading too far into Islam's different values, and understand that other cultures have unique social norms, like the veil, that do not imply anything more than the basic—in this case a religion.*

[Interview with U.S. male community member:] *He also expressed remorse at the prospect of an increasingly homogenized world culture, saying: "You can go to places in China, and it's just like Times Square in Manhattan." The advent of globalization brings with it the prospect of either a more equitable distribution of wealth and justice, or simply a continuation of centuries old disparity between the "modern" and "developing" world. I very much agree with X in that the most effective means of alleviating fundamentalist thought is to provide everyone in society with the assurance that their voice matters. . . . However, I do not feel that extending urgency to all people requires a strict assimilation of cultures into something homogenous.*

I observed a perceptible change when I compared the participants' opinions during the first weeks of class with those that they articulated in the analyses of their interviews. They were able to lay to rest many of the tensions and fears that the topic had initially evoked in them, and their willingness to *talk* about them was palpable. It was fascinating to see how they in turn heard and recognized similar fears and anxieties in the people they interviewed.

Participants used the final weeks of the semester to put together "clusters" of concerns, that is, to synthesize the various conversations and analyses in which they had previously engaged and condense them to half a dozen potential approaches to the issue of the headscarf (Belcher et al., 2002, p. 31). During the final week of the semester, they searched for further unifying aspects in their approaches and enunciated three that optimally framed the issue.[8] As a result, the 3/3/4/4 grouping that had characterized the class through much of the semester cohered to three distinct groups of 4/5/5. This cohesion did not imply compromise or consensus, as NIF emphasizes:

Deliberative dialogue is that form of talking that helps us to address differences of conviction. If we differ in conviction, we can't have consensus and we are very unlikely to compromise. What we do is find over-lapping self-interests that enable us to take action together. That behavior is common ground for action. (Franklin Pierce University, 2006)

The experience of being confronted by opinions different from or even dia-metrically opposed to their own within what they perceived to be an other-wise stable and shared framework (i.e., Middlebury College) resulted in greater sensitivity to "otherness." Deliberative dialogue facilitated the bridg-ing of gaps that would otherwise have remained or widened.

Each of the three approaches for the final deliberative dialogue had "contact zones"[9] that enabled interconnectedness—the "common ground" mentioned in the previous quotation. For the final deliberative dialogue, par-ticipants put together the following approaches. Accompanying each approach was an array of options that reflected carefully crafted collaborative efforts within the group:

> Approach One: *Discuss underlying oppressive structures in other patriarchal religions in order to stop the systematic, undifferentiated vilification of Islam.* All patriarchal cultures systematically value men more than women at all levels of society. Women are primarily seen as vehicles for procreation or as sex objects. Women's sexuality is acknowledged in all these cultures, but aggressively suppressed/contained in various ways. Media representations of men as strong and powerful and women as passive or sexually threatening/alluring perpetuate these attitudes. These stereotypes undervalue women, tolerate rape and domestic violence, and psychologically damage everyone, especially women who often struggle throughout their lives to find their own voice and to be recognized for their contributions.
>
> Approach Two: *Try to understand the differences between Islam and Judeo-Christian societies, even if we consider certain cultural practices to be oppressive to women.* Islamic legal doctrines are based on female–male differences. We cannot interfere with the strict segregation and pro-scribed forbidden spaces for women that Islamic religion requires, even if we consider such segregation to be discriminatory toward women. We have to ask what Western liberal values we may be unre-flectively validating in wanting "freedom" and "agency" for Muslim women. As long as we are writing for the West about "the other," we are implicated in projects that establish Western authority and cul-tural difference. We have to look more closely at terms like *modernity, secularism,* and *civilization* and their political significance in different cultures. Interference by organizations like the United Nations would

be justified only in cases of extreme violations of human rights that lead to torture and death.

Approach Three: *Modernity is a universal concept and is the only guarantee of enlightened progress. Consequently, we cannot condone the oppression of women in Islamic societies.* One must make sure that violence and oppression are not condoned under the mantle of cultural relativism. Islam condemns heterosexual relations as dangerous to the stability of the *umma*, that is, the Islamic community. Although more and more Muslim women are in the workplace, their work is seen as not as desirable or worth as much in the marketplace as work typically done by men. We have to guarantee that these women can be in public spaces without fear of harassment and discrimination. Our own secular societies have made major strides in providing equal opportunities for everyone. It is our duty as citizens of the most powerful nation in the world to warn recalcitrant societies that further disenfranchisement of women will not be tolerated.

Students had transformed what had begun as an acrimonious debate with a multitude of warring opinions and prejudices into common ground,

> that place (or those places) where participants can see how their goals are shareable, their values overlap and their interests intersect with those of others. It is the basis for win/win solutions to problems, where all parties in the dialogue have had their concerns and interests heard and accommodated to some degree in the decisions made. (Franklin Pierce University, 2006)

This process of accommodation continued during the final dialogue in the last week of the semester. Once each group had shared its opinions and recommendations with the rest of us, participants become more introspective. Group 3 (corresponding to approach three) began to revisit its insistence on an unconditional condemnation of the oppression of women in Islamic societies when it heard group 1 (approach one) advocating an investigation of non-Islamic societies for similar oppressive practices. Group 2 (approach two) consisted of students who had maintained all semester long what they perceived as a politically correct attitude. Keenly aware of Western ethnocentrism, these participants advised against interfering in the cultural practices of other societies, even if they considered these to be morally reprehensible and oppressive to women. They now realized that the line separating cultural relativism from human rights violations was sometimes indefensibly thin, and that oppression by any other name would smell as foul!

Two groups diagrammatically presented their recommendations for civic action. Group 1 drew a triangle and wrote "New Thought" at the apex, and "Patriarchal societies" and "Religious beliefs" at the two base points. In the middle of the triangle were the words "Our goal: less oppression."

Group 3 drew a triangle with the following recommendations at each point: "Political, economic incentives to initiate tax breaks for educational courses," "More education for women through mosques by men and women," and "Tax breaks for men and women (but mostly men) who attend dialogues led by Muslims; U.N. and similar organizations to offer educational opportunities through local embassies, etc., on women's rights." They drew arrows between the points to show their interconnectedness, and wrote "the triangle approach" in the center. Members of group 2 had requested to go last. They had rethought their position of cultural relativism and proposed looking once again at the following questions, which we had been debating over the semester:

- To what extent can or should one respect the cultural practices of others?
- What can one do to resist the gendering of public and private spaces?
- What is the source/intellectual history of terms like "freedom," "agency," "democracy," and "secularism"?

Some Concluding Remarks

By taking ownership of the issue, participants were willing and able to question and transcend the binary categories of traditional/modern, Islam/West, reactionary/ progressive, and ignorant/educated that continue to inform our discourse in the West. They listened to each other and went beyond debating and other adversarial ways of communicating, thus developing a public voice. Most important, deliberative dialogue became an integral part of the participants' approach to issues, allowing each exchange of ideas to be invigorating, productive, and potentially transformative. I believe that deliberative dialogue offered both students and educators a means to begin destabilizing the "collective programming of the mind," to use Hofstede's wonderfully creative phrase (1984, p. 51).[10]

Notes

1. Interview of Sister Olga Yaqob, a diocese hermit in the Roman Catholic Church and a campus minister at the Boston University Catholic Center, about her visit to Iraq.

2. Among the many organizations with social justice as their goal is the Paolo Freire Institute, established in 1992 as an international nonprofit institution. It has members from 24 countries, including the United States, and is dedicated to Freire's work (see http://www.thataway.org/exchange/categories.php?cid = 122&page_num ber = 5).

3. Merriam-Webster Online defines *discussion* as a "consideration of a question in open and usually informal debate" (Mish, 2008).

4. As of January 15, 2007, eight German states including Berlin have introduced legislation banning headscarves for teachers, seeing it as clashing with gender equality and as an affront to Christian values. Only Berlin has decided to ban all religious symbols in schools in its attempt to treat all religions on an equal basis.

5. http://www.emma.de/fundamentalismus_unter_uns_4_93.html

6. Nilüfer Göle, *The Forbidden Modern* (Ann Arbor, MI: University of Michigan Press, 1997); Fatima Mernissi, *Beyond the Veil* (Bloomington: Indiana University Press, 1987); Horrocks & Kolinsky, *Turkish Culture in German Society Today* (Providence, RI: Berghahn Books, 1996); Deniz Göktürk, David Gramling, & Anton Kaes (Eds.), *Germany in Transit: Nation and Migration, 1955–2005* (Berkeley: University of California Press, 2007); and Ibrahim Kalin "Western Perceptions of Islam" (*Islam-Online.net*, April 14, 2003. Retrieved April 14, 2003, from http://www.islamon line.net/english/Contemporary/2003/04/Article01a.shtml).

7. This was a documentary series produced by the Medienprojekt Wuppertal and supported by the Ministry for Family, Seniors, Women, and Youth, Federal Republic of Germany. It received the Erasmus-EuroMedia-Siegel award in Vienna on June 22, 2006.

8. Belcher et al. (2002) list some of the characteristics of a well-framed issue:

- The approaches are distinctly different, not just opposites of each other (because that would be the positive and negative image of the same approach).
- The approaches are persuasive enough so that they pull against each other: each has some appeal for different interests.
- Each approach is presented "best-foot-forward," and aspects of it might appeal to anyone.
- Each approach captures something truly valuable to people.

9. Mary Louise Pratt calls areas that reveal the intersection of two or more cultures "contact zones" in her book *Imperial Eyes: Studies in Travel Writing and Transculturation* (London: Routledge, 1992).

10. "Culture is the *collective programming of the mind* which distinguishes the members of one category of people from another" (Hofstede, 1984, p. 51; emphasis added).

I am in the process of putting together transcripts of all the interviews that the students conducted along with their analyses in the form of an "issue book." This will also become part of a more detailed account of my research and interviews in Turkey and Germany on the headscarf, tentatively entitled *To Veil or Not to Veil: Turkey, Germany, and the Shifting Boundaries of Alterity.*

References

Adelson, L. (2005). *The Turkish turn in contemporary German literature.* New York: Palgrave Macmillan.

Ashbrook, T. (Interviewer). (2008, February 11). An Iraqi nun's tale [Radio series episode]. In Wen Stephenson (Producer), *On Point.* Boston: WBUR. Retrieved September 3, 2009, from http://www.onpointradio.org/shows/2008/02/20080211 _b_main.asp

Belcher, E., Kingston, R. J., Knighton, B., McKenzie, R., Thomas, M., Wilder, J. C., & Arnone E. (Eds.). (2002). *Framing issues for public deliberation: A curriculum guide for workshops.* Retrieved September 3, 2009, from http://www.kettering.org/media_room/publications/Framing_Issues_for_Public_Deliberation

Byram, M. (Ed.). (2000). *Routledge encyclopedia of language teaching and learning.* London: Routledge.

Franklin Pierce University. (2006). *FAQs on deliberative democracy.* Retrieved September 3, 2009, from http://franklinpierce.edu/institutes/neccl/nec_deliberative.htm#whatsddial

Freire, P. (2000). *Pedagogy of the oppressed* (M. Bergman Ramos, Trans.). New York: Continuum.

Hofstede, G. (1984). National cultures and corporate cultures. In L. A. Samovar & R. E. Porter (Eds.), *Communication between cultures.* Retrieved January 12, 2007, from http://www.ac.wwu.edu/~culture/hofstede.htm

hooks, b. (1989). *Talking back: Thinking feminist, thinking black.* Retrieved on May 26, 2008, from http://www.chss.montclair.edu/english/classes/stuehler/engl105/ hooks.html#3rd

hooks, b. (2000). Racism and feminism. In L. Back & J. Solomos (Eds.), *Theories of race and racism—A reader* (pp. 373–388). London: Routledge.

Krashen, S. (2003). *Explorations in language acquisition and use*. Portsmouth: Heinemann.

Mish, F. (Ed.). (2008). *Merriam-Webster online*. Retrieved May 11, 2008, from http://www.merriam-webster.com/dictionary/discussion

Mitchell, G. (2000). *Racial and ethnic tensions. What should we do?* Dubuque, IA: Kendall Hunt.

New England Center for Civic Life (NECCL). (2008). *Academic policies CGPS*. Retrieved October 28, 2008, from http://franklinpierce.edu/academics/academic _policies_cgps.htm

Schulz, R., Lalande, J. L., II, Dykstra-Pruim, P., Zimmer-Loew, H., & James, C. (2005). In pursuit of cultural competence in the German language classroom: Recommendations of the AATG task force on the teaching of culture. *Die Unterrichtspraxis—Teaching German, 38*(2), 172–181.

Seyhan, A. (2001). *Writing outside the nation*. Princeton, NJ: Princeton University Press.

Tzortzis, A. (2003, October 10). Germany divided over hijab. *Christian Science Monitor* [Electronic version]. Retrieved December 4, 2004, from http://www.csmoni tor.com/2003/1010/p06s01-woeu.html

APPENDIX 13.A

Question Bank for Student Interviews

1. What role does your family heritage/culture play in your daily life? How do you respond when someone asks you about your culture, religion, and heritage? Of the three, with which one do you identify most?
2. How do you define secularism? Do you consider the United States to be a secular society?
3. What is your opinion about people who use clothing as a visual symbol of their beliefs (e.g., religious, political, etc.)? How effective is this way of communicating one's views? When does clothing become liberating or oppressive?
4. What do you think is really at stake when a woman decides to wear a headscarf or not to wear one?
5. Do you think that children should be treated differently in school because of their religious beliefs? Why or why not?
6. When you hear the word "Islam," how do you react?
7. To whom do we refer when speaking about Muslims in Europe? Is it a homogenous community? What are their social, socioeconomic, ethnic, and religious backgrounds?
8. Why do Muslims of second- and third-generation immigrants, most of them European citizens, often choose to identify themselves first as "Muslim" instead of "European"?
9. What efforts should be made (both by Muslims and by the host society) to address socioeconomic problems, discrimination, and racism against Muslim communities?
10. How should Europe respond to continuing, often Muslim, immigration?
11. How can Islam be reconciled with a secular society?
12. Are most Muslims willing to accept Europe's secular traditions, lifestyle, culture, and ideas?

AFTERWORD

I n the introduction to this book, Julia Alvarez serves as witness to our elite, White roots in the world of higher education, to the bias in our content and methods that did not include her "style and story." Her purpose is not to lay blame but to encourage us to imagine change, to dream. What could a new institution of higher education look like? Rather than divide our students into parts, how can we integrate their "body, mind, and soul"?

The previous chapters outline efforts in various disciplines, college offices, and schools to create more inclusive classrooms and institutions. Their focus on change points to the moment in time in which we find ourselves: In 2008 the word *change* defined a political movement in the United States characterized by the involvement of young people. Such a moment requires us to include the young in our conversations about education; they can tell us, now, what it took so many years for Alvarez to publically express.

For this reason we close with an essay by a first-year student, Zaheena Rasheed, who came to Middlebury College from the Maldives via the United World Colleges. Like Alvarez, she is a scholarship student from another country. Unlike Alvarez, she is not an immigrant to the United States but an international student. Rather than looking back, as Alvarez does, on experiences in educational institutions after 30 or so years of engagement, Rasheed reflects on a single year of college. For both, the process was halting, marked by their desire to avoid the task. Yet both were driven to put words to their experience.

Before Rasheed's essay, a few things about her: She returned home to the city of Malé after her first year of college to run an art education program for teenagers that raises public awareness of the environmental threats facing the island. A meter above sea level, the Maldives risk losing not only their coral reefs but, because of climate change and rising seas, the islands themselves. Rasheed applied for and earned a grant for her summer program for youth using arts-based environmental education and then stayed on in Malé in the fall to write for the only English-language news source, which covered the first election of a democratic president in the Maldives. On winning a first-year writing award for the essay that follows, she wrote in an e-mail explaining her leave of absence from the fall semester: "As a journalist, I am writing about political developments, social issues such as child abuse, the drugs trade, and economic problems. I've come to truly understand what it means when people say writing has the power to change hearts and minds." She goes on to remind us that this change remains a matter of life and death: "In November 2006, I was fired from my first job in the government because I called for the president's resignation. In April 2007, I was arrested for distributing balloons calling for reform. Many have been tortured in jail and beaten to death" (personal communication, September 17, 2008).

Given Rasheed's experience, one might ask: How do we recapture the relationship between the liberal arts and political reality? It is evident in the closing words of her e-mail that Rasheed is expecting a connection: "It is exciting to be in Maldives right now. But I am looking forward to returning to Middlebury College to complete my education. I believe an education is absolutely necessary for me to understand real world problems and to handle them with confidence" (personal communication, September 17, 2008).

Institutions, Alvarez reminds us, have to keep reinventing themselves. We propose that they do so in dialogue with the young.

AFTERWORD: OBLIQUE I AM

Zaheena Rasheed

When I moved into my dorm room as a first-year student at Middlebury College, I remember agreeing with my roommate on how small the room was. I shared in the idea that we both had a bigger, better furnished, and brighter life at home. Like my peers, I now participate in complaining about the cafeteria food, and I spend money on expensive clothes, eating out, and going out to music concerts and parties. The truth I hide from in shame is that my whole family of ten lives in a room the size of my dorm room. The truth is that, for me, home-cooked food is plain rice and fish soup—day after day. As a United World College Scholar, all my tuition fees and expenses are paid for—because my parents are so poor they cannot afford to pay for my flight ticket to get here. It surprises me, the ease with which I have gotten used to living this privileged life.

Reading Dorothy Allison, a lesbian feminist author born poor, for the first time the comfortable walls I built around myself have started to crumble. I realize I am here today because I spent my whole life running away from my home, my family, and my impoverished background. Like Allison (1994), I have grown up trying to deny the fact that I was born into poverty—"a condition . . . that society finds shameful, contemptible and somehow deserved" (p. 15). Looking in the mirror, I realize I have copied the dress, mannerisms, and attitudes, and, in some ways, ambitions of the girls I've met here. I try so hard to be part of this privileged community, so as to feel "real and valuable" (p. 22). What I did not recognize in my actions is that, like Allison, I am hiding, blending in for safety. The identity I have constructed has been at the expense of the fundamental me.

My family is from the rural south of Maldives. The south has been neglected by development efforts for decades as collective punishment due to a separatist movement in the 1970s. My family moved to the capital—

Malé—in the mid-nineties in the hopes of a better life with access to educa-tion, basic utilities, and health facilities. Moving to Malé was the end of my childhood; I was only five. I could not run in the streets or go crab hunting on the beach anymore. Confined to the suffocating walls of our very small house, I found escape in books and sleep. We shared a house with my uncle's family of seven. The house consisted of a small living space that functioned as a dining room and a bedroom at night, a kitchen, a single bathroom for seventeen people, and two bedrooms. The physical lack of space was to cause countless issues in the years to come.

The hardest thing about living in Malé was the realization that my fam-ily and I were different from other people. My first day in kindergarten, I cried all day because I could not communicate with my classmates, as they did not speak the same dialect that I did. I was different—the difference in dialect, the coconut oil in my hair, the mosquito bites that marked my legs and even the smell of my clothes made me stand out. I can still remember the smell of the coconut oil: rich, rancid, and a mark of the rural poor. My clothes used to smell like food because we hung our laundry to dry in the kitchen. I remember the perpetual itch and broken skin from the mosquitoes that breed profusely in the open well in the bathroom. I remember the lone-liness and shame in being the child left out. The early contempt and society's careless dismissal of me and my people led me to believe we were contempt-ible by nature—because we were poor and because we were from the South. I hide to this day because what could not be changed had to go unspoken. When I became old enough to plait my own hair, I did not let my mother and the coconut oil near it. I hid my legs and started tutoring in order to earn money to buy perfume.

Life in Malé is a continuous struggle to survive. With more than 130,000 people in less than two square kilometers of land, it is the world's most densely populated city. Land has become the most valuable commodity, with rents equaling prices in New York City. The landed elite charge exorbitant prices; the poor have no choice but to pay because there is nothing for us in the rural islands we come from. Most families spend more than 60 percent of their income on rent. I grew up never having enough. That feeling mani-fests itself in me in small ways even today; in my desire to load up my plate in the cafeteria and the desire to spend my paycheck the moment I receive it.

Poverty scars our souls. The outside markers of poverty can be remedied, but the emotional scars never really heal. "Suffering does not ennoble. It destroys" (Allison, 1994, p. 17). Combined with the contempt of society, it keeps us trapped in vicious cycles. We are the drug addicts, the pregnant teenagers, the sexually abused, the religious fanatics, the thieves, and the violent. We are also the silent and the oppressed. Growing up, I have seen poverty destroy so many of the people I love. It has nearly destroyed me. For me, reading Allison is the beginning of a long journey of self-confrontation that leaves me feeling raw, naked, and vulnerable. All these years, I too have believed "that all those things I did not talk about, or even let myself think too much about, were not important, that none of them defined me" (p. 16).

When I go back home, I sleep on the floor next to my sisters and parents. My brothers sleep on the bunk bed in our small room. We are like sardines packed into a can. A thin cotton curtain separates my parents from us and I used to wake up in the night to strange noises even though they tried to be quiet. I cannot imagine their indignity. Privacy is a luxury that only the rich can afford. The only time I was close to having a private moment was in the bathroom. But even in the shower, for the first sixteen years of my life I did not take off my underwear nor did I see myself naked in a mirror. I had neither the space nor the freedom in my mind to discover the woman I was becoming.

At 12, I was molested by one of my elder brothers. For a couple of nights, I gritted my teeth and let him grope my body. His hands were incredibly cold and alien on my skin, his breathing nervous and unsteady. When I could not stand it any longer, I wrote on his school book, "I know what you are doing. Please Stop." He did not touch me again and I repressed the memory. It came back years later, when I walked in on him molesting my cousin in her sleep. When I confronted him, he started to cry. He told me he was sick. Sometimes, he said, his body was overtaken by an uncontrollable urge and he didn't know how to deal with it—touching a woman made him feel better. I was shocked—at 23, I discovered, my brother had not masturbated once.

When I told my mother about my experience, her reply was a knife to my heart. "I know," she said, "You were sleeping next to me." I still do not know how to feel. How could she have let him molest me night after night and not done anything to stop him? How could she have kept silent? I was her daughter and a woman. Surely, she knows the violation and shame in an unwelcome touch? And him—how could he molest his own sisters instead of masturbating? How could he even compare the two avenues?

At the same time, I am full of empathy. My brother and my mother both are victims of the social forces that govern our lives. Tradition and religion are the refuge of the poor. When every day is a struggle to survive, when food, shelter, and money are never constant, we often turn to rigid rules. We blindly cocoon ourselves in their teachings because we do not have the freedom to question. Religion taught my brother that masturbation was a sin. Tradition taught my mother not to speak out for fear of shame and scandal. We live by what others think of us; hiding our secrets and putting on a face for visitors.

In the Maldives one in three women ages 15–49 report experiencing some form of physical or sexual violence at least once in their lives. One in six women in Malé and one in eight in the whole of Maldives report having experienced childhood sexual abuse under the age of 15. Yet the silence continues. In speaking out, victims get further victimized. Society views victims as "dirty" and "unpure," leading to further discrimination. The law based on the Islamic Shariah does not provide much protection. Sex offenders are not imprisoned but instead are banished to a different community with light sentences. Poverty silences our voices because we often do not have the resources or strength to fight for compensation or to find a solution.

After I told my mother about my cousin, she did take action—she told him to get married as soon as possible. I did not agree with her advice, but what could I have done? Marriage in my community is often a means to legitimize sexual relationships. Most people marry young while they are still economically and socially dependent—which is why the Maldives has the highest divorce rates in the world. There are 10.97 divorces for every 1,000 people. I tried to talk to my brother about seeing a counselor and I encouraged him to read some sex education materials. That was one of the hardest conversations of my life. I still remember how I had ended it when we could not deal with the awkwardness and tension in the air. I feel guilty for shrugging off the responsibility even when I struggle with the question of whether it is my responsibility to educate him.

The poverty I know is "dreary, deadening, and shameful" (Allison, 1994, p. 17). I straddle two very different worlds; a world of vicious poverty at home and a world of opportunity and wealth as a Middlebury College student. I am of both worlds, but I belong to neither. I wish I could share my life, and talk about the injustices. But who do I turn to? Among the people I know here, there is no one who can understand the hopelessness and fear I feel. We do not share a "common language to speak the bitter truths" (p. 32). I am scared of sharing the burden of my background with my wealthy peers. I am afraid that when I do, I might stop existing as a person to them. In the past when I have let them close enough to see, my intellectual self diminishes under the added layers of my poverty-stricken roots. Most respond with sympathy and pity. They end up feeling an obligation to pay for me in restaurants and at the movies, and every time I accept their pity, it chips off a little piece from my sense of self-worth. This is why I hide. I hide to survive, to preserve my self-confidence, to be considered an equal.

When I left home, I constructed a new identity by ruthlessly suppressing my background. Right now, I realize that to become whole I have to embrace and claim my roots. I have to be able to speak of home without hating the inevitable sympathy, and I have to be able to speak *at* home of my liberal worldviews without surrendering to cultural and social constraints. In its own right, being from these two worlds is a privilege. The two fabrics of my worlds are not spectacular in their own setting. It is only when the two are exported out of their setting that they become special. Being from a poverty-stricken, third-world existence gives me perspective in a first-world theory class. At the same time, having a first-class education adds authority to my voice in my community. I am only different and privileged because I can mix and match the two patterns to form my own unique pattern. I am lucky. I am one of the few who left a tin-box existence. Going away gives me the perspective I need to evaluate my own people and my own community; having the experience of both worlds enables me to come up with unique solutions.

Reference

Allison, D. (1994). A question of class. In *Skin: Talking about sex, class and literature* (pp. 13–36). Ithaca, NY: Firebrand Books.

CONTRIBUTORS

Neal Abraham came to DePauw University in 1998 after a long career as a research physicist, teacher, and faculty leader at Bryn Mawr College. He currently serves as executive vice president, while filling the roles of vice president for academic affairs, dean of the faculty, and professor of physics and astronomy. Dean Abraham continues his career-long interests in the study of chaos and nonlinear dynamics in lasers and other optical systems and in improvements in math and science education. His commitments at DePauw have included the enhancement of faculty opportunities and the recognition of faculty achievements in teaching and scholarly research, innovations in the uses of educational technology across the undergraduate curriculum, major building projects to upgrade DePauw's facilities for the study of science and the fine arts, recruitment and retention of a diverse faculty, gender equity, and mentoring of junior faculty. A past president of the Council on Undergraduate Research (CUR), Dean Abraham is also a long-time member of Project Kaleidoscope, a movement for the reform of math and science teaching in higher education. He has worked on professional society and National Research Council panels on undergraduate education, and has recently been named a director of the American Council of Academic Deans (ACAD). He has served on the Committee on the Status of Women in Physics of the American Physical Society. Work he and his colleagues did to increase the number of women physics majors at Bryn Mawr was recognized in 1998 by the Presidential Award for Mentoring.

Maurianne Adams is professor of education at the University of Massachusetts at Amherst where she teaches graduate classes on foundations of social justice education and on social identity development in the social justice education concentration. She co-edited *Teaching for Diversity and Social Justice* (Routledge, new edition 2007) and co-authored the chapters on pedagogy, religious oppression, and anti-Semitism. She also co-edited *Strangers and Neighbors: Relations Between Blacks and Jews in the United States* (University of Massachusetts Press, 2000), and *Readings for Diversity and Social Justice* (Routledge, 2000, 2nd edition 2010). Dr. Adams is editor of the journal

Equity & Excellence in Education and consults widely on social justice pedagogy, faculty development, and social justice and diversity issues on college
campuses. Her research includes social justice learning goals and outcomes,
and religious privilege/hegemony as an issue for social justice educators.

Meryl Altman has taught English and women's studies at DePauw University since 1990. She developed and directed the women's studies program for
much of that time, and is currently serving a term as faculty development
coordinator. Before coming to Greencastle, Dr. Altman taught at the College of William and Mary. She studied at Swarthmore and Columbia, where
she earned her Ph.D in English literature with a dissertation on modernist
American poetry. She has published articles about Djuna Barnes, H.D.,
Faulkner, William Carlos Williams, Sappho, metaphor, feminist theory,
gender equity, and queer theory, and writes periodically for the *Women's
Review of Books*. Her most recent publications focus on Simone de Beauvoir.

Julia Alvarez. Born in New York City in 1950, Julia Alvarez's parents
returned to their native country, Dominican Republic, shortly after her
birth. Ten years later, the family was forced to flee to the United States
because of her father's involvement in an underground plot to overthrow the
dictator, Trujillo. In the hardships of assimilating to the English language
and American life, Alvarez found comfort in the world of stories, fostering a
love for reading and writing. A versatile writer, Alvarez has written novels
(*How the Garcia Girls Lost Their Accent, In the Time of Butterflies, ¡Yo!, In the
Name of Salomé*, and *Saving the World*), collections of poems (*Homecoming,
The Other Side/ El Otro Lado, The Woman I Kept to Myself*); nonfiction books
(*Something to Declare, Once Upon A Quinceañera: Coming of Age in the USA*),
and numerous books for young readers (including *How Tía Lola Came to
Visit/Stay, Before We Were Free, Finding Miracles*, and *Return to Sender*). Alv-
arez has also taught English and creative writing at every level, from elementary schools to senior citizen centers. She is currently a writer in residence at
Middlebury College. In 1997, with her husband, Bill Eichner, Alvarez established Alta Gracia, a sustainable coffee farm–literacy center in the Dominican Republic.

Lee Anne Bell is the Barbara Silver Horowitz Director of Education at
Barnard College, Columbia University. Her research and writing focus on

pedagogical approaches to social justice in teacher education, how racial discourse affects teaching and learning, and ways to support new teachers as agents of change. As principle investigator for the Storytelling Project (Third Millennium Foundation 2004–2007), she brought together artists, teachers, university faculty, and undergraduates to explore ways to teach about race and racism through storytelling and the arts. This project is described in a forthcoming book, *Storytelling for Social Justice: Connecting Narrative and the Arts in Antiracist Teaching* as well as in two articles: "Flipping the Script: Analysis of Youth Talk about Race and Racism" (with Rosemarie Roberts and Brett Murphy) in *Anthropology and Education Quarterly* (2008) and "The Storytelling Project Model: A Theoretical Framework for Critical Examination of Racism through the Arts" (with Rosemarie Roberts) forthcoming in *Teachers College Record*. She is co-editor (with Maurianne Adams and Pat Griffin) of *Teaching for Diversity and Social Justice* (2007, Routledge) and author of "Expanding Definitions of Good Teaching" in *Everyday Antiracism: Getting Real About Race in School* (Free Press, 2008).

Terri Bonebright received her Ph.D. in psychology from the University of Nebraska in 1996 and currently serves as professor and chair of the Psychology Department at DePauw University. Her specialty areas are human cognition and perception, and research methodology, and her research focuses on human sound perception broadly defined. During her 13 years at DePauw, Dr. Bonebright has taught courses in these areas as well as specialty courses in areas such as intelligence and creativity, and has served two terms as faculty development coordinator. She also has an active research program in auditory perception and is currently working on using sound as a way to help people understand graphed information. Prior to entering academics, Dr. Bonebright had a variety of work experiences including owning a vegetarian restaurant, driving semi trucks for the entertainment industry, working for the railroad, and managing a mail sorting firm.

Priscilla Bremser has been teaching mathematics at Middlebury College for 25 years. Her mathematical interests include algebra and number theory, and she has published papers in finite field theory and related topics. Recently she has broadened her study of mathematics education, and is an instructor in the Vermont Mathematics Initiative, a professional development program for K–12 mathematics teachers.

Roman Graf is a professor of German at Middlebury College where he led diversity efforts for six years as Associate Provost and Dean for Institutional Diversity. In this capacity, beyond his contacts with his counterparts at peer institutions, he additionally introduced "Deliberative Dialogues" to the campus and has maintained connections with the leadership in this increasingly important field. With a Ph.D. in Comparative Literature from the University of North Carolina at Chapel Hill, Professor Graf has published primarily on 18th-century German literature. His research and publications focus on issues of sexuality and queerness from the 18th to the 21st century, and he presents and leads workshops on foreign language pedagogy and social justice issues in academia.

James E. Groccia is the Director of the Biggio Center for the Enhancement of Teaching and Learning and Associate Professor in the Department of Educational Foundations, Leadership and Technology at Auburn University. He is a former President of the Professional and Organizational Development Network in Higher Education (POD Network), the world's largest faculty and educational development organization. He received his doctorate in Educational Psychology and Guidance from the University of Tennessee. Over his career, Dr. Groccia has directed psychological and career counseling, health and orientation services and has coordinated faculty and educational development programs at Auburn University, the University of Missouri-Columbia, and Worcester Polytechnic Institute. He served for two years as Assistant Dean of the Graduate School at Missouri prior to going to Auburn in 2003. Dr. Groccia has presented at dozens of national and international conferences, conducted hundreds of workshops worldwide, has served as an advisor and consultant to institutions nationally and abroad, and has authored numerous articles and book chapters on teaching and learning issues. He is the author of *The College Success Book: A Whole-Student Approach to Academic Excellence* (1992) and co-editor of *On Becoming a Productive University: Strategies for Reducing Costs and Increasing Quality in Higher Education* (2005); *Student Assisted Teaching: A Guide to Faculty-Student Teamwork* (2001); and *Enhancing Productivity: Administrative, Instructional, and Technological Strategies* (1998).

Jeannette Johnson-Licon is the director of the DePauw University Women's Center. Previously, she served DePauw as the coordinator of Lesbian, Gay,

Bisexual and Transgender Services (July 1999 to June 2008), the Director of the Office of Multicultural Affairs (July 2000 to June 2008) and the Assistant Dean of Students (July 2004–June 2008). Originally from the southwest border region, Jeannette holds her bachelors degree from the University of Texas at El Paso and a masters in public policy from Duke University. She has worked at two private universities and one state college. After twelve years of professional employment in college administration, Jeannette is rediscovering her creative interests in writing and theater by taking courses at DePauw.

Chawne Kimber is an algebraist in the mathematics department at Lafayette College. For the past few years, she has served as co-chair of the Advisory Committee on Community-based Learning and Research and as co-principal investigator on several grants for a wide array of social justice and community-based research projects. Professor Kimber focuses on incorporating issues of social justice into the curricula of general education mathematics courses. She also mentors faculty in many disciplines in developing new service-learning courses or modifying course modules that enhance the understanding of the relevance of mathematics and develop students' quantitative literacy.

Glen David Kuecker is an associate professor of Latin American history at DePauw University, where he also holds a University Professorship. He received the Ph.D. in Latin American and global comparative history from Rutgers University, New Brunswick, and has a B.A. from St. Olaf College, Northfield, Minnesota. Professor Kuecker is co-editor of *Latin American Social Movements in the Twenty-first Century: Resistance, Power, and Democracy* published by Rowman and Littlefield in 2008. He does collaborative research with the Globalism Research Center, RMIT University, Melbourne, Australia, and with them explores community resistance to mining in Papua New Guinea. Professor Kuecker is co-founder of the Canary Institute (canaryinstitute.org), which engages in academic research and solidarity projects that focus on the topic of catastrophic systemic collapse. He is currently engaged in a series of journal publications on how community provides resilience to a catastrophically collapsing global system.

Barbara J. Love is an exciting speaker, presenter, consultant and writer on social justice education and critical liberation theory. Dr. Love is professor of social justice education at the University of Massachusetts-Amherst. Her education background includes teacher education and staff development, curriculum development, and multicultural organizational development, also with degrees in history and political science.

She consults nationally and internationally on organizational and individual empowerment and transformation. She has worked closely with schools and school systems throughout the U.S. and has served as chair of the local School Committee, as well as with faculties and administration at colleges and universities throughout the U.S. She has worked with organizations in the business and public sector in North America, the Caribbean, Europe, and Africa on issues of diversity and inclusion. She works from a unique set of assumptions about the nature of humans and the process of personal, organizational, and social change which participants have found empowering, enabling, and effectively motivating. Dr. Love is the International Liberation Reference Person for Black People in the International Re-Evaluation Counseling Communities (IRCC). She developed the Black Liberation and Community Development Project as a key forum for examining issues impacting the lives of Black people and a location for Black people to engage in healing the effects of internalized racism in their lives. She works with and leads delegations for United to End Racism (UER), a project of the IRCC at regional, national, and international forums and conferences. Dr. Love has published widely on social justice and liberation issues such as internalized racism, self-awareness for liberation workers, building alliances for change, and critical liberation theory. Dr. Love is greatly sought after as a keynote speaker for Forums and Leadership conferences.

Kamakshi P. Murti is professor (emerita) of German at Middlebury College. She has published on German Orientalism and minorities discourse, including two books *Die Reinkarnation des Lesers als Autor: ein rezeptionsgeschichtlicher Versuch über den Einfluß der altindischen Literatur auf deutsche Schriftsteller um 1900* (de Gruyter, 1990) and *India: The Seductive and Seduced 'Other' of German Orientalism* (Greenwood, 2000). Currently, she is working on a book-length manuscript about the Muslim headscarf entitled *Turkey, Germany, and the Shifting Boundaries of Identity*.

Carolyn F. Palmer is a developmental psychologist in the Department of Psychology and Program in Cognitive Science at Vassar College. She has served as the college's Director of Teaching Development for faculty, and has conducted many workshops on integrative learning processes, culture, and college student cognitive development. Professor Palmer's scholarship on the ecologies of human development, and the conditions supporting integrative, embodied learning, includes a fundamental social justice orientation. She interweaves the arts throughout her psychology and cognitive science teaching, which provides students with frequent and accessible practice discussing issues of viewpoint, culture, identity, gender, economics, and other social justice concerns.

Vijay Prashad is the George and Martha Kellner Chair of South Asian History and Director of International Studies at Trinity College. His most recent book is *The Darker Nations: A People's History of the Third World* (New Press, 2008). He is currently writing *Come Kalinga: A Meditation on India Today* (New Press, forthcoming, 2011).

Zaheena Rasheed grew up in the Maldives, studied at the Mahindra United World College in India, and is now a political science major at Middlebury College. A prominent member of the civil society movement in Male, in 2007 Rasheed won the first ever legal case against Gayoom's dictatorship for wrongful dismissal from a government project, and went on to become coordinator of the Maldivian Detainee Network. She served for two summers as a journalist for Minivan News during the country's historic multiparty elections, and earned a summer grant to educate Male youth about environmental issues facing the island. She is currently conducting fieldwork in the Maldives to understand and give voice to citizen perceptions of the changing role of government.

Rob Root has taught mathematics at the University of Delaware, Georgetown University, Vassar College, and—for the last 18 years—Lafayette College. He works in the mathematical modeling of fish locomotion, often engaging undergraduates in creating and interpreting these models. He has also published work on incorporating service-learning projects in the teaching of applied statistics. He looks forward to participating further in the exploration of connections between mathematics and social justice.

Kathleen Skubikowski (Ph.D. University of Indiana, Bloomington) is an associate professor of English, Assistant Dean of Faculty for Instruction, and

Director of the Center for Teaching, Learning, and Research at Middlebury College. Prof. Skubikowski brings to this project on social justice education her years of experience in faculty development as the director of both the writing across the curriculum and first-year seminar programs at Middlebury and of the New England Young Writers' Conference at Bread Loaf. She presents at conferences nationally and internationally each year; and she consults on faculty development, writing, first-year programs, and CTL's at liberal arts colleges across the country. Professor Skubikowski is currently a principal investigator on the New England Consortium on Assessment and Student Learning (NECASL) panel study of the class of 2010.

Karen L. St.Clair is Director of Emerson College's Center for Innovation in Teaching and Learning (CITL). As founding director, Karen has strategically planned to offer faculty, instructional, and organizational development opportunities for all teaching staff at Emerson. Before becoming an academic developer, Karen taught psychology for a variety of higher education institutions, many with diverse student bodies and faculties. She brings a liberal arts academic background (Wayne State University), the study of human psychological development and learning (Peabody College of Vanderbilt University), studies in counseling (North Carolina State University), and many years of teaching to her work as CITL Director at Emerson, an institution focusing on communication and the arts in a liberal arts context. Her advocacy for social justice education stems from her studies and research in the social sciences and her life-long spirit of volunteerism for humanity in need.

Sheila Weaver has taught mathematics and statistics at the University of Vermont for 25 years. She is especially interested in innovation in statistics and mathematics education. Over the last eight years, she has incorporated service learning in most of her college classes. In recent years, she has also taught professional development courses to middle and high school math teachers with Vermont Mathematics Partnerships; and she is a co-director of the Governor's Institute in Mathematical Sciences, a summer program for outstanding high school students in Vermont.

Catharine Wright, MFA in creative writing from the University of Michigan, draws on research and experience in the arts, social justice, educational technology, service learning, sustainability, and contemplative practice in her teaching in the writing and creative writing programs, English department, and women and gender studies department at Middlebury College. She has taught in and directed summer programs for first generation college students, served as Posse mentor and Queer Studies House liaison, and collaboratively organizes and facilitates roundtables for faculty on diverse pedagogies. Her publications include a non-fiction book on Vermont craftspeople, fiction in literary magazines, and articles on contemplative practice and the arts.

Arthur Zajonc, Ph.D., is the Andrew Mellon professor of physics and interdisciplinary studies at Amherst College, the director of the Academic Program of the Center for Contemplative Mind, and a senior program director at the Fetzer Institute. He is a co-founder of the Kira Institute, the former general secretary of the Anthroposophical Society in America, and past president of the Lindisfarne Association. He has served as scientific coordinator and editor for several dialogues with the Dalai Lama, including *The New Physics and Cosmology* held in 1997 and published in 2004, and was moderator for the 2003 MIT dialogue, published as *The Dalai Lama at MIT* (2006). Dr. Zajonc is also the author of *Catching the Light* (1993 and 1995), *Meditation as Contemplative Inquiry* (2009), co-author of *The Quantum Challenge* (2nd ed. 2005), and co-editor of *Goethe's Way of Science* (1998).

Abbot Academy
  absorption into Phillips Andover Academy, xxii
  education at, xvi–xvii
Abduction, 60
Abraham, Neal, xi, 100
AbuZayd, Karen Koning, 104
Academic development, 78–80
  as leader on campus, 80–81
  primary functions of, 81
Academic discourse, value of, xxiii
Academics, 178
  task of reconceptualizing fields, 13–14
  thinking about writing, 177–78
  view of personal, 178
Academic solidarity, analysis of, 51–52
Accountability, 46
Active learning, 14–15, 115, 156–57
Activism
  academic, 42–54
  environmental, 87
  political, 117–27
Activist scholarship, flaws in, 47
Adams, M., ix, x, 3, 5, 6, 7, 9, 10, 11, 12, 21, 23, 25, 29, 77, 89–92, 164, 169, 174, 178, 182, 188–89
Adams, Robert, 87
Adelson, L., 199–200
Advanced foreign language classroom, 157–60
Alienation, Marx's notion of, 51
Allen, Robert, 120
Allison, D., 188, 217–21
Allport, G. W., 4
Altman, Meryl, xi, 100
Alvarez, Julia, x, xii, 186, 215–16
American Friends Service Committee (AFSC), 141
Amherst College, xi

Anderson, J. A., 9
Anthropology, colonial, 121–22
Antiracist organization, creation of, 125–26
Antiracist teaching, focusing on preparation for, 27–28
Antonio, A. L., 5
Antonson, J., 189–90
Anzaldúa, Gloria, 49
Aristophanes, 106
Aristotle, 60
Arnold, G., 75
Arnone, E., 198, 202, 205, 209–10n8
Arts education, view of personal, 178
Ascendant Copper, 42–43
Ashbrook, T., 194
Asian Americans Students' Association, 122
Association for Retarded Citizens, 133
Austin, A. E., 78, 81
Authoritarian positions in educational framework, 154–55
Authoritative positions in educational framework, 154–55
Autonomy, 46, 88

Bacon, Francis, 65
Baker, Ella, 118
Bakhtin, M., 151, 152, 156, 160
Bakhtinean theory, 155
Baldwin, J., 95–96, 179
Banking model of teaching, 47, 48, 116n3
Barnard College, xi
Bartee, R. D., 5
Bartky, Sandra Lee, 109
Basij-Rasikh, S., 190
Bauman, G. L., 5
Beach, A. L., 78, 81
Beauboeuf, Tamara, 100n, 115
Belcher, E., 198, 202, 205, 209–10n8
Bell, L. A., x–xi, 5, 6, 9, 10, 11, 12, 13, 26, 28,

29, 70–71, 73, 90–92, 148, 164, 169, 172, 181
Bensimon, E. M., 5
Berger, J. B., 5
Berry, A., 54
Bertolini, M. E., 185
Bhaba, 179
Bhagavada Gita, 125
Bhan, Mona, 100*n*, 103
Biddle, B. J., 77
Biggio Center for the Enhancement of Teaching and Learning at Auburn University, xi
Bildung, 66
Bilmes, L., 141–42
Binarism, 179
Biographia Literaria (Coleridge), 60
Birnbaum, R., 71
Black Students Union, 122
Black studies movement, 127*n*
Black working class, racism and, 117–18
Blumoehr, F., 157
Bohm, David, 60
Bok, D., 3
Bok Center for Teaching and Learning at Harvard University, 87–88, 89
Boler, M., 32
Bonebright, Terri, xi, 100, 104
Border pedagogy, 49–50
Bordt, Rebecca, 103
Bowen, W. G., 3
Boyum, D., 140, 141, 144
Brahmin, 196
    worldview in India, 122
Bremser, Priscilla, xii, 131, 134–35
Brewer, M. B., 4
Brooks, David, 143
Brown, M. C., 5
Brown, R., 4
Brown v. *Board of Education,* 3, 4
Buffet, 141
Burgman, Ray, 103
Bush, George W., 143
Bustillos, L. T., 5
Byram, M., 151, 152–53, 195

Calculus, 132, 133
    reform movement in, 145*n*7

Cameron, Rich, 100*n*
Campus culture, using, 107–10
Campus outreach programs, 15
Campuswide, ethics-based approach, to social justice pedagogy, 100–115
Cantrill, T., 107
Capitalist market, higher education and, 47
Caraher, John, 107
Carlson, D., 184
Census Bureau, 138
Center for Teaching, Learning, and Research (CTLR), 94–96
    collaboration in, 94–96
Center for Teaching and Learning (CTL), 90
    mission of, 98
Chamberlain, M., 178
Chang, M. J., 4, 5
Change
    definitions of, 72
    factors for implementation, 73–74
    as noun, 77–78
    strategy for, to social justice education, 75–82
    theories and models for, 72–73
    as verb, 78–82
Chaucer's Wife of Bath, xxiii
Chesler, M., 4
Cisneros, Sandra, xxii
Citizen-scholar discourse, building, 177–91
Citizenships, components of, 46
Civian, J. T., 75
Civic engagement, 97
Civil Rights Movement, 124, 118, 119–120
Clarity of emotional experience, 168–69
Clark, B. R., 75
Classroom
    deliberative dialogue in, 201–8
    instructors in, 10–13
    students as active participants in, 8–10
Clayton-Pedersen, A. R., 5, 94–95
Cobb, C. E., Jr., 14, 132, 139
Cobb, P., 14
Cognitive development models, 10
Coleman, B. A., 189–90
Coleridge, S. T., 60
Collaborations
    around service-learning projects, 189–90

in Center for Teaching, Learning, and
    Research (CTLR), 94–96
in social justice education, 94–96
Collective ability, 88
Collective responsibility, 45
Colleges and universities. *See also* Higher
    education; *specific*
    core requirements for addressing diversity,
        4
    mission statements of, 164–65
Collegial development mode, 173–74
Colonial anthropology, 121–22
Color blindness, problems with, 32
Colvin, Claudette, 118
Commission of the European Communities,
    161*n5*
Community-based learning, xii
Community cultural wealth, 34–35
Community service
    learning programs for, 15
    in neoliberal higher education, 47–48
Concealed stories, 26–27, 30, 34–36
Contact hypothesis, 4
Contemplative inquiry, 65
Contemplative insight, cultivation of, 67–68
Contemplative traditions, 67–68
Context and Culture in Language Teaching
    (Kramsch), 151
Conventional morality, 63
Cooney, Elizabeth, 94
Cottrell, A. B., 184
Counter-storytelling community, creation
    of, 30
Course content
    curriculum in conveying to students,
        13–14
    delivery in pedagogical processes, 14–16
    variables in, 80
Crain, W. C., 59
Crary, Sharon, 100*n*
Creative writing programs, 179
Criminality, countering culture of, 126
Critical race theory (CRT), scholarship in,
    28–30
Crook, C., 143
Cullman, Joseph, Jr., 117
Cultural hegemony, power and, 52

Culture, political economy of, 125
Culture course, choosing text for, 157–58
Curricular change, x
Curriculum
    in conveying course content to students,
        13–14
    hidden, 155–56
    social justice education across, 87–98
Cytron-Walker, A., 4

Daly, H., 63
Davidson, J. E., 66
Dawkins, Richard, 62
Dean, M., 54
Deception, sources of, 66
Deduction, 60
Delgado Bernal, D., 12
Deliberative dialogue
    in classroom, 201–8
    defined, 194–95, 198
    Muslim headscarf and, 199–200
    as pedagogical tool for social justice,
        194–210
Della Piana, L., 28
Democracy, 46
Demographic gap, widening of, in diversity,
    5
Denison, ix
DePauw University, ix, xi
    campus culture at, 107–10
    Compton Center at, 102
    Environmental Policy Project of, 106
    faculty development at, 110–12
    first-year seminars and interdisciplinary
        programs at, 112–13
    Focus the Nation event at, 105–6
    humanitarian intervention at, 104
    Prindle Institute for Ethics at, 101, 115
    public events hosted at, 104–7
    social justice initiative at, 101–16
    Social Justice Institute at, 102–4
    women's studies at, 106
    workshop culture at, 101–2
    workshop model of faculty development,
        107–10
Development
    academic, 78–81

cognitive, 10
collegial, 173–74
educational, 78–80
faculty, 78, 88–89, 90, 107–12, 172–74
instructional, 78
organizational, 78, 80
Development workshop, faculty as explorers
    in teaching, 165–67
Dewart, Janet, 118
Dey, E., 4
Dialectical discourse, 180–82
Dialogical heteroglossia, 151
Dialogic principles, 151, 160
    application to foreign language classroom,
    151
Dianoia, 66
Dickinson, Emily, xxiii
*Die Gesellschaft der Bundesrepublik Deutsch-
    land*, 157
Differential equations, 131, 132
Dilworth, M., 27
Direct perception, 66
Discourse
    academic, xxiii
    citizen-scholar, 177–91
    dialectical, 180–82
    storytelling, 182
    student, 182–90
Discovery, 60
Discussion, 209n3
Diversity
    benefits of, 5
    educational benefits of, 3–4
    widening of demographic gap in, 5
Domination, patterns of social justice per-
    spective, 6–7
Donnay, Victor, 145n1
Dostoevsky, 155
Du Bois, W. E. B., 126, 179, 180–81, 191
Dudle, Dana, 100n
Dunkin, M. J., 77
Dykstra-Pruim, P., 197, 198
Dynamics of diversity change plan, 14, 24–25

Economic inequality, historical roots of pat-
    terns of, 6
Eddy, P. L., 78, 81

Education. *See also* Social justice education
    arts, 178
    authoritarian positions in framework of,
        154–55
    authoritative positions in framework of,
        154–55
    banking system of, 47, 48, 116n3
    higher, 47
    liberatory, 178
    social justice in foreign language, 148–61
    theory of, for marginalized people, 48
Educational benefits of diversity, 3–4
Educational change
    analysis of, 72
    types of, 72
Educational development, 78–80
Efficient cause, 60
Eighteenth Brumaire of Louis Bonaparte
    (Marx), 52–53
Einstein, A., 60, 61, 63, 67
Elder, J., 187
Elder, Larry, 141
Emerging/transforming stories, 26–27, 37–38
Emotional experience, clarity of, 168–69
Empathy, 46
Environmental activism, link to social jus-
    tice, 87
Episteme, 66
Equality, 46
Equity, 46
Erickson, P. E., 140
Ethnicity in postsecondary admissions poli-
    cies, 3–25
Ethnomathematics, 14
European Union's affirmation of multicul-
    turalism, 161n5
Everett, J., 100n, 105, 106, 107
Evolutionary game theory, 131
Eyes Wide Open exhibition, 141

Facilitating learning, 80–81
Faculty
    in cross-institutional settings, 13
    in designing curricula on diversity, 4
    in development of self-awareness, 12–13
    exploration of socialization, 9

as explorers in teaching development workshop, 165–67
lack of diversity in, 27–28
orientation sessions for new, 107–10
use of web-based communication, 15
Faculty development, 78, 110–12
in social justice education, 3–25, 88–89, 90, 172–74
workshop model of, 107–10
Feeling Power (Boler), 32
Feminism, 51–52, 126
Feminism Without Borders (Mohanty), 51–52
Feynman, Richard, 61
First-person narratives, 178, 183
Fish, Stanley, 53
Five Minority Perspectives on DePauw (documentary video), 103
Fletcher, J. J., 78, 81
Fontenelle, Bernard de, 60
Foreign language education. *See* Social justice in foreign language education
Formal writing, 182–90
Foucault, M., 54, 179
Four-quadrant analysis of teaching and learning, 7–16, 20–21
Frank, R., 139, 140
Frankenstein, M., 14
Freire, Paolo, 47, 48, 100, 114, 132, 149–50, 160, 178, 195, 197
Freire, Paolo, Institute, 209*n*2
Frequency distributions, 136
Fullan, M., 72, 74, 75, 76
Furman College, ix

Game theory, 133
Gamson, Z. F., 75
Gandhi, M. K., 58, 59, 122, 125
Ganley, B., 183
Gapminder Foundation, 137
Gardner, H., 169
Garewal, K., 190
Gentleness, 65
Geopolitics of knowledge, 52
German, teaching social justice education approach in, 159
Gini index, 137

Giroux, H., 47, 49, 50, 51
Globalism Research Center at RMIT University, Melbourne University, 45
Globalization, indigenous resistance to, 44
Goethe, J. W. von, 65, 66, 67
Goleman, D., 169
Gómez-Peña, Guillermo, 200
Goodman, D. J., 12, 91
Gordon, R., 28
Gore, Al, 143
Gornick, V., 181, 186
Gossen, G., 47
Governmentality, 54
Graf, Roman, xii, 148
Greene, Maxine, 177
Griffin, P., 5, 6, 9, 10, 11, 12, 29, 33, 90, 91–92, 164, 169, 172, 175*n*1
Groccia, J. E., xi, 70, 77, 79*n*
Grutter v. *Bollinger et al.,* 3–4
Guillermoprieto, A., 47
Gurin, G., 4
Gurin, P., 4
Gutstein, E., 132, 145*n*4
Gymnasien, 157

Habitus, 66
Hadlock, C. R., 133, 145*n*2
Hadot, P., 66
Halper, Nicole, 103
Hamilton, Lee, 101
Hardiman, R., 10
Harro, B., 11
Harvard Office for Race Relations and Minority Affairs, 87–88
Haverford College, 76–77
Helmholtz, H., 61
Henck, N., 47
Heteroglossia, 155
Hidden curriculum, 155–56
Hierarchy, countering culture of, 126
Higher education. *See also* Colleges and universities
academic development in, 78–79
capitalist market and, 47
change in, 72–75
models of governance in, 71

race and ethnicity in admissions policies and, 3–4
social justice education and, 71–72, 98
Hilliard, A., 35
Hines, S. M., 14
Hip-hop, 124–25
Histograms, 136
Hofstede, G., 209, 210n10
Hoggart, Richard, xix–xx
Holloway, John, 51
Holvino, E., 77
hooks, bell, 30, 103, 178–79, 185, 187, 195, 197, 203
Horowitz, D., 48
Hotel Rwanda (film), 87
The House on Mango Street (Cisneros), xxii
How Colleges Work: The Cybernetics of Academic Organization and Leadership (Birnbaum), 71
Humanitarian intervention, 104
Humphreys, D., 4
Hunger, 138
themes of, 136
Hunger of Memory (Rodriguez), xix
Hurtado, S., 4
Huusko, S., 190
Hydorn, Deborah, 133

Identification, 68
Imagination, 56, 60
secondary, 60
"I" narrative, 45
India, Brahmin worldview in, 122
Indigenous resistance to globalization, 44
Informal writing, 182–90
Innovative pedagogy, 114
Inquiry, contemplative, 65
Inquiry-based approach, acceptance of, in sciences, 114
Insight, 56, 66
role of, in science, 59–62
Institute on Social Justice Education, ix
Institutional change, x
Instructional development, 78
Instructional processes, 80
Instructors in classroom, 10–13
Intag Solidarity Network, 42–43, 44

Intercultural communicative competence, 151
Interdependence, message of, 88
Intimacy, 65
Intuition, 56
Irvine, James, 94
Ito, Aki, 184

Jackson, B. W., 10, 77
James, C., 197, 198
Janis, K., 190
Jim Crow racism, 118
Johnson-Licon, Jeannette, xi, 100
Jones, J., 169
Jordan, Vernon, 101
Judson, Olivia, 140
Julian, Percy, 101

Kailin, J., 28
Kanpol, Barry, 155–56
Kante, Babacar, 104
Kanter, S., 75
Kaufmann, Kelsey, 106
Keleher, T., 28
Keller, E. F., 68
Kelvin, Lord, 60, 63
Kenan, R., 181
Kendall, F., 91, 94, 96
Kezar, A. J., 72–73, 74, 75
Kimber, Chawne, xii, 131, 134
King, Jamesina, 109–10
King, Martin Luther, Day, 121
King, Martin Luther, Jr., 58, 59, 118–19, 122, 125, 127
Civil Rights Movement and, 119–20
Poor People's Movement and, 119
Southern Christian Leadership Conference (SCLC) and, 119
King, Michael, 117–20. See also King, Martin Luther, Jr.
King, P. M., 10
Kingsolver, Barbara, 101
Kingston, R. J., 198, 202, 205, 209–10n8
Kissinger, J., 189–90
Klass, G., 137
Klein, Joel, 145n5
Knighton, B., 198, 202, 205, 209–10n8

Knowing and Teaching Elementary Mathematics (Ma), 141
Kohl, Herb, 39–40*n*
Kohlberg, 59
Kotlowitz, Alex, 163
Kramsch, C., 151, 152
Krashen, S., 196
Krugman, P., 143
Kuecker, G. D., xi, 42, 43, 44, 100*n*
Kuh, G. D., 81–82
Kurlaender, M., 3

Lafayette College, 139
Lalande, J. L., II, 197, 198
Language teaching, structuralist approaches in, 148
La Raza, 122
La Voz Latina, 122
Learner variables, 80
Learning. *See also* Teaching
    active, 14–15, 115, 156–57
    community-based, xii
    community service, 15
    context variables in, 80
    facilitating, 80–81
    four-quadrant analysis of, 7–16, 20–21
    mathematical, xii
    outcomes variables in, 80
    process variables in, 80
    quantitative, 141
    service, xii, 47–48, 96, 133–34, 160
    social justice, 160–61
    style of, 9
    transfer of, 173
Learning institution, raison d'être of, xiv
Lears, T. J. J., 52
Leistyna, P., 177, 187
Leonard, J., 14
Lesser, L., 133
Levins Morales, A., 35
Lewis, Harry, 07, 178
LGBT Queer organizations, 126
Li, C., 190
Liberal arts
    math courses in, 132–33
    teaching, 174
Liberatory education theory, 178

Liberatory pedagogy, 114
Lindquist, J., 75
Liping Ma, 141, 143
Literary text, asking social justice questions using, 169–72
Literature
    asking social justice questions using, 167–69
    incorporating, in social sciences, 163–75
Logan, Ms., 39
London, H. B., 75
Lopez, Barry, 181
Lopez, G., 4
Lorentz, Hendrik, 61
Lorentz contraction, 61
Lounsberry, B., 81
Love, 58, 64, 67
    epistemology of, 64–67
Love, B. J., ix, x, 3, 7, 11, 13, 21, 23, 25, 29, 67, 89–90, 92, 148
Lowenstein, R., 137
Lucas, T., 27
Lynch, Richard, 100*n*

Macedo, D. P., 178, 189
Malée, life in, 218–21
Marchesani, L. S., 7, 10, 21, 25, 77, 188–89
Marginalization, xiii
    education theory and, 48
Marguerite, 59
Marx, K., 52–53
Mathematicians, thinking like, 144
Mathematics, xii
    Algebra Project in, 132
    in analyzing social issues, 131–32
    calculus in, 132, 133, 145*n*7
    epistemology, 14
    literacy in, 14
    regular courses in, 132
    social justice and, 131–44
        case studies, 136–44
        defined, 131–32
        examples of courses, 132–34
        MSJ network, 134–36
        thinking like mathematicians, 144
Mathematics in Service to the Community (Hadlock), 133

McCaig, Norma, 184
McClendon, S. A., 5
McClintock, Barbara, 68
McIntosh, P., 182–83
McKelvey, Steve, 133
McKenzie, R., 198, 202, 205, 209–10*n*8
McLaren, P., 47, 48
Mellen, D., 172
Mellon Institutes for Faculty on Social Justice Education, 89–90
The Merchant of Venice (Shakespeare), 163, 164, 165–66, 169, 173, 174
Merleau-Ponty, M., 66
Mexico Solidarity Network, 44, 50
Michie, G., 35, 39
Middlebury College, ix, xxii
    German classroom at, 158–59
    social justice education approach in teaching German, 159
    Social Justice Institute rubric developed at, 102
Milem, J., 4, 5
Miller, Andy, 132–33
Miller, R., 177, 179, 190
Mirror of Simple Annihilated Souls (Porete), 57–58
Mish, F., 209*n*3
Mitchell, G., 201
Modern Language Association, 2007 Ad Hoc Committee on Foreign Languages, 160
Mohanty, C. T., 51, 52
Monbiot, George, 107
Moral agency, 66–67
    necessity of personal experience in, 56–68
    question of, 62–64
Moral authority, 59
Moral insight, 56
Morality, conventional, 63
Moral relativism, 63–64
Moral sensibility, 63
Morehouse College, 117
Moreno, J. F., 5, 94–95
Morris, A., 118
Morrison, Toni, 31–32
Morson, G. S., 155, 156
Moses, R. P., 14, 132, 139

MSJ Network, 134–36
Multiculturalism, xi, 121–24
    benefits of, 5
    dynamics of, in teaching and learning, 8
    mathematics education and, 14
    social justice and, 89–90
Murti, Kamakshi P., xii, 161*n*4, 194
Muslim headscarf, deliberative dialogue and, 199–200

Nagda, B. A., 4
Narratives, 185–86. *See also* Stories
    first-person, 178, 183
    "I," 45
    study of, 178
    "We," 45
Nasir, N. S., 14
National Center for Educational Statistics (NCES), 5
National Conference on Race and Ethnicity in Higher Education (NCORE), ix, 96, 196
National Council on Education and the Disciplines, 140
National Issues Forums (NIF), 198
National Oceanic and Atmospheric Administration, 133
National Urban League, 118
Neoliberalism, 47
    community service and service-learning and, 47–48
Niederman, D., 140, 141, 144
Niemeier, S., 157, 158, 161*n*1
Nightenhelser, Keith, 100*n*
Noether, 61
Noun, change as, 77–78
Nussbaum, Martha, 95

O'Bannon, Brett, 100*n*, 104
O'Bear, K., 11, 13, 23, 148
Objectivity, 65
    divide between subjectivity, 47
Oldrieve, S., 167, 175*n*1
Once Upon a Quinceañera: Coming of Age in the USA, xv–xvi

Oregon State University's Difference, Power, and Discrimination Program, 76–77
Orenstein, P., 39
Orfield, G., 3
Organizational development, 78, 81
Orr, M., 107
Orwell, G., 180, 181, 191
Osborne, T., 54
Osler, Jonathan, 135, 145*n*1
Ott, Ursula, 199
Ouellett, M. L., 5
Öztürk, Emine, 199

Palmer, Carolyn F., xii, 163
Palmer, P. J., 66, 115
PA/NY Campus Compact Consortium's Learn and Serve America grant, 145*n*3
Paris Inquisition, 58
Parker, S., 5, 94–95
Parks, Rosa, 39–40*n*, 118
Participant self-awareness, 11
Participation, 65
Patrick, S. K., 78, 81
Pedagogical change, x
Pedagogy
    border, 49–50
    course content delivery in, 14–16
    deliberative dialogue as, for social justice, 194–210
    good as good, 113–14
    innovative, 114
    liberatory, 114
    relationship between solidarity and, 50–51
    social justice, ix–x, 100–115, 153–54
    transparent, 156
Perry, T., 35
Personal experience, necessity of, in moral agency, 56–68
Peterson, B., 145*n*4
Pettigrew, T. F., 4
Pfaff, T., 133, 145*n*2
Pharr, S., 12
Phillips Andover Academy, xxii
Physical desegregation, affirmation by *Brown v. Board of Education*, 4
Physics, great symmetry principles of, 61
Pierce, Charles, 60

Pierce, Franklin, University, 206, 207
Plurality of Worlds (Fontenelle), 60–61
Political activism, 117–27
Political economy of culture, 125
Polyculturalism, 124
    principles of, 124–25
Pope, Jeane, 100*n*, 105
Porete, M., 57–59, 63, 64, 67
    moral stance of, 59
Postsecondary admissions policies, race and ethnicity in, 3–4
Poverty, 138
    measuring, 137
    outside markers of, 219–21
    racialization of, 123
    themes of, 136
Powell, A. B., 14
Power
    defined, 50
    navigating relationships, 50–52
Practice as multidimensional, 72
Prashad, V., xi–xii, 117, 120
Pratt, Mary Louise, 210*n*9
Praxis, 195
    socially just university and, 52–54
Primitive superstitions, xviii
Prindle, Janet, 101
Prindle Institute, sponsorship of humanitarian intervention symposium at, 104
Prior socialization, 10
Probabilities, 136
Problem-posing approach, 132
Process, idea of in solidarity, 48–49
Process writing, 139–40
Professional and Organizational Development (POD) Network in Higher Education (n.d.), 78–79
Public space, relative freedom of, 117
Pythagoras, 156

Quantitative learning, 141
Quantitative literacy, 132, 139–40
Quantitative reasoning, 136
Quayle, Dan, 101
Question bank for student interviews, 211

Race
  learning about through story types, 26–40
  in postsecondary admissions policies, 3–25
Racialization of poverty, 123
Racism
  Black working class and, 117–18
  Jim Crow, 118
  learning about through story types, 26–40
Rainbolt, Martha, 100*n*
Random assignment to treatments, 136
Random sampling, 136
Rapunzel, story of, xiii, xv, xviii
Rasheed, Zaheena, x, 215–16, 217
Ravitch, Diane, 135
Rawls, J., 64
Reading the Mountains of Home (Elder), 187
Reform movements in math education, 141
Regular math courses, 132
Relativity, 61
Report of the Human Relations Committee, 96
Residential life programs, 15
Resistance stories, 26–27, 30, 36–37
Respect, 64–65
Rethinking Mathematics, 145*n*4
Rich, A., 100
Rilke, R. M., 64–65
Roberts, Catherine, 145*n*1
Roberts, R. A., 26, 29
Rodriguez, Richard, xix, xx, xxii
Rogers, J., 173
Rokey, E., 190
Root, R., xii, 131, 134, 139, 140–41, 143
Roper, L. D., 76, 78
Rose, N., 54
Rusesabagina, P., 87, 88

Said, 179
St. Augustine, 58
St. Clair, Karen L., xi, 70
St. Olaf College, 133
Sarris, G., 31
Sawyer, Amos, 104
Schaffer, A., 190
Schapiro, Steven, 91
Scholarship boy, xix–xx

Scholarship of teaching and learning
    (SOTL), 90
  mission of, 98
Schrödinger, E., 65
Schulz, R., 197, 198
Schwarzer, Alice, 199
Science, 67
  central role of insight in, 59–62
Scientific insight, 56
Scientific progress, factors in, 56
Scott, G., 72, 75
Scripps College, ix
  commitment to issues of diversity, 96–97
Secondary imagination, 60
Second-language-acquisition theory, 196
Seeing a Color-Blind Future (Williams), 32
Self-assessment
  instruments in, 12, 22–23
  of vulnerabilities in teaching, 22–23
Self-imposed silence, 190
Self-reflection in social justice education, 90–94
Sell, G. R., 81
Senge, Peter, 94
Service learning, xii, 96, 134
  courses in, 160
  integrating with social justice issues in
      mathematics courses, 133–34
  in neoliberal higher education, 47–48
Service-learning projects, 139
  collaborations around, 189–90
  in reinforcing classroom learning, 132
Seth, P., 190
Sexism, examining, 91–92
Seyhan, A., 200
Shakespeare, W., 150, 165–66, 171–72
"Shakespeare Meets Social Justice" work-
    shop, 165
Shape the agenda, 81
Shapiro, G., 135
Shapiro, J., 173
Shared sense of belonging, 46
Shelburne Farms, blue sky agenda item at,
    xxiii
Sherblom, S., 177, 187
Shuford, B. C., 10
Shulman, L. S., 77

Silko, 179
Singh, R., 190
Skin game, 120–21
Skubikowski, K., xi, xii, 87, 97
Slater, D., 51, 52
Sloan, D., 60, 66
Smith, Barbara Herrnstein, 150, 152, 156
Smith, D. G., 5, 77, 94–95
Smith, S., 94–95
Sobol, J. D., 181
Social capital, mobilization of, 42–43
Social change
  writing for, 177–91
    student discourse in informal and for-
      mal writing, 182–90
Social diversity, educational benefits of, 4
Social identity
  awareness of, 11–12
  models of, 10
Social inequality, historical roots of patterns
  of, 6
Socialization awareness, 11
Social justice, 140
  academic activism and, 42–54
  benefits of, 5
  defined, 70–71
  deliberative dialogue as pedagogical tool
    for, 194–210
  environmental activism link to, 87
  facilitation issues in, 12
  focus on broader contexts, 170–71
  integrating service-learning with, in math-
    ematics courses, 133–34
  link between higher education institutions
    and, 98
  mathematics and (*see under* Mathematics)
  multiculturalism and, 89–90
  as process idea and, ix, x
Social justice education, 70–71, 164–65
  across curriculum, 87–98
  challenge to, xx–xxi
  change in higher, 72–75
  collaboration in, 94–96
  commitment to, 77–78
  faculty development in, 3–25, 88–89, 165–
    67. *172–174*
  framework for, 6–7, 15

four-quadrant analysis of teaching and
  learning, 7–16, 20–21
higher education institutions and, 71–72
role of teacher in, 148–49
self-reflection in, 90–94
strategy for change to, 75–82
as term, xiii
Social Justice Education Workshop, Center
  for Teaching, Learning, and Research
  (CTLR), 91–94
Social justice in foreign language education,
  148–61
  advanced classroom, 157–60
  beginning classroom, 153–56
  learning, 160–61
  theoretical framework, 148–53
  transparent pedagogy, 156–57
Social justice issue awareness, 11–12
Social justice learning, 160–61
Social justice pedagogy, ix–x
  campuswide, ethics-based approach to,
    100–115
  principles of, 153–54
  support of, by workshop culture, 107–10
Social justice questions, asking
  using literature, 167–69
  using specific literary text, 169–72
Social justice work as interruptive, 97–98
Socially just university, praxis and, 52–54
Social relationship, solidarity as, 45
Social sciences, incorporating literature in,
  163–75
Social sensibility, 160
Society of the Federal Republic of Germany,
  158
Socratic method, 115
Solidarity, 45–48
  culture of, 118, 126
  idea of process in, 48–49
  as process of crossing borders, 49
  relationship between pedagogy and, 50–51
Somerville, Siobhan, 109
Sophocles, 110
Sorcinelli, M. D., 78, 81
Southern Christian Leadership Conference
  (SCLC), 118, 119
Spearing, E., 57–58

Special relativity, 61
Stahler-Sholk, R., 44
Statistics, 132
Steele, C., 35, 114
Steinbring, H., 14
Stereotyping processes, 169–70
Stern, S., 145n5
Sternberg, R. J., 66
Stiglitz, J., 141–42
Stirling, G., 173
Stock stories, 26–27, 33–34
Stories. *See also* Narratives
   concealed, 26–27, 30, 34–36
   emerging/transforming, 26–27, 37–38
   resistance, 26–27, 30, 36–37
   stock, 26–27, 33–34
Storytelling discourse, participating in critical, 182
Storytelling Project Model, 26–31
   effectiveness of, 39
   focusing on preparation for antiracist teaching, 27–28
Story types
   illustrating, in seminar for student teachers, 31–38
   learning about race and racism through, 26–40
Structuralist approaches in language teaching, 148
Student discourse in informal and formal writing, 182–90
Students
   as active participants in classroom, 8–10
   curriculum in conveying course content to, 13–14
Student-teachers
   illustrating story types in seminar for, 31–38
   relationship of, 149
Subcomandante Marcos, 46–47
Subjectivity, divide between objectivity, 47
Subordination, patterns of social justice perspective, 6–7

Tatum, B., 92, 123, 169, 179, 187
Taylor, K. L., 80–81

Teacher, role of, in social justice classroom, 148–49
Teacher variables, 80
Teaching. *See also* Learning
   banking model of, 47, 48, 116n3
   four-quadrant analysis of, 7–16, 20–21
   liberal arts, 174
   self-assessment of vulnerabilities in, 22–23
   structuralist approaches in language, 148
   transfer of, 173
Teaching to Transgress (hooks), 47
Ten Commandments, 63
Tenure, xxii
Teraguchi, D. H., 5, 94–95
Terms of engagement, 30
There Are No Children Here (Kotlowitz), 163
Thomas, M., 198, 202, 205, 209–10n8
Thompson, P., 178
Thoreau, H. D., 58, 59, 125
Transformation, 66
Transformative idea of praxis, 53
Transparent pedagogy, 156
Triesman, U., 114
True moral agency, enablement of, 56
Tse, T. M., 141
Tyagi, A. E., 139

Undernourishment, 137
Understanding White Privilege (Kendall), 91–94
Universality, xiii
Universities. *See* Colleges and universities; Higher education
Upward mobility, 123–24
Useem, R. H., 184
The Uses of Literacy (Hoggart), xix

Valenzuela, A., 35
Vanden, H., 44
Vassar College, ix
   Office of Teaching Development at, 165–67
Verb, change as, 78–82
Vermont Campaign to End Childhood Hunger (VTCECH), 137, 145n8
Vermont Folklife Center Apprenticeship Project, 189–90

Vila, H., 179, 183
Vilas, C., 46
Villalpando, O., 12
Villega, A. M., 27
Virtues, 63, 64
Voice, message of, 88
Vulnerability, 65

Wall of Remembrance, 142
Warren, E., 139
Washington, S., 13, 92, 148
Weaver, S., xii, 131, 136, 138, 139, 145*n*2
Web-base communication, faculty use of, 15
Weinstein, B., 92
Weinstein, G., 23, 92, 148, 172
Weinstein, J., 11, 13
"We" narrative, 45
West, Cornell, 105
Western civilization, 121–22, 123
What Is Ancient Philosophy (Hadot), 66
What Price the Moral High Ground? (Frank), 140
What the Numbers Say, 140–41, 143–44
White privilege, 97
White supremacy, 121, 123
White teachers, socialization of, 28
Wijeyesinghe, C. L., 10
Wilder, J. C., 198, 202, 205, 209–10*n*8
Wildman, S. M., 12
William of Paris, 58
Williams, D. A., 5
Williams, P. J., 32
Williams, T. T., 87, 88, 98

Wilson, E. O., 62
Wise, Tim, 96
Women and Global Peace, 96
Women for Global Peace organization, 190
Women's Center, 126
Woodrum, A., 177, 187
Woolf, Virginia, 109
Workshop model of faculty development, 107–10
Wright, Catharine, xii, 177
Writing
   creative, 179
   process, 139–40
   for social change, 177–91
      student discourse in informal and formal writing, 182–90
   thinking about, 177–78
Writing Across the Curriculum (WAC), 88
Writing at the End of the World (Miller), 177–78

Yaqob, Olga, 209*n*1
Yosso, T., 34–35
Young, I. M., 12
Young and Muslim in Germany (film), 204

Zajonc, A., xi, 56, 64, 65, 68
Zeilinger, A., 61–62
Zimmer-Loew, H., 197, 198
Zinn, Howard, 95
Zorrilla, Carlos, 42–43
Zúñiga, X., 4

Also available from Stylus

Getting Culture
Incorporating Diversity Across the Curriculum
Edited by Regan A. R. Gurung , Loreto R. Prieto

How do we educate our students about cultural diversity and cultural differences, and eliminate cultural ignorance, stereotyping, and prejudice? What are the conceptual issues involved in reaching this goal? How can we integrate these perspectives in disciplinary and diversity courses, and the curriculum?

This book is a resource for answering these questions. Within the framework of current scholarship and discussion of essential concepts, it offers practical techniques and empirically proven "best practices" for teaching about diversity. It is intended for faculty integrating diversity into existing courses, and for anyone creating courses on diversity. It can also serve to inform and guide department chairs and other administrators in the design and implementation of diversity initiatives.

Driving Change Through Diversity and Globalization
Transformative Leadership in the Academy
James A. Anderson
Foreword by **Ronald A. Crutcher**

"On rare occasions one finds a book that reframes prior visions. Anderson's is such a book. The first three chapters provide a framework for understanding diversity and globalization, which moves beyond the limits of affirmative action, ethnic studies, and overseas study tours. The theoretical discussion is rooted in the premise that universities' (read also society's) ability to work with diversity and globalization will determine the nature of their futures. Following a discussion of principles, Anderson moves from theory to practice, giving illustrations of campuses that have embraced some facet of this new vision applying it either in terms of teaching strategies and methods, curricular organization, and/or student development. The fact that Anderson is able to draw on working applications gives credence to his theoretical propositions."—***Irene Hecht, Director,*** *Department Leadership Programs, ACE*

Sentipensante (Sensing/Thinking) Pedagogy
Educating for Wholeness, Social Justice and Liberation
Laura I. Rendón
Foreword by **Mark Nepo**

"What would happen if educators eschewed the silent agreements that govern institutions and established a new set of working assumptions that honor the fullness of humanity? In this visionary study, Laura Rendón lays the groundwork for a pedagogy that bridges the gap between mind and heart to lead students and educators toward a new conception of teaching and learning. Grounding her work in interviews of scholars who are already transforming the educational landscape, Rendón invites the reader to join a burgeoning movement toward more inclusive classrooms that honor each learner's identity and support education for social justice. Her book is vital reading for anyone seeking to create more inclusive institutions for students and teachers alike."—***Diversity & Democracy (AAC&U)***

22883 Quicksilver Drive
Sterling, VA 20166-2102

Subscribe to our e-mail alerts: www.Styluspub.com